CW00825856

V

Chen Erjin

Verso

China:
Crossroads Socialism

Translated by Robin Munro

**British Library
Cataloguing in Publication Data**

Chen, Erjin
   China.
   1. Zhong guo gong chan dang
   I. Title
   324.251′075   JQ1519.A5

First published 1984
© Chen Erjin

Verso Editions and NLB
15 Greek Street London W1V 5LF

Filmset in Bembo by
PRG Graphics, Redhill

Printed in Great Britain by
The Thetford Press Ltd
Thetford, Norfolk

ISBN 0 86091 062 8
    0 86091 762 2

Contents

Translator's Note and Acknowledgement

Any work of translation entails a certain amount of textual interpretation, but the particular style and nature of Chen Erjin's writing has made this especially true in the present case. The author's highly agglutinative prose style in many ways stretches the grammatical resources of the Chinese language to the limit, and often quite simply goes beyond those available under the rules of proper English usage. Drastic translation remedies have therefore sometimes been required, notably the introduction of new English coinages. While these may well offend the guardians of English purity, they have at least partially solved otherwise intractable problems, and are in my view further justified by the often highly inventive nature of Chen's own terminology. The only deletions which have been made are of non-significant textual repetition, excessive 'socialist kitsch' imagery, or heavily mixed metaphor (so beloved by Chinese writers in general) which would jar with the English reader. In general I have attempted to forge an English prose style which conveys the dignity and austerity of the original text, without glossing over or concealing its occasional shortcomings.

I would like to thank Frank Wilson for his considerable help and support during the preparation of an earlier draft of this translation, and Hugh Lathrop and Liu Xiangheng for so carefully checking my final draft against the original Chinese. Also, I would like to acknowledge the valuable assistance of the Contemporary China Institute, London in providing me with a one-year Research Fellowship, during which much of the work on this book was completed. My sincere thanks go out to Professor Stuart R. Schram and Charles K. Maisels for many hours of fruitful discussion and useful comment upon my own introduction to Chen's text. Finally, I would like to stress that it has not been possible to obtain the author's permission to produce this English edition of his work, and I can therefore only hope that he would indeed welcome its appearance in the West.

Introduction

Chen Erjin and the Chinese Democracy Movement

by Robin Munro

1. The Context of Chen Erjin's Work

Chen Erjin's extraordinary work of political analysis, originally entitled *On Proletarian-Democratic Revolution*, is the first major un-official critique of 'existing socialism' to have reached the West from China. In attempting here to interpret and evaluate this work, two very different periods in the recent history of the People's Republic stand out as immediately demanding of our attention. First: autumn 1976, when the death of the 'Great Helmsman' Mao Zedong was followed in a matter of weeks by the arrest of four of his closest political allies: Zhang Chunqiao, Yao Wenyuan, Wang Hongwen, and his own wife Jiang Qing—the so-called 'Gang of Four'. Second: winter 1978, when the historic 3rd Plenum (of the 11th Central Committee) saw the decisive victory within the Communist Party of China (CPC) of the pre-Cultural Revolution 'old guard' headed by Deng Xiaoping, over the interim 'bureaucratic left' leadership headed by Mao's chosen successor Hua Guofeng. This victory led, in short order, to official termination of most of the radical policies of the previous two decades, and to the initiation of a new 'general line' for China's socialist development—one consisting, in essence, in an eschewal of class struggle, and a firm emphasis upon economic construction and modernization as China's primary task in the last decades of the twentieth century.

Winter 1978 also witnessed the spontaneous and dramatic emer-gence, in several of China's major cities, of a numerically small yet politically vibrant movement of grassroots writers and activists, dedicated to the promotion, from below, of the new leadership's professed aim of democratically renewing China's social and poli-tical system. This—the 'Democracy Movement'—was organized primarily by socially conscious young workers and students from the so-called 'lost generation' created by the Cultural Revolution. A whole series of unofficial journals and bulletins recorded the outpouring of political, sociological and literary self-expression by these moral and intellectual survivors of that unique political generation.

Chen Erjin's work *On Proletarian-Democratic Revolution*, completed some three months before Mao's death but unpublished until the appearance of a *samizdat* edition six months after the 3rd Plenum, in many ways acts as a unique bridging-text between these two very different periods, prefiguring at the level of theory and ideology a degree of continuity and development which starkly contrasted with the overt rupture and discontinuity. For Chen's work can be seen as a synthesis of certain key aspects of Maoist Cultural Revolutionary theory with those new elements in China's political and social thought which, taken together, provided the dominant ethos and rationale for the policy direction and social order ushered in by the 3rd Plenum. On the one hand, revolutionary transformation, class struggle, erosion of the division of labour, direct mass action and the building of genuine organs of workers' power; on the other, constitutional integration, stability and social harmony, economic rationality, individual freedom, and institutionalized democracy and legality.

The fact that Chen wrote this work more than two years before the 3rd Plenum, at a time when ideas such as institutionalized democracy, legality and free speech were regarded as uniquely unwelcome by the authorities, testifies both to his prescience and to his personal courage. Somewhat ironically, however, official CPC ideology would today still regard the two halves or elements of Chen's synthesis as irreconcilable and virtually antithetical, the victory of the new policies having been predicated upon a total repudiation (made official in October 1979) both of the Cultural Revolution experience, and of its underlying theoretical rationale. Before we consider how successful is Chen's attempt to marry these apparently divergent conceptions of socialist development, it is first of all necessary to examine in more detail the overall situation obtaining in China during each of the two periods mentioned above—the first of which provided the context of the book's composition, the second the context in which it was published and began to exert a social influence. We must see, that is, how the events of 1976 led to the events of 1978.

The last year of Mao's life must have been one of unremitting bleakness, disillusionment and loneliness for him. Almost a decade of Cultural Revolution strategy, designed to transform social relations in a way that would pre-empt and avert in China what he saw as the 'revisionist' Soviet restoration of capitalism, had resulted in massive alienation from the regime on the part of China's population, and chronic internecine strife within the party leadership itself. Mao's sketchy and undeveloped ideas on the danger that a new ruling class might pervert the course of China's development—ideas first identifiable in the post-'Great Leap Forward' period of the late 1950s—had also led to sweeping intra-party purges, involving an unprecedented mobilization of the masses against the party bureaucracy as a whole. However, this mass mobilization—described as 'extensive democracy'[1] by Mao—was irredeemably marred by populist and quasi-fascist characteristics, such as the use of fanatical, inexperienced youth (the Red Guards) and later the army, as the principal agencies of political change. Far from liberating the masses and allowing them to become more individually autonomous and self-determinant, it generated an insidious and ever-increasing sense of fear and distrust at all levels of Chinese society. By the mid-1970's, the leading group around Mao (later dubbed the 'Gang of Four') had developed the various fragmentary elements of his Cultural Revolution theory into a harshly authoritarian doctrine of unremitting class struggle—the principal 'bourgeois' targets of which seemed, more often than not, to be ordinary members of the working class. Despite the sweeping purges of the late 1960's, a process got underway from 1972 onwards, in the wake of the Lin Biao affair,[2] whereby many of the pre-Cultural Revolution party 'old guard' were rehabilitated and restored to positions of authority—thanks largely to the efforts of Premier Zhou Enlai. By the time of Zhou's death in January 1976, these figures (including the present *de facto* party leader Deng Xiaoping) had regained sufficient influence to be able to

1. For a sample of Mao's writings on 'extensive democracy' (*da minzhu*), see his *Selected Works* Vol. 5, pp. 343–7, and pp. 357–8.
2. Marshal Lin Biao, second only to Mao in the party hierarchy during the Cultural Revolution, is said by the Chinese to have died in a plane crash in Outer Mongolia in September 1971 while attempting to defect to the Soviet Union.

constitute an (as yet largely silent) opposition to the ultra-left group around Mao which probably reflected majority opinion within the party. Popular and intra-party opposition to the regime came together in a dramatic and unexpected way in early April 1976, around the time of the Qing Ming festival, when Chinese traditionally pay their respects to the dead. In Tian An Men Square in the centre of Peking, hundreds of wreaths laid by work-units and ordinary citizens at the foot of the Monument to the People's Heroes in commemoration of Premier Zhou were suddenly removed by police and militia on the night of the Qing Ming festival. This was evidently at the behest of the ultra-left leadership, who had waged a series of thinly-veiled campaigns against Zhou Enlai during the last years of his life. Public outrage at this blatant slur on the enormously popular Zhou led to the occurrence, in Tian An Men Square the following day, of the first spontaneous mass demonstration in the history of the People's Republic. This protest, by hundreds of thousands of ordinary citizens, was brutally suppressed by the authorities and declared to have been a counter-revolutionary disturbance. Deng Xiaoping, as the leading representative of the intra-party opposition, was dismissed from all his posts, and went into internal exile. The infirm Mao, by now reduced to sporadically issuing cryptic and ambiguous 'supreme directives' to the nation from his self-imposed confinement in the old Imperial Palace, was faced in his last months with the knowledge that his 'revolution to touch men's souls' had received the thumbs-down from the Chinese masses.

One month after the 'Tian An Men Incident'—as the shadows of authoritarian repression fell across the land, and as the political crisis entered its final and most severe stage—Chen Erjin completed the writing of his work *On Proletarian-Democratic Revolution*, which he had begun the previous year, in spring 1975, in response to Mao's call to the nation to study the theory of proletarian dictatorship.

Few definite facts are known about Chen Erjin's personal history. Unlike other prominent figures in the unofficial Democracy Movement of 1978-81, he had few meetings with foreigners and published virtually nothing of an autobiographical nature in the unofficial press. It is clear, however, that his ideas exerted a steadily increasing influence within the ranks of the Democracy Movement, from the time of the publication of his book, in June 1979, in a special edition of the unofficial Peking journal *April 5th Forum*. From the little information available[3], the following very rough outline of Chen's life can be constructed.

Chen was born in 1945, in Yunnan Province in south-west China. He is of middle-peasant class origin. His formal schooling comprised five years of primary education, and he worked as a peasant for the first few years thereafter. In the early 1960s, he worked for a short period as an unskilled labourer, and was then admitted to a teacher-training college in Kunming, capital of Yunnan Province. Just before the outbreak of the Cultural Revolution in 1966, after two years' study, he graduated as a teacher. He played an active part in the Cultural Revolution as leader of a 'Rebel' Red Guard group in Kunming, and on two or three occasions undertook extensive journeys across the country to 'exchange revolutionary experiences' (*geming chuanlian*). He was in Peking in the autumn of 1966, and participated in one of the historic mass rallies in Tian An Men Square at which Mao Zedong addressed hundreds of thousands of visiting Red Guards from all over the country. He produced a few short pieces of writing during the Cultural Revolution, but regards these as having been of little importance or value. Apparently, he took no part in the widespread armed struggle between Red Guard factions which characterized the period from 1967 to 1968. At the end of this period, which in certain areas had meant virtual civil war, he was invited to join the newly established Yunnan Provincial Revolutionary Committee, but for reasons unknown declined to do so. Around 1968 he worked for a short time as a teacher in the large industrial city of Shenyang in north-east China. He then returned to Kunming, and continued his teaching work in a school run by a local coal mine. From the early 1970s onwards, he worked as a statistician in the same mine, and it was during this period that he wrote *On Proletarian-Democratic Revolution*. In early 1978 (eighteen months after the fall of the 'Gang of Four'), he was arrested after he had submitted the work to official publishing bodies. He spent ten months in prison, during which time he was beaten and tortured. While in jail, however, he refused to renounce any of the views expressed in his book. The verdict upon him, as on countless others,

3. This information comes primarily from an informant who has met Chen Erjin and wishes to remain anonymous, and secondarily from Chen's own 'Introduction of 1979', included in the Chinese edition of this work but omitted here for reasons of space.

was officially reversed in early 1979 as a result of the policy changes initiated at the 3rd Plenum, and he was thereupon freed and declared to have been a victim of the 'Gang of Four'. Chen is married and has three children. He has no knowledge of any foreign language, but has read extensively the Marxist classics in translation. Like most of the more recent unofficial writers, he appears to be largely unfamiliar with Western Marxist thought since the time of Lenin, and entirely so in the case of the various 'New Left' schools of Marxism. He is thought to have read one or two works by Trotsky in the course of 1980. His only known hobby is playing Chinese chess. He impresses others as being strong-willed, of incisive intellect, and a tactful and experienced political organizer.

Shortly after his release from prison, Chen went to Peking with the aim of having his book published officially, but he met with no success. He there made contact with the six-month-old Democracy Movement (and, in particular, the *April 5th Forum* unofficial publishing group), and at this point his own story converges with that of the Democracy Movement as a whole.

The Democracy Movement began in mid-November 1978. In the course of that year, a major power-struggle had been developing between the Hua Guofeng leadership, and the recently reinstated Deng Xiaoping and his supporters. The former (subsequently dubbed the 'whateverist' faction[4]) had a strong vested interest in upholding the legacy of Mao and the Cultural Revolution while sharply distancing itself from the ultra-leftism of the fallen 'Gang of Four'; the latter (subsequently dubbed the 'practice' faction) sought nothing less than an overt repudiation of the entire Cultural Revolution, and a decisive break with Mao's radical leftist line which, with only brief respites, had dominated policy-making in China since the late 1950s. The confrontation, in which the 'whateverists' were clearly placed on the defensive, was skilfully channelled through a series of political and philosophical debates—the most significant of which centred on the proposition of vanguard members of the 'practice faction' that 'practice is the sole criterion for verifying the truth'. By challenging the dominant role ascribed to theory by the 'Gang of Four' in their general epistemology, this proposition paved

---

4. The nickname derives from this faction's purported adherence to the principle that whatever Mao said or did was intrinsically correct.

the way for a total deflation of Maoist dogma and orthodoxy from the period of the Cultural Revolution. A series of policy victories by the 'practice faction' culminated, in November 1978, in the dramatic official reversal of the verdict on the Tian An Men Incident, which was now declared to have been a 'wholly revolutionary action'. The public popularity of Deng Xiaoping and the 'practice faction' soared to new heights, as the people came to see him as their champion, as one who would lead them forwards from the long dark years of arbitrary violence, factional intrigue and bureaucratic tyranny. At the same time, the official reversal of verdicts on major past historical issues opened a Pandora's box of still more fundamental questions—for the frank admission by the authorities that the party had committed grave errors of judgment and political line served, on one level, to undermine the party's own legitimacy and claim to higher wisdom. Policy was in a state of almost complete flux, and for a time in late 1978 a 'secret speech'-type denunciation of Mao seemed a quite likely outcome. The party bureaucracy had few solid guidelines on the permissible limits of criticism and debate, and as the Central Work Conference of November met in Peking to prepare for the crucial 3rd Plenum of December, there was a momentary political vacuum and a marked slackening of political control at grassroots level. At this unique historical juncture, with successes in the offing for the 'practice faction', the kind of ordinary citizens who had risen in protest in Tian An Men Square in April 1976 took to the streets once more—only this time not in a spirit of confrontation.

One of the earliest signs that something unusual was afoot came on 19 November, when a wall-poster claiming that Mao had committed errors in his later years appeared on a drab stretch of wall in central Peking close to the official residence of the top party leadership. This incident, reported across the world, was closely followed by the appearance of a whole series of other posters on 'Democracy Wall', expressing citizens' criticisms of individual party figures and of the various oppressive features of the social order which had arisen in China in the course of the Cultural Revolution. On 24 November, Peking citizens were treated to the astonishing sight of a giant 94-page wall-poster, entitled 'God of Fire Symphonic Poems',[5] being pasted up on a high fence along one side of Tian An Men

5. For a selection of English translations of these poems, see *Coming Alive: China After Mao*, by Roger Garside (Andre Deutsch 1981), pp. 287–296.

Square, directly opposite the Mao Mausoleum. The author of these poems was a young man from Guiyang City, in south-west China, named Huang Xiang. That same day, again at Tian An Men Square, Huang and seven of his friends proclaimed the founding of the Enlightenment Society—an unofficial organization dedicated to the ideological modernization of China—and distributed to the public copies of their own privately mimeographed journal. The following day, large numbers of citizens who had come to read the Democracy Wall posters spontaneously formed into groups and began discussing their aspirations to a more democratic social system. In marked contrast to the xenophobic spirit which had become so widespread in Chinese society since the Cultural Revolution, a warm invitation to participate in these discussion groups was extended to any foreigners who happened to be present. This reflected a widespread resurgence of interest in the alternative values and social systems of the West, prompted both by the favourable news coverage given to the USA by the Chinese media in the run-up to the normalization of Sino-American diplomatic relations, and by such factors as President Carter's professed support for the cause of human rights, all of which served to foster a new, democratic image of the West among the Chinese people.

Two days later, on the evening of 27 November, five thousand citizens gathered at Democracy Wall to hear impromptu speeches by young poster-writers and others. The atmosphere was one of exhiliration and confidence, and a report from a Canadian journalist that Deng Xiaoping had earlier that day expressed his basic approval of the activities at Democracy Wall,[6] gave rise to unrestrained joy and euphoria. The crowd began to march down the broad, imposing Avenue of Eternal Peace towards Tian An Men Square, where they sang the Internationale and the national anthem in front of the Great Hall of the People, and then divided into groups to discuss issues ranging from the advantages of Yugoslav-style socialism to the benefits of a US-style separation of powers. Further mass discussion meetings took place in the Square on the following two nights, and, as news of the dramatic happenings in Peking spread to other parts of the country, a similar pattern of events began to form in other major

6. This strange episode, in which John Fraser of the Toronto *Globe and Mail* played a complex role as intermediary between Deng Xiaoping and the crowd at Democracy Wall, is vividly recounted in *Coming Alive* (op. cit.), pp. 223–5.

cities, particularly Shanghai where criticisms of the lack of liberty in China, and of the social system in general, were perhaps more forceful and extreme than in Peking.

But the publication and successful distribution of the *Enlightenment* journal had suggested to the activists of Democracy Wall a more effective, enduring and in some ways less provocative form for the promotion of what had now been dubbed the 'Democracy Movement' (or the 'April 5th Movement', in recognition of the underlying continuity with the Tian An Men Incident of 1976). By early December crudely mimeographed journals, some extending to several dozen pages in length, began to appear on Democracy Wall alongside the profusion of wall-posters. The first issue of one of the earliest such journals—*April 5th Forum*—bore no details of the identity of its authors, but when no attempt was made to remove the journal from Democracy Wall, other titles soon began to appear (*Peking Spring, Exploration, Science Democracy and Legal System*, and so on) carrying publishers' names and contact addresses. A small but committed number of writers and activists—or 'democracy fighters', as they became known—gradually joined together in groups centred on specific unofficial journals. In the course of the next two and a quarter years, a total of more than 150 such journals were established throughout the country, with some thirty-five in Peking alone, as well as more than forty semi-official student publications, mostly of a literary nature. These journals formed the organizational and ideological core of the movement, publishing a broad mixture of political, social and economic commentary and analysis in which the dominant concerns were democracy, legality, and such civil liberties as freedom of speech, publication and association. The great majority of journals adopted a broadly Marxist framework of analysis, with only a very few embracing overtly capitalist or anti-socialist ideas. The sizeable number devoted to literary themes fostered a powerful new *genre* of short-story and poetry writing that sought to expose the 'dark side' of society and to explore the inner world of the emotions. The journals were produced by a laborious and primitive process of stencilling and screen-printing, but print-runs ranged from a few hundred to more than a thousand and they were all sold openly on the streets of China's cities. The grassroots writers and activists firmly rejected the 'dissident' label from the outset, regarding themselves instead as the natural allies, the demotic counterparts, of the new reforming leadership.

The extent to which Deng and his colleagues were prepared to share this view was by no means clear. They were committed to a policy of establishing socialist democracy and legality, and redressing social injustices after two decades of leftist domination; indeed, they had been promoting their own official democratic reform movement—the 'movement to emancipate the mind' (*jiefang sixiang yundong*)— since early 1978. Moreover, the Democracy Movement served them as a vanguard force in raising such issues as the re-evaluation of the Cultural Revolution, and of Mao himself. But as they steadily consolidated their control over the party, in the aftermath of the 3rd Plenum, the Dengists began to give clear indications that they regarded the voice of the streets as at best a nuisance, and at worst a serious threat to the 'stability and unity' for which they had been appealing to the nation since mid-November.

For, besides the urban-based publishing and demonstration activities of the Democracy Movement, in which the main participants were young workers and students, two parallel grassroots movements had arisen during the winter of 1978: first, large numbers of peasants from all over China began arriving in the capital, ragged and starving, to petition the central authorities about the persecution and sufferings inflicted upon them by local cadres during the years of the Cultural Revolution; second, large numbers of 'sent-down' urban youth, transferred to remote rural areas after 1968 as part of the 'down to the countryside' campaign and as a means of coping with the problem of urban over-population, began to return illegally to the cities, angry and disillusioned now that the remaining Maoist ideological justifications for their banishment had been officially overturned. In January 1979 a large demonstration of petitioning peasants ('against hunger and oppression, for democracy and human rights', as their banner read) took place in central Peking. Shortly afterwards a young woman named Fu Yeuhua, who had helped to organize the peasants, was arrested and eventually sentenced to two years' imprisonment. The unofficial journals of the Democracy Movement rallied to her defence, and this in turn helped to forge a greater sense of organizational solidarity between them. The illegal young returnees from the countryside, for their part, quickly established quite militant networks in the cities, and staged rallies and demonstrations in support of their demand for urban household registration. In Shanghai in early February, for example, the returnees occupied the main railway station and disrupted the flow of trains for a whole day.

The subsequent war with Vietnam, along with the growing social unrest, seems to have produced a temporary resurgence of leftist influence within the party, and to have hardened opinion within the 'practice faction' against continued toleration of the independent grassroots activity symbolized by the Democracy Movement. By April 1979 the authorities had had enough, and a number of leading writers and activists were arrested—notably Wei Jingsheng of *Exploration*, and Chen Lü and Ren Wanding of *The China Human Rights Alliance*. (Significantly, just prior to his arrest, Wei Jingsheng had published a long article entitled 'Democracy or New Autocracy?' in which he distinguished himself by being the first in the Democracy Movement openly to criticize Deng Xiaoping.) The early euphoria of the movement evaporated, but this by no means put an end to the determination of those involved to continue the struggle, to test with their own persons and their own actions the sincerity of the new regime's commitment to the democratic reformation of Chinese socialism. June saw the publication of Chen Erjin's *On Proletarian-Democratic Revolution*, and in the summer months, as more and more peasant petitioners flooded into Peking, a series of new unofficial journals were founded. However, sporadic repression and harassment by the authorities continued, together with a media barrage against 'ultra-democracy', 'ultra-individualism' and 'anarchy'. In October 1979 Wei Jingsheng was sentenced to 15 years' imprisonment, on the twin charges of revealing state secrets (about China's war with Vietnam) to a foreign journalist, and publishing 'counter-revolutionary' articles. Once more, the movement rallied to defend a fallen member, even though Wei's strongly pro-Western views tended to clash with those of the majority. In November, Liu Qing—a leading member of the *April 5th Forum* group—was arrested for distributing a transcript of Wei's trial at Democracy Wall. Later that month, Democracy Wall was closed down by municipal proclamation, and transferred to a remote corner of a park where would-be poster-stickers were required to register their names and addresses with an attendant official.

By early 1980 most unofficial journals had been forced to close down, but many groups and individuals continued to produce short regular bulletins, intended for circulation among themselves rather than for sale to the general public. The danger here was clearly of a drift towards the marginality and isolation of Soviet-style dissidence; however, precisely at this critical moment in the movement's history, a heaven-sent opportunity presented itself. In June 1979 the 2nd Plenary Session of the 5th National People's Congress (China's parliament) had passed several new laws, one of which was the Electoral Law. This stipulated not only that all democratic parties and popular bodies could put forward candidates for the direct prefectural, district and work-unit elections to local People's Congresses (the legislative branch of local government), but also that any individual member of the electorate could stand for election provided that three people could be found to propose the nomination. Local elections began in the spring of 1980, and the opportunity to re-direct their activities into an officially sponsored channel was seized upon by many participants in the Democracy Movement. These included: Fu Shenqi, a 25-year-old worker at the Shanghai Power Plant and editor of the unofficial journal *Voice of Democracy*; Gong Ping and He Defu, both workers at a Peking chemicals factory, and editors of the pro-Soviet journal *Peking Youth*; and Zhong Yueqiu, a 23-year-old smelting-plant worker from South China, and editor of *Voice of the Commoner* and *North River*. But conditions for independent electoral activity proved to be most favourable on the university and college campuses: in Peking University alone, candidates for election to the local People's Congress included Wang Juntao (22 years old) and Han Zhixiong, both editors of the unofficial journal *Peking Spring*, and both alternate members of the Central Committee of the Communist Youth League; Fang Zhiyuan, Peking liaison representative of the Canton journal *Voice of the People*, and chief architect of a nationwide campaign to promote an unofficial 'Draft Publication Law'; and Hu Ping, 33-year-old editor of *Fertile Soil*.

The overall picture which emerged was one of considerable worker and student support for Democracy Movement candidates (several of whom actually *won* election), with, however, widespread interference by local leaderships. Dramatic incidents such as the outbreak of a mass student protest and hunger-strike at the Hunan Teachers' College against bureaucratic manipulation of the local election did not help matters overall, even though in this particular instance the central authorities intervened in favour of the protesting students. In early 1981 an official campaign was launched against 'ultra-democracy', 'anti-Party and anti-socialist activities' and 'dissidence', and in the course of the year this broadened out into a general party offensive against 'bourgeois liberalization'. Although this had to be virtually abandoned, owing to extensive opposition from the intelligentsia and media, and even from such high-ranking party figures as Chen Yun, it nonetheless succeeded in putting an end to the independent grassroots initiatives which had occurred during the election campaigns. Indeed, the media had for some time been trying to depict the Democracy Movement activists merely as latter-day counterparts of the detested Red Guards. In September 1981, while summarizing the course of direct elections over the previous year and a half, the Minister of Civil Administration and Chairman of the National County Election Office, Cheng Zihua, stated: 'In these elections, a tiny minority of people made use of the opportunity afforded by the election of people's representatives to carry out so-called "election contests", in which they disregarded the socialist legal system, spread anarchy and ultra-individualism, conducted secret "link-ups" (*chuanlian*), and expressed outrageous and inflammatory views, openly contravening the Four Basic Principles . . . We must resolutely oppose this.'[7]

However, the Democracy Movement had not put all its eggs in one basket. More or less concurrently with the independent electoral initiatives of some of its activists, others in the movement (particularly in South China, where more enlightened provincial leaderships made it possible for unofficial publishing to continue to a greater extent than in the north) had been attempting to bring about organizational unity between unofficial journals from the different regions. The summer of 1980 marked the high point of the official reform movement. Major speeches in August and October, by Deng Xiaoping and Liao Gailong (a senior party historian and policy researcher), contained sweeping proposals for reform of the cadre system, greater separation of the roles of party and state, and a more

7. See *Zheng Ming* No 48 (Oct. 1981), p. 78. The 'Four Basic Principles', issued by the party in March 1979 as forming the primary articles of faith from which no deviation can be permitted, concern the need to 'uphold party leadership, the socialist path, the dictatorship of the proletariat (now termed "the people's democratic dictatorship"), and Marxism-Leninism-Mao Zedong Thought'.'

independent role for 'mass organizations' such as the trade unions. This firm reassertion of the reforming policy direction gave fresh hope to the Democracy Movement: new journals were set up, some old ones recommenced publication, and in August 1980 the move towards a degree of organizational unity reached fruition. In that month, shortly after the arrest and brief detainment of several of its leading proponents, an 'All-China Association of the People's Press' was founded. (Chen Erjin, using the pen-name 'Lu Ji',[8] wrote an article commemorating the event in the Shandong unofficial journal *Theoretical Banner*, of which he appears to have been the editor.) The Association soon comprised a membership of nearly thirty unofficial journals from all over China—Shanghai, Shandong, Kaifeng, Changsha, Changchun, Ningbo, Anyang, Wuhan, Qingdao, Guiyang, Wenzhou, Shaoguan and other cities—and went on to publish at least nine issues of a new national unofficial journal entitled *Zeren* ('Duty'). Some months later, a second organization centred in Peking, the 'North-China Association of the People's Press', was also established.

The founding of a nationwide organization of unofficial journals coincided with the outbreak of the Polish Solidarity movement. Events in Poland had a dual effect in China: they were a source of great inspiration and encouragement for those in the Democracy Movement, but at the same time they hardened the attitude of the party leadership against any tendencies towards autonomous action at the grassroots. In the winter of 1980, three thousand Taiyuan steel workers (supported by the local unofficial journal *Wind against the Waves*) united to protest against their harsh living conditions. Their leaders were quickly arrested. In early 1981, the official press in Wuhan reported that a small group of students had led moves to establish Polish-style free trade unions, and warned that the aim of such people was to lead the country into chaos by shaking off the party's leading role.

The authorities moved swiftly and decisively to counter this supposed threat to law and order. Sometime during the first weeks of 1981, an official 'Document No. 9' was issued by the leadership calling upon the party to put an end to all 'illegal organizations and

8. I must stress that there is no *definite* proof that 'Lu Ji' and Chen were one and the same person, merely a considerable amount of circumstantial evidence (too complex to itemize and explain here) which in my opinion points clearly to this conclusion.

publications'. The arrests began immediately after the fifth anniversary of the Tian An Men Incident, and within two weeks almost thirty of the leading writers and activists of the Democracy Movement were behind bars. The movement was thus decapitated, and any remaining activities were soon driven completely underground. During the summer of 1982, news began to leak out that certain key figures in the movement had been brought to trial. The sentences were appallingly severe: 14 years imprisonment for Wang Xizhe, 15 years for Xu Wenli (chief editor of *April 5th Forum*), 10 years for He Qiu, and Liu Qing's sentence was increased from 3 to 10 years. What happened to the other detainees is anyone's guess. Chen Erjin is thought to have gone into hiding around the time of the arrests, and his present circumstances and whereabouts are unknown.

2. Chen Erjin's Theory: The Search for a New Revolution

The theoretical output of the Democracy Movement, through the many thousands of pages of the unofficial journals, was astonishingly diverse. The analyses of China's social formation, class structure and politico-economic characteristics varied greatly from one writer to another, and it would therefore be quite wrong to depict Chen Erjin either as a typical ideological representative of the movement, or as its crowning figure. In certain respects, it could even be said that Chen's work belongs more properly to the period in which it was written—the closing years of Mao's life—than to the very different era which followed the fall of the 'Gang of Four' and gave birth to the Democracy Movement. In a sense, however, it provides a crucial point of linkage between the two. For on the one hand, it seeks to inherit the militantly anti-bureaucratic and emancipatory socialist content of Cultural Revolution theory, while exposing its inherent limitations and insufficiencies. And on the other, it prefigures in a remarkable way many of the central concerns of the later period, of which the Democracy Movement formed a part. For some time following the actual publication of Chen's work, the Democracy Movement as a whole—having arisen as the vanguard of the repudiation of the Cultural Revolution—did not really know what to make of Chen's qualified yet frequently fervent espousal of Cultural Revolutionary ideas. The attempted synthesis must have come as a stunning surprise to many. However, as the movement developed, and became increasingly radicalized by its own experience of repression, Chen's views attracted correspondingly greater interest and support.

As a citizen with little social status, Chen was well aware of the negative consequences of the Cultural Revolution, and his main aim was, precisely, to attempt a major reworking and development of Cultural Revolutionary theory such as might show the way towards a resolution and transcendence of the evident disasters of Cultural Revolutionary practice. The 'Gang of Four' also, in their own way, attempted to develop the theory, but of course it was largely they who bore responsibility for the practice; it is therefore of the greatest importance that we carefully distinguish Chen's ideas from those of the 'gang'. A historically specific reading of the former shows any affinity with the latter to be almost entirely superficial, and attributable to the simple fact that both were, of necessity, expressed in terms of the dominant political discourse of the day. As Chen states in his 'Introduction of 1979': 'Although the argument in the present work is based upon the same sentence from Marx as that upon which Zhang Chunqiao based his argument,[9] namely the sentence from *The Class Struggles in France: 1848-1850* in which Marx first employed the concept of proletarian dictatorship, we nonetheless arrived at diametrically opposed conclusions upon the matter.' The real paternity of Chen's theory is highly complex and, in the best sense of the word, eclectic. Essentially, he was concerned to develop theoretically the radical anti-bureaucratic component which had been present in Mao's thought from the late 1950s, but which Mao himself eventually came to regard as posing too great a threat to the post-revolutionary order. In this project, Chen was the direct successor of groups such as the 'Sheng Wu Lian' Red Guards from Hunan, who in 1967, in a radical manifesto entitled *Whither China*, had argued that the logical outcome of the Cultural Revolution would be a state structure of the Paris Commune type; and the 'Li Yizhe' authors of the famous 1974 Canton wall-poster 'On Socialist Democracy and Legality', who first formulated the now officially accepted critique of the Cultural Revolution as a period of 'feudal-

9. Chen is referring to Zhang's now notorious article 'On Exercising All-Round Dictatorship Over the Bourgeoisie', see *Peking Review*, No. 14, April 1975.

fascist dictatorship'. Mao categorically rejected the Sheng Wu Lian proposals, on the grounds that such a state structure would negate the role of the party, and would in any case be unrealistic since leaders and figures of authority would always be required. The 'Li Yizhe' themselves, denounced at the time by Li Xiannian (now President of the People's Republic) as 'extremely reactionary', were rewarded for their views with several-year prison sentences. To a considerable extent, Chen succeeds in overcoming the limitations of all three of these positions: the anarchic ultra-leftism of Sheng Wu Lian, the vaguely conservative oppositionism of 'Li Yizhe', and the theoretical inconsistency of Mao.

Mao had posited the existence in China of a new bourgeois class whose leading representatives, located at the summit of the Communist Party, were bent on carrying out a 'capitalist restoration' such as was claimed to have already occurred in the Soviet Union. Whereas Sheng Wu Lian, developing the analysis, termed this the 'red capitalist class', Chen provides a highly significant twist to the analysis by redefining the new ruling class not as capitalists, but as the representatives of qualitatively different exploitative relations of production. In so doing, he imparts to the concept of 'revisionism' a specificity which it lacked in Mao's theoretical framework.[10] For Chen, the danger is not of a reversion to pre-socialist relations of production, of a turning back of the political clock by a conspiratorial minority within the party, but rather of an unchecked *forward* development—under the impetus of defects inherent in single-party dictatorship—towards an authentically new exploitative mode of production.

Chen divides his work into four parts. The first—'History'—is an account of full-blown revisionism, with the Soviet Union serving as the paradigmatic case. The generous provision of political hyperbole

---

10. Chen's borrowing of the term 'revisionism' to denote Soviet ideological heterodoxy reflects, on one level, a desire (prompted by political necessity) to legitimize his theory by cloaking it in the terminology of mainstream Maoism. But on another level, it achieves the opposite effect, in that his drastic redefinition of the term manifestly implies that Mao got things all wrong. The crucial point here is that whereas the Maoist 'anti-revisionist' struggle of the early 1960s to mid-1970s served, in an important sense, as a rearguard defence of aspects of Stalinism (against Khruschev's denunciation of the latter and 'revision' of Marxist theory), Chen's 'anti-revisionism' comprises a defence of true democratic socialism against virtually the entire legacy of Soviet-style socialism.

here tells us much about the uninformed and distorted perception of the Soviet Union on the part of ordinary Chinese (and many in the party leadership) during the Cultural Revolution. However, the true function of this part of the book is to provide, not so much an accurate picture of the Soviet Union itself, but rather a *dystopia*, a vision of everything which Chen hopes fervently will not come into existence in China. Indeed, it could be plausibly argued that this was the role which the 'Soviet Union' played for Mao himself.

Chen analyses revisionism as follows: in the Soviet Union public ownership of the means of production has been usurped by a new ruling class—the 'bureaucrat–monopoly privileged class'—and turned into a new, 'collective' form of private ownership.[11] The commodity nature of labour-power has been fully re-established, with the important difference that it is now stripped of the market rights (i.e., to negotiate the place, time and terms of exploitation) which it enjoyed as a commodity under capitalism. It can thus be exploited in a totally unrestricted fashion. Ideology plays a crucial role here, for the appropriation of the terminology and theory of socialism allows the new ruling class (partially, at least) to confuse and deceive the workers as to the true nature of the system. The workers remain the nominal owners of the means of production, but are in reality reduced to the status of mere slaves. The functional equivalent of money-capital in this exploitative system is 'privilege-capital': the power exercised by those who administer the post-revolutionary state becomes 'privilegized', and privilege itself capitalized. At first sight, this identification of *power* as the organizing principle of the new mode of production appears problematical, even idealist; however, in his attempt to construct a rudimentary political economy of revisionism, Chen traces the roots of this new modality of the capital-relation squarely back to the system's economic base. In his view, the special feature of the post-

11. This term, 'the bureaucrat–monopoly privileged class', seems clearly to be Chen's modification of the term commonly used by CPC ideologists, since at least 1970, to denote the Soviet ruling stratum: namely, 'the bureaucrat-monopoly capitalist class' (see, for example, *Leninism or Social Imperialism?* (Peking 1970, p. 15). However, Chen's substitution of the word 'privileged' for 'capitalist' reflects his fundamental departure—as discussed below—from the official anti-revisionist theory of the day. The derivation of the *officially* used term may be traced back to Mao's pre-'49 writings on 'bureaucrat-capital' in China: see, in particular, his *Selected Works* Vol. 4, (Peking 1969), pp. 167, 237, 398, 417–420. See also, in this general connection, footnote 9 of Chapter 5 below.

revolutionary transformation to 'social production under public ownership' lay in the assertion, by the party, of an administration over the whole by means of a fusion, or 'unicorporation' (*yitihua*), of the twin powers of political leadership and economic control. A monopolistic system of politico-economic development was thus created, and the resultant loss of the individual specificity of politics and economics provided the highly distinctive conditions which led to the emergence of privilege-capital. Moreoever, says Chen, the process itself entailed a 'primitive accumulation' of this new form of capital by the embryonic new ruling class. This theme was enthusiastically embraced by several other Democracy Movement writers (and related in a more direct manner to the experience of China itself):

'The Chinese Communist Party, relying upon the force of its political power, began the primitive accumulation of capital: this, precisely, was the "three great transformations". The form for this primitive accumulation was, in industry the system of state ownership, and in agriculture the system of rural collective ownership. Because this primitive accumulation was carried out through direct reliance upon the resources of political power, there naturally was created, simultaneously, a special kind of economic system—politico-economic unicorporation.'

What is more: 'There is thus created a special form of capital: power. Power becomes the form of continuance of capital. This power–capital is able to propagate itself, assume material form, and circulate.' (Zhu Jianbin). And finally: 'If we call Western capitalism "money capitalism", then we should call Eastern "socialism" – "power capitalism".' (Wang Yifei)[12]

12. Lest all this be dismissed as merely a typically exotic example of Chinese voluntarism, its close correspondence with certain Western schools of Marxist thought should be noted. In *The Alternative in Eastern Europe*, Rudolf Bahro describes the Stalinist terror as having been the historically necessary form for the primitive accumulation of capital. Even more pertinent are the following remarks by Harry Cleaver: 'In fact, *we can define capital as a social system based on the imposition of work through the commodity form* . . . This understanding of the nature of capital is obviously markedly different from that of bourgeois economics and some interpretations of Marx, which see capital in a reified manner, that is, as simply things: means of production, profit, investible funds. These are indeed moments in the organization of the social relation but must not be mistaken for the relation itself' (*Reading Capital Politically*, 1979, p. 72). And, in this sense, there is 'no real difference between a "capitalist" accumulation of capital and a "socialist" accumulation of capital' (ibid., p. 105).

In Chen's view, as a result of these structural tendencies, proletarian dictatorship eventually degenerates into revisionist, social-fascist dictatorship by the new ruling class, and the primary social conflict becomes that between privilege and labour.

So much for the 'Soviet Union'. But what of China itself? In the second part—'Necessity'—Chen explores in detail the transition from post-revolutionary socialism to revisionism, and puts forward a materialist analysis of those elements brought into existence by the former which lead, 'necessarily', to the creation of the latter. Necessity is, however, conditioned and contained in Chen's schema within a theory of contradiction: there exists a 'basic contradiction'[13] in the post-revolutionary order which circumscribes the sphere of necessity, but this contradiction can be resolved, through conscious political action, in one of two ways. A bifurcation (rather than a 'back-tracking') of history is possible—either towards full socialism, or towards revisionism. China, in Chen's view, stands at present at the nodal point in this bifurcation, and may therefore be described as a 'crossroads' socialist society. But what is the nature of this basic contradiction? 'The capitalist mode of production is characterized by the existence of a fundamental contradiction between the *socialization of production* on the one hand, and *ownership by private individuals* on the other. In the case of crossroads socialist society, the basic contradiction in the mode of production resides in the following: the incompatibility between, on the one hand, *highly organized and politico-economically unicorporate social production under public ownership*, and, on the other, *coercive monopolization of power by the minority.*' (p. 87)

The analogistic strand in Chen's methodology—transposition and modification of categories found in Marx—stands out clearly in this passage. However, the formulation as a whole provides Chen with a solid and consistent framework for his subsequent exposition of the developmental tendencies of 'crossroads socialism'. Chapter 4 is devoted to an analysis of the first aspect of the contradiction (abbreviated in the present translation to 'unicorporate publisocial production'[14]). What this term signifies, in essence, is the particular social

13. In the Maoist tradition, contradictions are regarded not only as providing the motive force of historical progress, but as constituting the very essence of both social and natural existence.
14. See *Translator's Note,* p. 87.

configuration of the productive forces (broadly conceived as both the means/instruments of production *and* labour-power) resulting from the transformation to public ownership. Historically progressive because of its great productive efficiency, it constitutes, says Chen, the 'socialist organism' of the new society. However, this 'socialist organism' is marred from the outset by state-capitalist attributes, which in turn derive from the system of management: the division of labour between producers and administrators makes possible an exploitation of the social labour process by the latter, and public ownership consequently comes to assume more of a formal than a real character. Since political power is the dominant element within the configuration, it is the division of labour *in the exercise of power* (*quanli fengong*) which ultimately determines the outcome of the tension between the 'socialist organism' and the 'state-capitalist stone' which it contains.

Chen then proceeds, in chapter 5, to consider the second aspect of the contradiction: 'coercive monopolization of power by the minority'. This aspect—which appears to refer not merely to the superstructural expression of the new relations of production, but also, in a certain sense, to these relations themselves—is viewed in a diachronic perspective. In the early post-Liberation period, the party's imposition of a fixed monopoly of power was entirely necessary, for purposes both of countering imperialist hostility and of waging the class struggle entailed in the transformation to public ownership. During this period, the party substituted for the proletariat and exercised dictatorship on its behalf, and true proletarian democracy was not possible.[15]

Subsequent, however, to the establishment of public ownership over the means of production, this fixed monopoly comes increasingly to act as a fetter upon the growth of the productive forces, primarily through its negative effects upon the human element in the latter—labour-power. Henceforth, it can only be maintained by *coercive* means. Crucially, as both the agency and embodiment of the fixed monopoly of power, the party itself undergoes a parallel transformation. Chen identifies four features or formal elements of

15. Chen's constant use of the term 'proletariat' is somewhat misleading, suggesting as it does an *ouvrieriste* bias clearly inappropriate to an industrially underdeveloped country such as China. Actually, though, he sees the population as being divided into two broad strata—producers and administrators—and the term 'proletariat' refers, essentially, to *all* the former.

the superstructure as being the vehicles for a possible evolution of the party into a new ruling class (in both a political and an economic sense): 'the system of appointment to office, the hierarchical order, the autonomization of the state organs, and the sanctification of the party'. A sustained and vitriolic denunciation of each then follows, with a quotation from Engels providing an appropriately combative conclusion: 'For [the dialectic], nothing is final, absolute, sacred. It reveals the transitory character of everything and in everything; nothing can endure before it except the uninterrupted process of becoming and of passing away, of endless ascendancy from the lower to the higher.' (p. 108.)

At the same time, of course, the dialectic requires human assistance in order to become operative. Political intervention—the 'proletarian–democratic revolution'—is needed to prevent the basic contradiction from driving crossroads socialist society towards revisionism. And, although the roots of the skewed power–relationship between party and people lie within the economic base (above all in the division of labour between producers and administrators), it is nonetheless in the superstructure that the degenerative process is primarily centred. The 'proletarian–democratic revolution' is therefore to be *a political revolution within the superstructure*, a social reformation aimed at the transference of power from the party minority to the workers as a class, but carried out for the underlying purpose of converting merely *formal-juridical* ownership by the latter into true ownership with actual power of disposal. This dialectical view of the reciprocity between base and superstructure, with the latter functioning as the 'leading edge', is a characteristically Maoist one. The conception as a whole, however, represents a distinctive development of Mao's own 'two stage' approach to the socialist revolution, which also called for the transformation of the economic base to be succeeded by an appropriate reformation of the superstructure.

At this point, before proceeding to a consideration of Part 3—'Actuality'—where Chen specifies and elaborates upon the nature of this new revolution, we must digress somewhat from his own line of exposition and briefly examine Part 4—'Rationality'. For the latter provides, in a single chapter, the entire philosophical underpinnings of the former. In itself, the term 'proletarian–democratic revolution' signifies much more than a simple eclectic blending of the two terms which, for both Lenin and Mao, denoted the successive stages of

national and social revolution: the 'bourgeois–democratic revolution', and the 'proletarian–socialist revolution'.[16] As we have seen,
Chen structures his ideas within a dialectical framework of contradiction, but in so doing he places special emphasis upon a particular
moment of the dialectic which had, for the previous two decades, all
but disappeared from the theoretical armoury of Chinese Communism: namely, 'sublation', or synthesis. It is this reinstatement of
the dialectic which provides the rationale for his attempt, in Part 3, to
appropriate the bourgeois–democratic state structure for the proletarian cause. Initially (although this is not made explicit by Chen)
the two confront each other as thesis and antithesis, but in the course
of struggle a synthesis can be achieved whereby the bourgeois-
democratic state form is raised to a higher level, and invested with
proletarian content.[17] It is worth noting the extraordinary theoretical
courage which such a formulation, made as it was during the high
point of the 'Gang of Four', implies. Chen's admiration for the
American system—which he in effect regards as the ideal-type of the
bourgeois state—would have been less surprising if expressed in late
1978, when moves towards a normalization of Sino–US relations
were in full swing; in 1976, however, workers throughout China
were still using pictures of American GIs for target practice in militia
training. Indeed, the mere espousal of democracy as a worthy political ideal was at that time, despite Mao's sporadic advocacy of
'extensive democracy', regarded with the deepest suspicion. For the
'Gang of Four' in particular, the key to combating revisionism lay in
the relentless exercise of 'all-round dictatorship over the bourgeoisie', and one of their most frequently quoted political formulas
in this connection was: 'old cadres = democrats = capitalist-
roaders'. In other words, democracy itself was viewed as irredeemably bourgeois in nature.

Maoist 'ultra-leftism' invariably stressed contradiction (opposition) as the dominant factor in the dialectical process, while syn-

---

16. For a definition and brief analysis by Mao of the different types of revolution, see
his *Selected Works* Vol. 2, pp. 326–7 and p. 329.
17. Overall, Chen's work would present most awkward problems of categorization
for any party ideologist seeking to criticize it: is he an 'ultra-leftist', on account of his
emphasis on Cultural Revolution-type theory, or, conversely, an 'ultra-rightist', on
account of his great interest in the American governmental model? For a tentative and
partial solution to this dilemma, see my discussion of Chen as a 'left-wing de-
radicalizer', pp. 38–9 below.

thesis, or 'negation of the negation', was consigned to academic oblivion.[18] The reasons for this had more to do with the politics of the day than with philosophy. At the Eighth Party Congress of 1956, class struggle in China was said to have basically been brought to an end as a result of the successful establishment of public ownership. The following year, however, Mao made a significant first move away from this view in his article 'On the Correct Handling of Contradictions among the People', where he stated that contradictions and class struggle still existed under socialism. His thinking quickly became still more radical, and, with the fragmentary emergence of his 'new class' theory, class struggle on the ideological level between the people and the new representatives of the bourgeoisie was given ever greater prominence. The Maoist philosophical codephrase for this renewed emphasis on class struggle was 'one divides into two' (stressing opposition), while that of his opponents in the party was 'two combine into one' (stressing unity). In the run-up to the Cultural Revolution, this latter perspective was condemned as somehow providing a theoretical justification for Khruschevite revisionism, and the concept of sublation became tainted by association along the way. But as Chen argues forcefully in chapter 13, the absolutization of either opposition *or* unity leads to a false and incomplete conception of the dialectic. In his view, the methodological formula 'one divides into two' acquires validity only when supplemented by a second term denoting synthesis—the subsequent dialectical stage in which the contradiction is resolved, and succeeded by a new opposition. Rejecting the formula 'two combine into one' as signifying merely a metaphysical *denial* of opposition, he advances the new term 'two struggle and produce a third' (*er dou chu san*) to fill this epistemological gap.

On the political level, Chen's critique of the 'two kinds of neo-

18. 'Engels talked about the three categories, but as for me I don't believe in two of those categories . . . The juxtaposition, on the same level, of the transformation of quality and quantity into one another, the negation of the negation, and the law of the unity of opposites is "triplism", not monism. The most basic thing is the unity of opposites. The transformation of quality and quantity into one another is the unity of the opposites quality and quantity. There is no such thing as the negation of the negation. Affirmation, negation, affirmation, negation . . . in the development of things, every link in the chain of events is both affirmation and negation.' (Mao, August 1964, in *Mao Tse-tung Unrehearsed*, ed. Stuart Schram, Harmondsworth 1974, p. 226). In 1958, Mao even went so far as to assert the existence of a 'law of the negation of the affirmation' (*kending fouding zhi guilü*)!

metaphysician' amounts to a rejection both of the pre-Cultural Revolution old guard within the party (and this might also apply to the present leadership, to the extent that it maintains an unqualified insistence upon 'stability and unity'), and of the Cultural Revolutionary left (the 'Gang of Five', if one includes the later Mao). Here we have perhaps the clearest indication of a project which runs throughout the book: namely, the search for an independent, 'true left' position whose legitimacy would not be sought by reference to any of the existing leadership factions, and, indeed, for a qualitatively new form of radicalism reflecting the interests and aspirations of the people rather than one or other section of the bureaucracy, left or right. It would thus be a total misapprehension to regard Chen either as a closet 'Gang of Four' supporter, or even as, in some sense, standing still further to the left of the political spectrum. Viewed in the light of the historical context in which Chen was writing, what is remarkable about his appraisal of the Cultural Revolution is not the affirmative component, but rather the fact that he was bold and original enough to begin to raise serious and far-reaching *criticisms* of the movement. Writing further upon this subject in late 1980, when the official volte-face had secured sanction for even the most extreme denunciations of the Cultural Revolution, Chen again elaborated an independent critique, which went further on the negative side than had his earlier position, and yet affirmed the unique value of certain social and ideological *by-products* of the movement:

'Since the Great Proletarian Cultural Revolution (GPCR) was not the creation of Mao Zedong the individual, I feel that it is incorrect to maintain that "with the death of Mao, the GPCR was in all senses finished". In my view, the GPCR was a failed [movement of] petty-bourgeois left-wing reform. The reasons for its failure were twofold. First, the proletariat itself was not yet sufficiently mature: proceeding from simple-hearted emotion and illusion, it ended up blindly "protecting this" and "vowing to die for that"; similarly, it . . . was split and undermined by the reactionary theory of class origins (the division of society into poor peasants, rich peasants, landlords, the rebel faction, the conservative faction, etc.), and failed to determine the target, content, nature and task of its own revolution. Second, Mao Zedong himself, who monopolized the power of leadership in this revolution, could only, because of his class position and the limitations of his time, propagate a line of petty-bourgeois left-wing reform, a line proceeding from the defence of his own ruling position and aimed at purging the persons and line of his [former] comrades-in-arms. The reason that the movement, once started, developed so rapidly and fiercely was, precisely, that it meshed with the anti-bureaucratic aspirations of the people. It could not, however, represent their fundamental interests. . . Although the GPCR was brought to an end by the defeat of the petty-bourgeois left-wing reform, it nonetheless nurtured within itself the seeds of a new, thorough revolution: the proletarian-democratic revolution.' ('Lu Ji'.)

The notion of 'petty-bourgeois left-wing reform'[19] appears to represent a further development and integration by Chen of two seminal ideas first expressed in his 1976 text: the exposure of the 'idealization of existing society by petty-bourgeois socialism', and the critique of 'left-wing reformism'. It should be observed in passing that despite his exploratory attempt (via the discussion of the 'two kinds of neo-metaphysician') to transcend the notorious 'two lines' conception of China's alignment of political forces, Chen nonetheless remains, to a considerable extent, enmeshed in the Manichaean worldview imposed during the Cultural Revolution—a worldview religious in its insistence upon seeing everywhere a battle to the death between the forces of light (Mao/Marxism) and the forces of darkness (Liu/revisionism). For Chen, the two aspects of the basic contradiction are represented politically by the Marxist line and the revisionist line, and are irreconcilable in nature. The 'reformist line', however, defines itself by *avoiding* the contradiction, and is thus doomed to failure from the outset. Given the generally accepted image in the West of the present Chinese leadership as 'moderate', 'pragmatic', and so on, it might well be supposed that Chen's charge of reformism was directed at those who, in the event, proved triumphant in the intra-party power struggle. This, again, would be a serious misconception. A close reading of the relevant section of the book reveals the 'reformists' to be none other than the eponymous 'Gang of Four': 'The reformist critique of revisionism is similar to the utopian-socialist critique of capitalism—indeed, the

19. Although this tantalizing theme is left undeveloped in the article quoted above, it suggests a potentially fruitful new line of approach for the current official analysis of the Cultural Revolution as an era of 'feudal-fascist dictatorship'.

blueprint for "continuing the revolution" which they have devised bears fair comparison with the *phalanstères* of Fourier! Reformists of this variety possess all the characteristics of the petty-bourgeoisie, *the most prominent of which is the pernicious tenacity of small-scale production.* On the one hand, they possess revolutionary fanaticism, and on the other they may easily turn to the right ideologically' (pp. 122-3). It would be hard to find a more impressive prefiguration than this of the post-1976 official analysis of the ultra-left tendency: the idea of a peasant economy giving rise to the 'feudal-fascist dictatorship' of the Cultural Revolution, the idea of the 'theory of continuing the revolution under the dictatorship of the proletariat' as being mere reactionary utopianism, and the idea of the radical tendency in the party as being ' "left" in form but right in essence'.[20] Finally, Chen makes an incisive observation as to the isolated position of the ultra-left in China, and accurately (though somewhat over-graphically) predicts the circumstances of their future demise: 'They fail to understand that the "restriction of bourgeois right", when carried out under the overall control of the bureaucrat class, can amount to nothing more than an empty phrase. They are placed in an extremely dangerous position, being not only divorced from the mass of the people, but at the same time hated by the bureaucrat class as a whole. At the decisive juncture, the bureaucrat class will assuredly drown them in their own blood.' (p. 123). But perhaps what is of greatest significance here is that Chen identifies the future conquerors of the ultra-left not as Marxist saviours, but as 'the bureaucrat class'. In his view, an enlightened party leadership might indeed play a major instrumental role in resolving the basic contradiction—hence the possible scenario for a 'peaceful carrying out of the proletarian-democratic revolution'; but in the last analysis, nothing short of a true revolution in the superstructure carried out by the people themselves—a radical reorganization of the entire 'division of labour in the exercise of power'—will suffice. In his *Introduction of 1979* Chen expressed the hope and expectation that Deng Xiaoping, and the 'older generation of proletarian revolutionaries' as a whole, might prove to be just such an enlightened leadership, and that the peaceful carrying out of proletarian-democratic revolution might even, by late 1978, have already begun.

20. Ultimately, in the course of 1978, this latter assessment was officially dropped, in order to allow a direct and far-reaching criticism of the leftist line as such to take place.

We shall assess this issue presently, in the context of a further discussion of the general ideology of the Democracy Movement.

If the part of Chen's book dealing with the 'Soviet Union' may more properly be regarded as presenting a dystopian vision, a nightmare of the future, then Part 3—'Actuality'—may justifiably be regarded as his Utopia. This is not to suggest that there is anything inherently unrealizable in the state structure proposed by Chen; certainly, he himself is quite confident as to its practicability: 'It should on no account be thought that all this is mere pie in the sky, some insubstantial fantasy that can never be realized. It belongs entirely to the realm of the possible, and will begin to become a reality as soon as the proletariat and working people as a whole both recognize it, and begin to act upon it' (p. 196). Certain of its aspects clearly *are* somewhat 'utopian', although there is a sense in which they contribute to the picture of the ultimate goal or 'maximum programme'. Above all, however, it is the absence in the text of any real outline of the minimum programme, of a specific programme of transition to the new state form, which gives the account as a whole its 'utopian' dimension.[21] In view of the high degree of practical detail in which Chen describes the new state form itself, this absence is at once conspicuous and remarkable. An explanation may lie in the following circumstance. In the June 1979 *samizdat* of Chen's work—the only known edition and hence the one from which the present translation has been made—certain parts of the manuscript, notably the whole of (the original) chapter 13, were excised by the unofficial publishing group *April 5th Forum*, apparently (as indicated by Chen in his *Introduction*) for reasons of political caution.[22] It seems eminently probable that this chapter was considered so controversial as to be unpublishable precisely because it specified means and

21. The first three sections of chapter 12 do address certain issues which might fall under the heading of 'minimum programme', but not those more central issues which I subsequently allude to as forming 'the problem of the state'.
22. An editorial note in Issue No. 2 (1980) of 'Lu Ji's' unofficial journal *Theoretical Banner* announced a plan to republish Chen's work in a revised edition which would include certain of the sections deleted in the *April 5th Forum* edition. However, it is not known whether this new edition was ever actually produced. It should also be noted here that in his *Introduction of 1979*, Chen specifies two sections of his original plan for this work which remained uncompleted: 1) a chapter on 'The dual nature of modernized production and the planned economy, and the problem of developing a science of management'; 2) a full discussion of the various philosophical issues which he tentatively raises in the final chapter.

measures by which the proletarian–democratic revolution might actually be implemented—how, for instance the 'second communist party' (which appears fully formed, from nowhere as it were, in chapter 10) is actually to be created and organized; what its social basis is to be; how it is to achieve strategic parity with the existing party, and so forth. Furthermore, what kind of time-scale should we envisage for this transitional process—surely one or several decades, at least? Most likely, *April 5th Forum*'s editorial decision to omit chapter 13 was based upon a perception that, under China's 'cross-roads socialism', apparently idealistic utopias are less threatening to the authorities than nuts-and-bolts proposals for action and organization, no matter how gradualist and incremental the overall perspective within which these are contained.

The quote from Engels with which Chen concludes chapter 12— '. . . and in the place of moribund reality comes a new, viable reality: peacefully if the old has enough intelligence to go to its death without a struggle, forcibly if it resists this necessity'—suggests that chapter 13 might also, or instead, have dealt with the question of precisely how proletarian–democratic revolution is to be carried out in the absence of an enlightened party leadership, willing to embrace the new cause—in the event, that is, of a need for violent confrontation and struggle with the existing authorities. Not having seen the original chapter 13, we can only speculate as to how, in Chen's view, this 'unfolding of violent revolution at a still higher level' (p. 222) would actually proceed. (In certain respects, it would be remarkable if even one as bold as Chen had been intrepid enough to broach such an issue in any detail.)

Chen bases his blueprint for the proletarian–democratic state upon the principle of a tripartite separation of powers. Quoting directly from Montesquieu, he advocates a clear division between the legislative, the executive and the judiciary, and, particularly in the description of upper-level organs of power such as the presidency, he relies heavily on the American governmental model. A number of scattered comments would suggest that it was mainly the Watergate Affair which aroused Chen's interest in the US system. In common with many Chinese, he was deeply impressed by the spectacle of the impeachment and removal from office, by constitutional means, of the supreme leader of the most powerful state in the world. At the same time, however, he shows a sober recognition of the essential nature of the American system. What he admires most about it is not its supposedly broad social-representative qualities, but the way in which, by institutionalizing opposition within the bourgeoisie, it both consolidates and stabilizes the dominance of that ruling class within society as a whole. It is the form, not the content, which attracts Chen, and he posits the possibility of transferring this form—by a process of sublation—to the context of the post-revolutionary state, as a means of consolidating and stabilizing the *proletariat*'s new-found position as ruling class.

In their various writings on the form and organization of the future proletarian state, Marx and Engels tended to oscillate between advocacy of the Paris Commune model ('direct', participatory democracy, fusion of executive and legislative powers, etc.) and of the parliamentary democratic republic (representative democracy, separation of powers, etc.). Detailed scrutiny of Chen's proposed state form reveals only a partially successful attempt on his part to synthesize these two contradictory models. Here, once again, we see him seeking to sustain aspects of Cultural Revolutionary radicalism, while at the same time anticipating the themes of institutionalized representative democracy and separation of powers that were to emerge so forcefully in both official and unofficial thinking from the 3rd Plenum of 1978 onwards.

The basis of the state form is provided by the two separate (but parallel and horizontally-linked) pyramids of representation of the legislative and the executive, each extending from grassroots level to the summit of state power. To the extent that Chen has opted for a separation of legislative and executive, his stress on the value of the Paris Commune model becomes somewhat rhetorical.[23] And yet, although what he proposes is essentially a parliamentary system, it is by no means simply a copy of that found in the West. Rather, it is a multi-layered pyramid of representation through 'people's conferences', with direct election operating from the grassroots (factory and rural councils) to the county level, and indirect election (or a combination of indirect nomination and direct election) operating from levels higher than the county to the level of the supreme legislative organ, the 'National People's Conference'. The multi-tiered structure, the electorate's power to recall and dismiss strictly

---

23. 'The Commune was to be a working, not a parliamentary body, executive and legislative at the same time.' (Marx, *The Civil War in France*).

mandated delegates, the need to reduce the social division of labour, the extensive powers of self-government and self-management given to local and workplace conferences—these are all features drawn by Chen from the Paris Commune model. Overall, his programme for state reform represents a valuable contribution to the extensive left-wing literature on workers councils (from Pannekoek to Gramsci), most of which tends towards syndicalism in its failure to discover the level of the state power.[24]

Particularly in the light of recent official reforms in China, whereby the direct election of people's representatives has been extended to the county level, Chen's 'system of people's conferences' might appear to be little different from the existing system of people's congresses. But it is in the role of the legislature in relation to the power structure as a whole that important differences emerge. As Chen says: 'The people's conference would be, both in name *and in fact*, an organ of legislative power' (p. 175, emphasis added). The central issue here concerns the long-standing claim of the CPC (in common with other ruling communist parties) to exert 'unified leadership' over all spheres of state and society. By contrast with the situation under liberal democracy, the party is supposed to stand separate from the state, and to exercise control over it in all important matters. There thus exists, in effect, a *four*-power separation: party, legislature, executive and judiciary, with the state proper comprising only the latter three instances. The structural ambiguity to which this 'four-power' model gives rise, namely the question of whether it is the party or the legislature which constitutes the ultimate source of power and authority in the land, exists of course only on the level of theory. In practice there has never been any real contest: the party formulates policy and law, and the National People's Congress then ratifies it in rubber-stamp fashion. Indeed, the generalized incidence since 1949 of concurrent holding of party and state posts led to a virtual fusion of the two spheres, with the state being reduced to the mere formal structure through which party policy was expressed. Since 1980, as part of the post-Mao leadership's attempt to re-establish more constitutional forms of government, major reforms have been underway aimed at a separa-

---

24. For an interesting account of workers' council movements in the Eastern Bloc countries, see chapter 7 of Neal Ascherson's *The Polish August*, Harmondsworth, 1981.

32

tion of the functions of party and state. In some Western discussions of this subject, one finds the implicit suggestion that the current redefining of the party's role as one of overall political and ideological guidance, with lessened involvement in day-to-day administrative affairs, means that the party should to all intents and purposes act as the legislature, while the state should assume the role of the executive. This confusion serves merely to highlight the true extent of the structural ambiguity mentioned above. The current reforms may indeed resolve the important problem of personnel overlap, but success here would surely serve to confirm and stabilize the existing four-power configuration, thus preserving the subordinate status of the formal legislature.

This is not to suggest that there is anything inherently unworkable about the four-power structure, or to invest the three-power separation characteristic of liberal democracy with universal and exclusive validity. Taking the most charitable perspective, one could argue that the party's political and ideological guidance involves the exercise of proletarian *hegemony*: an ideological contextualization and delimitation of legislative power, such as occurs in all societies, in order to ensure that legislation and policy-making serves the overall interests and aspirations of the ruling class. While Chen does not express himself specifically in these terms, and has almost certainly never encountered the ideas of Antonio Gramsci, it would seem that this is broadly what he conceives as the essential and indispensable purpose of 'party leadership'.

In line with his 'two-stage' conception of proletarian dictatorship, however, Chen advocates a change from the overt and personalized form of direct party rule to the more institutional and impersonal modality of a written Marxist constitution, for which the party (or rather the 'two' parties) would serve as a mere vehicle of implementation. Again, we perceive the idea of a development and maturation of the post-revolutionary state, implying a shift from *coercive to consensual* means for the exertion of proletarian hegemony. Inevitably, such a shift would involve resolution of the ambiguous four-power model in favour of the more clear-cut 'three-power' model. For despite Chen's opaque and tortuous argument (pp. 165–166), to the effect that the Marxist constitution would itself embody and, so to speak, preserve at a higher level the leading role of the party (a line of argument made necessary by the party's total insistence on obedience to the doctrine of 'unified leadership'), the unavoidable implication is that the party would in practice be entirely divested of its supra-state role and credentials, to be absorbed into the state structure as an integral but subordinate part of the formal legislative machinery. The doctrine of 'unified leadership' is thus, in effect, boldly jettisoned as having outlived its historical usefulness, and a radical solution is advanced to the classic power dilemma of 'existing socialism' arising from the party-state duality.

Now, it should be recognized that this absorption of the party into the state, while resolving the in-built ambiguities of the four-power model, might itself tend to resuscitate the old problem of the party supplanting the state—only this time from inside, as it were. For while single-party participation in elections to the various levels of the state legislative pyramid, with candidates from the same party campaigning on different tickets, is quite conceivable (and would certainly, in the short term, be a more feasible and practicable measure than the introduction of any kind of party pluralism), it would imply a potential for democratic self-reformation on the part of the CPC which Chen's earlier analysis (pp. 110–113: 'The Change in the Communist Party') suggests does not actually exist. *External intervention by the masses* is seen as the only means by which the pernicious evolution of the party subsequent to its assumption of power might be disrupted. However, drawing the lessons from the destructive and anarchic aspects of the Cultural Revolution ex-perience, Chen proposes an institutional framework through which such mass intervention might reasonably be mediated: namely, elec-toral choice between two separate communist parties. Moreover, he identifies certain distinctive features of China's recent political for-mation (some of which appear rather fanciful, while others have a definite ring of truth about them), as revealing an already incipient development towards a two-party system (pp. 171–175). In his *Introduction of 1979* he writes:

'Historical progression towards this, in a pattern of development similar to that followed by the bourgeois party political system, is assured . . . The bourgeoisie had to search over a period of many decades before finding the optimum form for the development of capitalist society. The proletariat, however, by following the principles of Marxism, learning from the lessons of history and grasping its own laws of motion, can accelerate the course of

history and arrive at the optimum form for the development of
socialist society in a comparatively short period of time. *Is the
socialist path really viable, and communism in fact realizable? The
answer to this will depend, precisely, upon our success or otherwise in
achieving a major breakthrough on the question of the form of proletarian
dictatorship, and on the question of party leadership.'*

After affirming the need, in the 'elementary form of proletarian
dictatorship . . . for the implementation of a single-party system
and dictatorship through the concentration of power', Chen
continues:

'Exactly when the transition from lower to higher form will take
place will be determined by the movement of the economy and by
the course of history. As to whether it takes place peacefully or
not—this will depend upon the level of awareness within the
governing communist party. Provided that the power of party
leadership has not fallen into the hands of revisionists . . . and
provided that the party foreswears, once and for all, the disastrous
and interminable internecine conflict which forms the inevitable
outcome of the single-party system and of dictatorship through
the concentration of power, then it will be possible for the transition to be carried out wisely and peacefully.'

And finally:

'There are those who regard the progression from the bourgeois
two- or multi-party system to the proletarian single-party system
as constituting the requisite path to the withering away of political parties. Sadly, however, such is not the case. For historical
development never proceeds in a linear fashion; indeed, it more
often than not moves in an ascending spiral fashion, seeming to
effect self-closure and a return to the old. Hence, from the bourgeois two- or multi-party system to the proletarian single-party
system, and then from the latter to a proletarian two- or multi-
party system—this alone constitutes the truly requisite path
towards the withering away of political parties.'

Significantly, Chen concludes this remarkable passage with the
caveat: *'My humble views on this particular topic are recorded herein for
reference purposes only'.*

For Chen party pluralism would serve, under socialism, a quite
different function than that which it serves under capitalism. In the

latter case, different parties represent different classes or social strata, whereas the distinguishing feature of single-party socialist states has been, precisely, that the party undertakes the task of integrating and harmonizing the divergent interests of all social strata (excluding of course the former exploiters)—a tradition which, having now become an inseparable feature of socialist states, would be sustained under communist-party pluralism. The principal function of the two parties, in Chen's schema, would not be to represent different social bases, but rather to put forward different strategies and policy proposals towards the consensual attainment of common goals, as prescribed in the 'written Marxist constitution'. In other words, the main purpose of the two-party system would be to provide an institutional safeguard for communist opposition.

The whole question of how to handle (indeed, whether even to *allow*) such opposition has proven to be the most divisive and destructive one in the entire history of the international communist movement, and nowhere more so than in the case of China since 1949. By the closing years of the Cultural Revolution decade, when Chen penned the following, the handling of both intra- and extra-party opposition had sunk to a veritable nadir of intolerance and brutality: 'The two-party system would provide a rational form for the containment of . . . contrast and struggle. It would supply the requisite conditions and platform for the public expression, discussion and testing of opinions contrary to those of the ruling party. The written Marxist constitution would, in turn, allow the opinions, views and policies of the ruling party to be integrated, on a correct basis and orientation, with those of the party in opposition' (p. 168). At that time, it would have been perfectly clear to any Chinese with an ounce of political sophistication that there was little chance that the authorities would regard such a proposal as anything other than naked counter-revolution. Moreover, while the party has changed drastically since 1976 in its leadership personnel and overall policy direction, and while a considerable diversity of views is now to be found within its upper ranks, there is no reason to suppose that it has departed so radically from the monolithic tradition as to be now prepared even to consider the notion of an organized extra-party opposition. Chen may be something of a political dreamer, but he certainly possesses this modicum of practical *nous*. But although he did not *expect* the party to accept such a proposal, Chen's pessimistic analysis of the status quo had led him to conclude that such radical reforms as the introduction of party pluralism represented the only alternative to, on the one hand, an unchecked development towards 'revisionism', or, on the other, violent popular revolution as the means of checking that development. And precisely because the alternatives are so dire, the party must be given every encouragement and opportunity to embrace the peaceful option—no matter how radical or 'utopian' it might seem to be, and no matter how great the party's own apparent unwillingness or inability so to do.

Clearly, both in the theory and in the reality which it describes, Chenist 'history' and 'necessity' have at this point entered into a crisis of disjunction, and the 'actuality' posited as their cumulative outcome now threatens to elude us entirely. Democracy—institutionalized opposition and electoral choice—is identified as the indispensable means by which hostile or erroneous political views may be exposed to public scrutiny and debate, and so be peacefully deflected. But the central 'problem of the state', as encountered by the Polish Solidarity movement in December 1981, remains unsolved. How, precisely, is such democracy to be instituted in the first place? Can it ever be possible 'peacefully to disarm' in this way a ruling communist party which has every interest in maintaining the status quo? Few Marxist dissidents from other socialist countries have had much success in attempting to solve this problem of the state, which paradoxically looms even larger in their own societies than in the capitalist world. Here again, we can only regret the absence in Chen's text of any real outline for a minimum programme. Chen, the reconstructed Maoist, does offer us a certain perspective on how the peaceful option might be accomplished, and it is a characteristically voluntarist one.[25] But before considering this perspective on the solution, we must first examine how Chen theorizes the problem.

25. This is not meant in any derogatory sense, as will become apparent in the latter part of this article, where further attention is given to the 'voluntarist-determinist' dilemma which has posed itself so acutely for all those who have sought to make socialist revolution in underdeveloped countries. And, as Stuart Schram points out: 'It is worth recalling . . . that the word "voluntarist" has been extensively used and abused in anti-Chinese polemics by the Soviets, who have conveniently forgotten that it was originally put into circulation 30 years ago by Western scholars to characterize what Lenin did to Marxism.' ('To Utopia and Back: A Cycle in the History of the Chinese Communist Party', *The China Quarterly*, Sep. 1981, p. 429, fn.)

His treatment of this theme, in chapter 11, takes the form of an analysis of the nature and purposes of the proletarian dictatorship; and it is here that he makes perhaps his most significant contribution to the Marxist analysis of the place and role of democracy under socialism. As noted earlier, it was Mao's call to the nation in 1975 to study the theory of proletarian dictatorship which first prompted Chen to embark upon the writing of his book. Chen's views remained unknown, however, and instead it was those of Zhang Chunqiao and Yao Wenyuan—both of 'Gang of Four' fame—which were spread throughout the nation, and became established for a time as orthodoxy.[26] But why, precisely, was a campaign to study the proletarian dictatorship deemed necessary? In Mao's view: 'Lack of clarity on this question will lead to revisionism.' Since approximately 1974, a couple of years after the Lin Biao affair, a noticeably rightward drift in party policy had been underway—in particular, the moves presided over by Premier Zhou Enlai and Deng Xiaoping towards a stress on economic modernization as the main focus of work, the introduction of meritocratic criteria for educational and occupational advancement (as opposed to the former political, or 'virtuocratic' ones[27]), and a de-emphasis upon class struggle. Mao smelled revisionism here, and the articles by Zhang and Yao emerged as secondary representations—how faithful these were to his own thinking on matters we may never know—of Mao's final bid to roll back the tide of de-radicalization. In essence, Zhang and Yao called for *further* radicalization as the means of countering this challenge, and this meant, in the context of the late Cultural Revolution, an intensification of authoritarian dictatorship: tighter ideological controls and harsher suppression of dissidence, a relentless hunt for 'bourgeois' habits amongst ordinary Chinese citizens, vicious personalized attacks on suspected 'capitalist-roaders' within the party, and the creation in effect, of an anomalous situation of *intra*-class struggle whereby worker was pitted against worker, while the overall structural disposition of power within society (that between party and people) remained virtually untouched. Chen also

---

26. See: 'On the Social Basis of the Lin Piao Anti-Party Clique', by Yao Wenyuan, *Peking Review* 7/3/75; and 'On Exercising All-Round Dictatorship Over the Bourgeoisie', by Zhang Chunqiao, *Peking Review* 4/4/75.
27. For a highly interesting analysis of 'virtuocracy', a term originated by Susan Shirk, see her *Competitive Comrades*, University of California Press, 1982.

38

insisted on the need to uphold and consolidate proletarian dictatorship, but his developmental conception of the latter led him towards very different conclusions as to how this might best be achieved.

Evoking once more the theme of synthesis, we might even describe Chen, in this connection, as a 'left-wing de-radicalizer' (to contrast him both with the party ultra-left, and with the rightward-leaning party majority). 'Left-wing'—firstly in that he calls for firm adherence to the 'Marxist theory of the state' (the view that all states are essentially dictatorships whereby the ruling class imposes its will upon the subordinate classes, that the idea of a 'state of the whole people' is thus a contradiction in terms,[28] and that the state will 'wither away' only in tandem with the disappearance of antagonistic classes); secondly, in that he incorporates Mao's idea of a gradual shift in the *object* of dictatorship from 'external' enemies (the big bourgeoisie and the foreign imperialists) to 'internal' ones (those in the party pursuing a revisionist line). But he is at the same time a de-radicalizer, for he entirely repudiates mere intensification of the existing form of dictatorship as a means of dealing with internal enemies, and calls instead for a fundamental and qualitative change in the form itself. In illustrating this project, Chen draws an illuminating parallel between past historical development and the desired transition from 'feudal fascism' to proletarian democracy:

'It is precisely *because* proletarian legality, democracy, dictatorship through the separation of powers, and safeguarding of human rights 'bear a certain resemblance' to their bourgeois counterparts that these things do indeed amount to new and pioneering historical creations! . . . Just as the elementary form of proletarian dictatorship is bound to be somewhat 'similar' to feudal despotism, so, too, the advanced form of proletarian dictatorship is bound to be somewhat 'similar' to the bourgeois democratic republic. Such is the dialectic of history, and so must it be!' (p. 225)

This division of the proletarian dictatorship into two distinct and successive forms and stages follows in direct logic from his dia-

28. In criticizing Khrushchev during the early 1960s for his concept of a 'state of the whole people', CPC ideologists seem completely to have overlooked the fact that it was first introduced by Stalin, who enshrined it in the famous 1936 Soviet Constitution.

chronic conception of the power relationship in crossroads socialist society. The party's fixed monopoly of power—though entirely justified in the initial stage—becomes increasingly dysfunctional and reactionary, and stands in contradiction with the main task of the dictatorship in its 'second stage': the assumption of power by the workers themselves.

Finally, Chen appears as a de-radicalizer in the additional sense that (somewhat selectively relying upon the theoretical prestige of Lenin) he defines the essential characteristic of true proletarian dictatorship as being the creation of 'a new and higher type of the social organization of labour'—rather than, as the 'Gang of Four' held, the ruthless exercise of political force. This feature of the theory has a certain close affinity with current official interpretations of the state form (now once again given the more benign-sounding title of 'people's democratic dictatorship'), and brings Chen firmly into the camp of the economic modernizers.

Further scrutiny of Chen's account of the advanced form of pro-letarian dictatorship soon reveals, however, an apparent contradiction between his identification of the main enemies in the later period as 'internal' (and hence, presumably, more insidious and dangerous than the previous ones), and his prescription of less forcible, more consensual means for the resolution of the ensuing social antagonism. Surely the 'Gang of Four's' authoritarian conception of proletarian dictatorship meshed more easily with the Maoist theory of internal enemies, the 'new class' theory to which Chen also subscribes? His attempt at a synthesis here encompasses both the recognition of a historical need for force and party despotism (by contrast with the Trotskyist thesis of 'tragic betrayal') during the first stage of dictatorship, and a belief in the possibility and rationale of hegemony by consensus and democracy, with the advent of the second stage. For Chen, it is the very fact that the main enemies of the revolution are now located *within* the party, and that the struggle must therefore proceed primarily within the realm of political line and ideology, which renders the overt use of force so outmoded and inapplicable in this later stage. Indeed, the coercive nature of the four main features of the existing state is such, in his view, that the use of force as a means of eliminating internal enemies would serve merely to exacerbate the self-destructive tendencies which the system already displays—the crucial point being, of course, that the aim is not to destroy the system (for then the 'socialist organism' would also be lost), but rather to redeem it, by means of a radical *restructuring* of state power. Once more, we see Chen battling to reconcile key elements of Cultural Revolutionary theory with aspects of the new, and as yet only dimly perceived, 'spirit of the age': institutionalized democracy, consensual social order, and rule by law in place of rule by man.

With this, however, the tension between 'history' and 'necessity' reaches its maximum limit, and the problem of the state swells to a climax. For the laying down of the Word, the establishment of the law, is a supremely voluntarist act, an act of man. Chen now raises his eyes to the saviour. He petitions Mao.

This section of the book—'Considerations on the Failure of Napoleon and the Success of Washington', with its pointed discussion of the moral and political qualities of famous historical figures— is in form very similar to the exhortatory type of essay frequently submitted to the emperor by scholars and government ministers during the dynastic period. Its inspiration, however, derives from the long-standing Chinese Communist stress upon the vital importance of the political quality of individual leaders. For Chen, as for Mao, success in the revolution can still be achieved, even in the face of sizeable reactionary opposition within the party, provided that supreme leadership power remains in the hands of 'true Marxists' rather than revisionists. In what is really an 'Open Letter to Chairman Mao', Chen contrasts the achievements of the two major representatives of the bourgeois revolution in a manner reminiscent of Hannah Arendt's work *On Revolution*. As with the latter, the French Revolution becomes the precursor of the Leninist revolutionary movement, with the Bolsheviks appearing as the natural successors of the Jacobin tradition. By means of this historiographical device (although the comparison is drawn in the most circumspect of language), Napoleon is presented by Chen as a figure whose life and experience contain lessons directly pertinent to the career of Mao: 'How utterly contradictory . . . is it not, that Napoleon, a representative of the bourgeois revolution, should have proceeded in the end to institute a feudal autocratic system and have himself crowned and proclaimed emperor!' (pp. 239–240)

The implication in Chen's subsequent discussion is that Mao, if he wishes to avoid becoming known as China's Napoleon, should take a leaf out of Washington's book, and set about building a stable system of constitutional government and democratic representation—in other words, that he should lend his personal prestige and authority to the cause of proletarian–democratic revolution.[29]

When in May 1976 Chen had completed his book, he dedicated it to Mao, and on two occasions wrote to him expressing the wish that he should read it. Mao, of course, probably never received or read the book. Indeed, one suspects that if he had, the shock might well have advanced the hour of his death, which occurred only four months later. And yet, one also suspects that Mao might have found much with which he could identify in Chen's thinking. In any event, it is highly doubtful whether it would still have been politically feasible for Mao to play the role of China's Washington; the unquestioning loyalty shown to him by the masses in 1966, the unique popular support which had enabled him to set in motion his last great experiment in social engineering—the Cultural Revolution—had diminished steadily in the course of the decade that followed, as the experiment itself went further and further awry.

None of Mao's successors is likely ever to attain the god-like status which he once enjoyed, and which would be an almost necessary credential for anyone aspiring to play the role outlined by Chen. Perhaps the events which followed Mao's death have in any case rendered the role less necessary. Whereas Mao was once hailed as 'the reddest, reddest sun in our hearts', wall-posters in Shanghai in the winter of 1978 proclaimed Deng Xiaoping to be 'the moon in the people's hearts'—a change in popular symbolism expressive of a widespread and deepening desire for change in the whole style and nature of political leadership in China. Despite his final, desperate appeal to the authority of Mao, Chen intimates this tendency. For, in becoming 'Washington', 'Napoleon' would reshape his own role; and in leaving behind a consensual and democratic system of pro-letarian self-government that no longer revolved around a 'red sun', he would have effected a revolutionary synthesis of the antithetical traditions of communist East and capitalist West. In this contradictory picture, where a lingering faith in Mao's essential omnipotence and sagacity is expressed side by side with a growing sense of

29. This theme has itself a certain history in China; a *Liberation Daily* article of 4 July 1944, for example, specifically compared the CPC struggle to that waged by George Washington.

42

betrayed trust and disillusionment as to his actual potential, we
perceive perhaps the tail end, the last dying embers, of the Mao
personality cult. As a final word on the matter, Chen issues the
following dire and poignant warning: 'Truly, he who serves as
supreme leader of the revisionist party and state suffers a wretched
fate indeed: in terms of power, he is but a temporary god; by his own
people, he is viewed as an eternal enemy; in his personal existence, he
is but a prisoner, stripped of all freedom; and in the context of
history, he stands nailed to the pillar of shame, and is condemned
down the ages' (p. 242).

This brief passage may fulfil the additional purpose of preparing
the reader for the singular and probably unfamiliar style in which
Chen's ideas and analysis are couched. It suggests, moreover, a
degree of inappropriateness in applying terms such as 'dissidence'
and 'oppositionism' to his work. Instead, words borrowed from the
religious tradition, words such as 'heterodoxy' or even 'apostasy',
somehow spring to mind. And, insofar as all such thinking arises as a
cognitive reflex against the dominant ideology, his work as a whole
serves as both a clear demonstration and an oblique yet weighty
indictment of the 'monist' worldview which Mao took such great
personal pride in having imposed upon modern Chinese society.
Lastly, applying Chen's own insistence upon a dialectical view of
reality, we may note the presence within that worldview—in unity
with its own opposite—of a pervasive dualism, reflected most
clearly in the historical disparity between the emancipatory project
of Chinese socialism, and the largely coercive political form in which
it has thus far been expressed.[30]

3. The Democracy Movement and the 'Fifth Modernization'

Given the inevitable, a *priori* official rejection of such ideas as party
pluralism, and the complete lack of any indications in China today of
a trend towards violent social revolution, it may appear that Chen
would now regard China as sliding inexorably down the path
towards 'revisionism'. The options facing the nation at the time
when he wrote his book did seem to him to be quite stark and
irreconcilable. However, the political crisis of 1976 was resolved in a

30. More tangibly, perhaps, this inherent dualism is reflected in the 'Manichaean'
cosmology which underlay so much of Cultural Revolution practice.

way that few could have foreseen, and it is clear from Chen's *Introduction of 1979* that the intervening changes caused him to move cautiously towards a less uncompromising assessment of the available options:

'China, whose four great inventions supplied such immense impetus to the progress and civilization of mankind, has an enormous potential to fulfil. Provided the Communique of the Third Plenum is put into effect, and democracy is given genuine legal and institutional form, then an era of emancipated thinking, great blossoming of ideas and far-soaring development must surely now follow. We need only consider the Spring and Autumn period and the era of the Warring States, when the "hundred schools of thought" contended in such splendid fashion, to see that the Chinese have never lacked talent and ability. The Xin Hai Revolution of 1911, led by Sun Yatsen, brought about a faint reappearance in China of such intellectual diversity and contention. Sadly, though, such factors as the frailty of the Chinese bourgeoisie and China's long experience of feudal despotism prevented this faint glimmer from once more becoming a brilliant beacon.'

In common with most other Democracy Movement writers, Chen realized that a new 'reform faction' had emerged within the party since the time of the Cultural Revolution (not to be confused with the 'left-wing reformists' mentioned above). It was implied by some writers that this faction was not entirely coextensive with the Dengist leadership group, and that its real core force comprised a sizeable body of progressive-minded social scientists, party theoreticians, and senior journalists and editorial staff—a high-level but minority stratum dependent for its existence upon patronage by the Deng group. In his *Introduction*, Chen does not draw this particular distinction:

'The awakening of the people is historically inevitable—this much goes without saying. But as for the party, all hope for its regeneration and further growth lies with the older generation of proletarian revolutionaries, they who are alive and holding power at the present moment . . . They are no longer the men they were prior to the Cultural Revolution: they have been tempered by their experience in it, and their affinity with the people has been strengthened. No longer do they see merely the good points of the existing system—bitter personal experience has brought them to a close awareness of its grave disorders as well. They have awoken to the realization that what has been presented as socialism is nothing else than a system of feudal despotism . . . The revolutionary qualities they have begun to display in the aftermath of their escape from the cruelty and repression of Lin Biao and the "Gang of Four", the position which they now occupy and the role which this allows them to perform, all presently provide China with the possibility—indeed the reality—of *peacefully* undergoing the proletarian-democratic revolution.'

However, continues Chen: 'What they most of all require at the present time is support in the realm of theory. And such support will certainly not be forthcoming from our ivory-tower scholars, they who stand aloof and divorced from reality, nor even from our worldly-wise and play-safe heroes. It is destined to come from the people alone.'

What, then, formed the overall ideological content of the Democracy Movement—a movement of 'people's theory' if ever there was one? For reasons of space, it is possible only to give a meagre indication here of the rich diversity and wide span of ideas which it encompassed. This will then be followed by a brief evaluation of the diverse ways in which the movement responded to Chen's radical thesis.

Although the more sober and down-to-earth Marxist current, represented by such journals as *April 5th Forum* and *Peking Spring*, was present from the movement's earliest days in winter 1978–79, this period also saw the emergence of ideological currents which were more directly iconoclastic in nature. Significantly, these also tended to be the most abstracted and divorced from actual realities in China, and ultimately, to offer least in the way of practicable prospects for real change. The *Enlightenment* group, for example, tended to espouse the classic Western liberal concepts of natural law and justice, and the transcendental values of universal brotherhood and equality; relatively little attention was paid to such problems as the dependence of political goals upon economic realities, or the possible disjuncture between formal political equality and actual social inequality. However, the emphasis upon European Enlightment thought seems to have had an authentically inspirational effect upon many of the early participants in the Democracy Movement. Under-lying this response was an increasingly widespread feeling that because of the lack of an independent capitalist phase of development in China, the present struggle for democracy was actually, in large part, a struggle against *feudal* ideology and social remnants; and since the democratic revolution had not been accomplished in proper sequence, it would therefore, one way or another, have to be carried out under conditions of existing socialism. Furthermore, although some of these early currents of thought, such as the ideological mélange of Rousseau, Sun Yatsen and Christianity advocated by the *Thaw* group may now seem a little quaint and exotic, they none-theless played at that time an important psychological role. For such a dramatic widening of the limits of political debate and ideological discourse was in itself a liberation: previously internalized prohibi-tions and notions of heterodoxy began to dissolve, and to lose their force as sources of self-censorship.

The raising of the human rights issue, notably by the *Chinese Human Rights Alliance* in its famous '19-point Declaration' of January 1979, played a similar role; however, the movement as a whole soon proceeded consciously to reject the 'human rights' approach, partly because it saw it as leading in the direction of unnecessary confronta-tion with the authorities, and partly because it wished to elaborate a more sophisticated and historically specific view of the civil liberties question. From the outset, a majority within the movement was more concerned with identifying and eradicating the *structural* sources (political, social or economic) of inequality and oppression in China.

Undoubtedly the trauma of the Cultural Revolution had also generated a widespread 'crisis of confidence' in Marxism itself, and this manifested itself within the Democracy Movement in a twofold way. Firstly, writers such as Wei Jingsheng of the *Exploration* group, adopting a stance of 'political agnosticism', tended to regard the structural sources of inequality and oppression as the product of the whole theory and practice of Marxism. At the same time, however, Wei's conception of political democracy as the 'fifth modernization', and the one upon whose realization the success of the official Four Modernizations[31] programme would depend, became a corner-

31. The 'Four Modernizations' is the term officially used to denote the current programme for the economic development of agriculture, industry, national defence, and science and technology.

stone of all subsequent Democracy Movement thinking. Secondly, even the majority who continued to search for a Marxist analysis of the problem suffered indirectly from this crisis of confidence. It was manifestly incumbent upon them, as upon the official theoretical circles of the CPC, to prove that the problem—particularly during the 'ten years of chaos' of the Cultural Revolution—had originated in a distortion and misapplication of Marxism, rather than in the doctrine itself. For the first few months of its existence, the Marxist wing of the Democracy Movement produced little in the way of independent theoretical analysis of this complex issue. Having once initiated the open condemnation of the Cultural Revolution, it tended to follow closely the subsequent official party line, which maintained a categorical distinction between the 'correct' Marxism which had prevailed until the late 1950s, and the 'erroneous', ultra-left Marxism which had then gained the ascendant. The main distinguishing features of the movement in its early days (apart from its obviously dramatic social form) were the championing of civil liberties and the demands for socialist democracy and legality—the conception of which remained, however, rather vague and nebulous. In a sense, the movement attempted at this time to provide a spur to the moral conscience of the new reforming leadership.

Two major implications flowed from the official party position to which the movement by and large adhered: firstly, that it was necessary to return to more orthodox conceptions of Marxism, and in particular to the primacy of the economic base over the superstructure; secondly, that the Cultural Revolution had essentially been a 'man-made tragedy', resulting from subjective misconceptions on the part of Mao, and from ill-intentioned manipulation of the historical process on the part of Lin Biao and the 'Gang of Four', rather than a necessary outcome of the social and economic dynamic of the preceding period. Subsequently, Democracy Movement writers began to perceive these two implications of official theory to be mutually inconsistent: the stress on a return to orthodoxy seemed to be negated by the almost voluntarist explanation of the Cultural Revolution, by the lack of any *structural* conception of its origins. The publication in mid-1979 of Chen Erjin's book, in which the Cultural Revolution was unequivocally declared to have been an inevitable outcome of the first 17 years of the history of the PRC, prompted a gradual disruption of the convergence between official and unofficial analyses of past events.

However, the departure from the official line on the Cultural Revolution was not made in a uniform direction by the Democracy Movement—several divergent views emerged on the matter, and the earliest of these poured scorn on the notion that the Cultural Revolution had been in any way necessary or inevitable. Indeed, the consensus within the movement remained broadly anti-Cultural Revolution throughout. Wang Xizhe from Canton, for example, in his long essay 'Mao Zedong and the Cultural Revolution', in some ways simply produced a much more extreme version of the official analysis: he argued that Mao's ultra-leftism had consisted in his attempt to accelerate artificially the socialist transformation of the relations of ownership and production, thus overriding the view of Liu Shaoqi and the rest of the party, who considered a further consolidation and prolongation of the semi-capitalist period of New Democracy to be necessary. Wang, striving to recover an orthodox Marxist view of the dependence of politics upon economics, saw the premature curtailment of this latter period as having been deeply inimical to the fostering in China of any consciousness or tradition of democracy. In his view of Mao the man, however, Wang departed drastically from the party line, which condemned the Cultural Revolution as 'erroneous' while maintaining that Mao himself had merely been wrong, rather than ill-intentioned. For Wang, Mao had been 'the greatest Stalinist of them all'—his acknowledged political conviction and integrity notwithstanding; for his purpose in carrying out the Cultural Revolution had simply been to purge all his opponents within the party, so that he would be left free to impose upon China a 'utopian dream of agrarian socialism'.

In fact, Wang wrote 'Mao Zedong and the Cultural Revolution' as a direct rebuttal of a new school of thought within the Democracy Movement, one which both affirmed the basic sincerity and correctness of Mao's militant assault on bureaucratism and the defects of the superstructure during the Cultural Revolution, and insisted upon the continued relevance for China today of this 'valuable thinking of Chairman Mao in his later years'. To a certain extent, however, the hostility shown towards this Chenist theme by Wang and other members of the movement's more orthodox Marxist wing reflected a partial misunderstanding on their part of what Chen and his fellow-thinkers were actually saying.[32] For they were by no means conferring a blanket endorsement upon Mao's Cultural Revolution. The following passage gives us a somewhat clearer indication of the consensus of opinion within this new school of thought:

' . . . Mao Zedong *was*, in the last analysis, a great leader of the proletarian revolution. Following the Soviet Union's shift to bureaucrat-capitalism, he promptly put forward his theory of assault upon the superstructure, mobilized for the Great Proletarian Cultural Revolution, and thereby dealt a shattering blow to the system of bureaucratic despotism which had remained dominant in China for the past several thousand years. Although he failed to solve the problem, and, indeed, left behind a legacy of devastation, he nonetheless succeeded in rearing and tempering a new revolutionary generation, one whose historic mission it is to carry out the proletarian–democratic revolution. His historical achievements will endure for all time'.

Thus, the idea was that the real 'value' of Mao's later thinking had lain not so much in the thinking itself, but rather in the way in which, by stimulating mass-based anti-bureaucratic activity, it had contributed in an indirect yet crucial sense to the formation of a new political generation, one with the capacity and will to devise a truly appropriate and effective strategy for dealing with the superstructural disorders of Chinese socialism. This wing (and in a more general sense the whole) of the Democracy Movement saw itself as the vanguard of the new political generation. However, it by no means shared a unified view as to precisely what that strategy should be; and while the concept of 'proletarian–democratic revolution' appears to have been widely accepted, several distinctive analyses soon emerged. The main participants in this debate either openly acknowledged their fundamental indebtedness to Chen's pioneering work,[33] or else, without comment, simply appropriated certain of

32. There are even indications that 'Jin Jun', to whom Wang specifically addressed his article, was none other than Chen Erjin himself. A full English translation of Wang's article has been published by Plough Publications, Hong Kong (1981).
33. Dong Fang, for example, writes: 'Comrade Chen Erjin, as the one who pioneered the theory of proletarian–democratic revolution, has made a major contribution to the birth of this [Dong's own] theory. My views were developed primarily on the basis of

his distinctive theoretical categories and ideas for use as central elements in their own construction of alternative theories. There was much redefining of, and juggling with, both the various stages of the revolution and their various inter-relationships; but far from sliding into mere abstraction, the debate as a whole succeeded in identifying and shedding light upon several major problems in socialist theory. Significantly, the author of the passage quoted above, a young sales worker in a hardware factory in Hebei Province named Wang Yifeng, writing under the pen-name 'Dong Fang' ('The East')[34], proved to be Chen's most trenchant critic, and we shall therefore focus here upon his ideas. But first we should summarize the general drift of the debate.

The first appraisal of Chen's book was written by Shi Huasheng,[35] a prominent theoretician in the movement, and one of the few who appears to have had any familiarity with contemporary Western Marxist thought. Shi begins by evoking the famous Lenin–Kautsky debate on the timing and content of the Russian Revolution, and makes the pregnant observation that 'the significance of this was extremely complex, and far from being as simple and straight-forward as we have hitherto supposed'. With memories of the Cultural Revolution still fresh in the mind, Kausky's eloquent warn-ings of the danger that proletarian dictatorship in backward Russia might degenerate into a party-bureaucratic dictatorship over the people struck a powerful chord of recognition in several of the participants in the debate, and, perhaps unsurprisingly, the Second International theme of 'economic determinism' proved strongly influential. In a qualified critique of Chen's emphasis upon super-structural change, Shi argued that since the base had in reality only been converted to state (rather than public or social) ownership, Chen's programme might result in the emergence of a form of democracy little different in essence from that of the capitalist

the materials and ideas which he supplied, and it is essential to state this point quite clearly.'

34. This information on the real identity of 'Dong Fang' comes from an article included in Gregor Benton's excellent anthology of Democracy Movement writings: *Wild Lilies, Poisonous Weeds*, London 1982, pp. 102–105. Apparently, Wang Yifeng was only 26 years old at the time of his participation in the debate summarized here.

35. 'Lun women guandian zhi tong yu yi', by Shi Huasheng, *Si. Wu Luntan* No. 11, August, 1979, pp. 39–46. See also 'Zuoqing luxian he wuchanjieji minzhu geming', same author, pub. in *Si.Wu Luntan* No. 12.

world.[36] In Shi's view, the stress should rather be placed upon the creation of a system of worker-management designed to give real content to the workers' formal-juridical ownership of the means of production. This call for further change within the relations of production was extended by other writers, and turned into a primary emphasis upon the development of the productive *forces*. Crucially, this entailed a rejection—outright or otherwise—of Chen's 'bifurcatory' conception of China's present potential, and a resuscitation of the more orthodox Marxist theory of the 'unilinear' succession of historical forms.[37] Correspondingly, Lenin's belated recognition of the need in Russia for a period of state-capitalist development *after* the revolution was cited as powerful proof of the historical inevitability of such a phase in China's development. However, clear differences of view emerged as to China's precise location on this 'unilinear' trajectory. Perhaps the most uncompromising view was set forth, in a highly complex article entitled 'Establish People's Capitalism, and Move Towards Socialism', by Huang Shi (a man intriguingly described in the unofficial press as 'an old Bolshevik', and apparently the object of considerable veneration within the movement).[38] Huang divided the world economy into three distinct and geographically distributed types of capitalist com-

36. As was observed earlier, however, Chen himself insists upon the need for further transformation within the base. In the following passage, written in 1980, he gives us the distillation of his thinking upon the 'twofold nature' of public ownership: 'After completion of the transformation to public ownership of the means of production . . . the wielding of power by private individuals is an unavoidable fact, and one which produces a tug-of-war between the public ownership system on the one hand, and private ownership power on the other: either the public ownership system will, as a consequence of private ownership power, undergo a change in nature and begin to follow the dead-end road of revisionism; or else the public ownership form, being unable to support the content—appropriation of power by private individuals—will generate a new revolution, a revolution for communal power, and will (as China is now about to do) embark upon the bright road towards socialist society.' ('Lu Ji')
37. As Maurice Godelier demonstrates in his path-breaking article of 1964—'The Concept of the "Asiatic Mode of Production" and Marxist Models of Social Evolution' (in *Relations of Production*, David Seddon, ed., CASS 1978)—the 'unilinear' theory, which maintains in *a priori* and ahistorical fashion that social development everywhere either has passed or will pass through the specific series of stages and modes of production characteristics of European development, was mainly Stalin's creation. The Democracy Movement modified this theory at will, and the melting-pot of ideas was such that, paradoxically, its resuscitation led to an interest also in the 'Asiatic mode of production'—a concept which Stalin's 'unilinear' theory was, for mainly political reasons, specifically designed to ban.
38. 'Jianli renmin zibenzhuyi, tongxiang shehuizhuyi', by Huang Shi, *Ren* (Jan. 1981), pp. 37–49.

modity production, the most backward being the planned-economy systems of Russia and China (the 'ossified model of total state monopoly'). In order eventually to reach socialism, he argued, China would first have to emulate the most advanced model of commodity production: the 'petty-governmental' system of free market capitalism found in Japan. Another writer, Zhu Jianbin (a young steel worker from Wuhan, and editor of *Sound of the Bell*), determined China to be an 'intermediate formation' lying somewhere between feudalism, capitalism and socialism. How, he asked, could such an 'unthinkable and ahistorical phenomenon', this 'thing which is neither fish nor fowl', ever have come into existence in the first place? 'In all such countries, the "intermediate formation" arose not as a natural consequence of economic development but as a result of the class which had won victory in the class struggle availing itself, in accordance with its own will, of the counter-active force of the superstructure (primarily, state political power).'[39] Zhu implied that China had paid heavily for this heterodox reliance upon the 'counter-active force of the superstructure': the representatives of the proletariat—the CPC—had for all their fine and sincere intentions merely changed places with the former exploiters, who then joined the proletariat at the bottom of the class ladder where it had remained throughout. As a result, economic development had been arrested at a largely pre-capitalist stage, and the only way forward for China now lay in the implementation of Lenin's state capitalism. In terms of theory, all this would appear to be light-years away from Chen Erjin. Remarkably, though, Zhu's analytical description of present-day Chinese society reproduces, in almost every respect, the distinctive concepts first elaborated by Chen: for example, 'politico-economic unicorporation', and the idea of a new political economy in which members of a bureaucratic ruling class extract profits differentially on the basis of their individual political power. For a theoretical synthesis of the different overall perspectives of Chen and Zhu, we must now turn to the writer Dong Fang.

In a major article of October 1980 entitled 'On Socialist Revolu-

---

39. 'Zhongjian xingtai jiqi fazhan qushi', by Zhu Jianbin, in *Minzhu Zhonghua*, Hong Kong 1982, pp. 439–457. This debate as a whole in many ways resumed (consciously or otherwise), in the clear light of 25 years' subsequent historical experience, a major official debate of the mid-1950s centring upon such issues as the speed and stability of the period of transition to socialism (with terms like 'state capitalism' and 'intermediate stage' being openly discussed), and whether or not to extend and prolong the period of New Democracy.

52

tion—A Special Transition Period', Dong made a convincing
attempt to bring together the formerly dislocated emphases upon
economic development and superstructural change, and to integrate
the apparently divergent formulations of 'state capitalism' and
'proletarian–democratic revolution'.[40] As we observed earlier,
Chen's was a transitional text caught between the political discourse
of the mid-1970s and a newly-emerging worldview which began to
discover its own distinctive means of expression only towards the
end of the decade. For Dong, however, it was necessary to discard
the whole notion of 'revisionism', whether in its Maoist or Chenist
form:[41]

> 'Comrade Chen Erjin's [erroneous] identification of the Soviet
> Union as a "revisionist" country stems from his insufficient
> understanding of the special laws of [this] socialist revolution.
> Like Mao Zedong, he makes the mistake of seeing state owner-
> ship as public ownership, and the intermediate formation as a
> socialist society. Although they both perceived the discrepancy
> between theory and reality, neither were prepared thoroughly to
> repudiate [the theory]; [Chen Erjin] strains the theory still further
> with his introduction of the awkward and erroneous concept
> 'crossroads socialism'. This methodology, of searching for truth
> not in the socio-economic base, and of reaching conclusions after
> only having grasped the existential phenomenon of ideology,
> must now be discarded.'

In Dong's view, because of both the overall lack of development in
the economic base, and the persistence over more than two millenia
of a despotic superstructure such as existed only briefly in the West
during the transition from feudalism to capitalism, the transformation from the old society to socialism in China could only be
accomplished in the course of a 'two-stage special transition period'.
After its initial assumption of power, the proletariat's main task was
to bring into being the requisite material and economic basis for
socialism, and this it could do only by creating and developing state
capitalism. (Confusingly enough, in view of Zhu's definition, Dong

40. 'Lun shehuizhuyi geming—teshu guodu shiqi', by Dong Fang. Article dated 14
Oct 1980, no other details available.
41. By 1980, the Chinese leadership had entirely dropped the use of the term
'revisionism' in the official analysis of the Soviet Union.

terms this early phase of the special transition the 'intermediate stage'.) Only the full development of state capitalism, argued Dong, would make possible that genuine superstructural transformation which was the necessary prerequisite for a qualitative transformation of the economic base (relations of production) and, hence, for the inauguration of socialism. Owing to the continued presence of a despotic superstructure inherited from the old society, this 'second stage' of the special transition would have to involve a second revolution carried out on the basis of the first. Moreover, 'because this [second] revolution has the twofold task of not only abolishing capitalist relations of production, but also abolishing the system of bureaucratic despotism, there emerges a special form of the world communist revolution: proletarian-democratic revolution.'

Thus, while Dong constructs a quite different theory and typology to account for and describe the historical course of the Chinese revolution, he nonetheless arrives at the same conclusion as Chen Erjin as to the nature of its present task. His theory is at once more economically determinist than Chen's (by virtue of the 'state capitalist' emphasis) and more politically radical—for the proposed revolution manifestly confronts, in his schema, a doubly daunting task! We are caught up here in something of a terminological time-warp, a conceptual chaos which is, in my view, directly reflective of profound and unresolved problems and ambiguities in the whole Leninist theoretical project of elaborating a design for socialist revolution in the underdeveloped world. In practice, not the least of these problems has been the fact that while political power, and the superstructure as a whole, *had* to be the dominant factor in the Chinese and Russian revolutions, the relative autonomy which the state thereby acquired proved to have catastrophic implications for political democracy. In the search for a 'fifth modernization', the voluntarist-determinist dilemma poses itself with a vengeance.

Dong's attempt to resolve this problem emerges most clearly in his treatment of the issue of class struggle. His primary contention is that a modified form of class struggle is still appropriate in China today, not because (as Mao held) there emerges under socialism the twofold problem of a 'new bourgeoisie' and the continued dominance of old bourgois ideology, but, precisely because China is *not yet* socialist. He therefore rejects Mao's famous doctrine of the continuance of class struggle throughout the historical period of socialism—a doctrine informing much of Chen Erjin's analysis—as an idealist fallacy rooted in Mao's erroneous assessment of the present nature of Chinese society. On the same grounds, he dispenses with Chen's definition of democracy—'an advanced stage of proletarian dictatorship'. Dong's argument is worth quoting at some length: 'The proletarian-democratic revolution, being a second revolution carried out on the basis of a previous [proletarian] revolution, has as its immediate aim the abolition of the bureaucratic machine. Because of this, the outcome of the revolution will be, not a dictatorship by the proletariat, but rather the total abolition of dictatorship and the implementation of complete democracy.'

But why, precisely, should this be so? Dong explains the matter further:

'The intermediate formation—the result of the first revolution—brings about, through the transformation to state ownership of the means of production, the destruction of the fundamental basis for the production and existence of classes. In train with the gradual creation of a state[-owned] economy, classes in the original sense of the word cease to exist. The new-style exploiting and oppressor class—the bureaucrat class—is entirely the creature of the changeover period between the two stages of the special transition. Rather than calling it a class, it would be more appropriate to describe it as being a big-bureaucrat stratum floating, unsupported, in mid-air. It is quite unlike the monopoly-capitalist class, for it possesses no firm and extensive social basis. Instead, it carries out exploitation and oppression solely by means of its *power* of ownership.[42] Today's bureaucrats, as soon as they lose their power, will become proletarians with nothing to call their own. This is a situation which could never obtain in the case of the proletarian revolution in capitalist countries. Once the revolution has completely smashed the bureaucratic machine, all people will simultaneously become proletarians; they will become classless people. Thus, the process of revolution is one of carrying out dictatorship, while the process of carrying out

42. Dong's term 'power of ownership' (*zhanyou quanli*) appears to apply in broadly the same sense as Chen's term 'private ownership power' (*siyou quan*), as used by him in the passage quoted in footnote 36 above, in which he counterposes juridical right against actual power.

democracy is one of the withering away of democracy.'

The question which seems to underly this passage as a whole may be posed as follows: If, as orthodox Marxism maintains, democracy is a state form and the state itself is an instrument of class domination, then what, if anything, can the idea of 'socialist' or 'proletarian' democracy actually mean? Lenin's answer, and subsequently Mao's too, was in certain respects rather too obvious: democracy would apply among the working people, and dictatorship against the former exploiters would provide a state form guaranteeing the exercise of that democracy. This conception stood in clear contradiction to Lenin's alternative insistence (following Marx) upon the inescapable need for the proletariat to *smash* the existing state machine, instead of simply taking it over and using it for its own purposes. For the proletarian state as thus conceived would in its essential features be little more than a mirror image, the symmetrical inverse, of the bourgeois state, rather than its qualitative repudiation or negation. The Kautskyan theory of 'pure democracy', of freedom predicated upon absence of dictatorship, can rightly be charged with having left unanswered the central problem of political and class power. Equally, however, the Leninist theory of a symbiotic relationship between dictatorship and democracy can well be seen as having served, in the period since the October Revolution, to obscure the emergence of relations of domination quite different from those which the proletarian dictatorship—as originally devised—was meant to express.

Perhaps the most distinctive aspect of the above passage is that 'state capitalism' (synonymous in Dong's view with state ownership) is seen—insofar as it removes the juridical and social basis for the existence of an economic ruling class—as developing not only (as Lenin thought) the material preconditions, but also the *political* preconditions for socialism. Furthermore, insofar as state capitalism generates a 'class struggle' between the workers and the non-class of bureaucrats—a struggle in which the aim of the former is to appropriate that *de facto* power which alone gives the latter its cohesiveness and makes the dictatorial state form still necessary—it is seen as developing the political preconditions for an *abolition of dictatorship* and for the emergence of 'complete' or classless democracy: 'All former products of the private ownership system—classes, dictatorship, political parties, etc.—would entirely and forever disappear as a result of the victory of the proletarian-democratic revolution and the total abolition of the bureaucratic machine. A portion of mankind would inscribe upon its banner: "free communism" (or rather its lower stage, socialism).'

This conception reinstates—albeit within the framework of a quite different series of revolutionary stages—the maximalist definition of democracy which can be found in both Marx's and Lenin's more speculative writings: namely, that 'complete democracy' will arise only in tandem with the withering away of the state; that, in a sense, 'democracy' only becomes possible with the *destruction* of democracy as a state form. While convincing and original in certain respects, however, Dong's conception of democracy has a curiously static, indeterminate and even millenialist quality about it. A primary characteristic of millenialist thinking in general is its attribution, at the level of ideology, of a certain *imminence* to projects whose realization is in fact entirely impossible under prevailing social conditions. Practical politics is rendered largely superfluous, and appeal to the 'moral necessity' of the project serves as spiritual compensation for the actual political impotence of its advocates. Additionally, the more 'purified' the project itself becomes, the more morally necessary does it appear to be, while at the same time the link with reality becomes ever more tenuous. The maximalist definition of socialist democracy—that which depicts it as being in no way coextensive with bourgeois democracy—performs a somewhat similar ideological function.[43]

Dong's claim that the approaching proletarian-democratic revolution will result in the total disappearance of classes, dictatorship and political parties can only, in view of present social and economic realities in China, be regarded as pure wishful thinking. Democracy has all of a sudden become the millenium, and proletarian-democratic revolution the apocalypse which ushers it in. In short, a voluntarist leap has become necessary in order to redeem and radicalize the determinist analysis. By comparison, Chen's programme for a pluralist system of socialist democracy, one which would be contained within a definite state form appropriate to an

43. Significantly, a variant of this definition can be found in official Chinese and Soviet discussions of socialist democracy: the socialist system is declared to be 'one hundred times more democratic than bourgeois democracy' and 'entirely different in nature', etc.

'advanced stage' of proletarian dictatorship, appears as eminently practicable and reasonable. Chen, and Mao, may indeed (as Dong argues) have made false extrapolations on the basis of a mistaken assessment of the nature of present society, but at least they both perceived that the future society would contain, and need to resolve, fundamental conflicts of interest between different groups, strata or classes. As Chen states in his *Reply to a Letter from Dong Fang*: 'Anyone who imagines the future society to be some kind of fabulous paradise has been well and truly fooled.'

Dong had attempted, in effect, to stand Chen 'on his feet': to place both the anti-bureaucratic radicalism and the utopian-visionary element in Chen's thinking upon a more firm and orthodox theoretical basis that fully asserted the primacy of economic factors. In the process, Mao himself was made to undergo a similar postural inversion. However, the resultant theory—which one could perhaps describe as 'radical determinism'—was far from being a complete success. For although the attempts of Dong and the other 'state capitalists' to purge Chen's theory of its more voluntarist aspects did indeed yield very valuable and worthwhile insights, they did not in the end lead to any real *dissolution* of the voluntarist-determinist dilemma, merely to its re-emergence at a more advanced level of theory.

Determinism, it appears, consigns both socialism and democracy to the millenium, while the practice of voluntarism (which in Chinese means 'by will alone') serves to subvert Marxist assumptions as to how history *should* proceed, and results in the emergence of social formations which largely defy conventional Marxist analysis or description. One thing is certain, however, and that is that voluntarism *has* succeeded in producing drastic social, political and economic change in societies throughout the world. To accuse it, as did Zhu Jianbin, of having done so 'in defiance' of 'objective economic laws' seems to be largely meaningless, for the accusation itself calls into question the objective validity of such 'laws'. Even in China today, despite the extensive downplaying of the role of ideology, the return to a more economic-determinist strategy of development (as reflected in the current reforms) has been made as a direct result of the flexing of a particular *political will* by those at the top. In China, the political line still by and large determines everything, and no doubt will continue to do so. Chen Erjin was surely correct in maintaining that the 'system of proletarian democracy' could only be brought into existence by an extraordinarily bold and imaginative act of political will, and that such an act would have, primarily, to be the work of the masses. Neither the development of the economy (vital though that is) nor the democratic reforms now being carried out by the party leadership can substitute for this act. That the horrendous trauma and suffering of the Cultural Revolution should have led—as in the suppression of the Democracy Movement—to a virtual proscription of self-generated forms of mass-based politics in China, is to my mind the most pernicious of all the long-term consequences of the Cultural Revolution, and one which seriously diminishes the prospects for the development in China of a more democratic form of socialism than that which exists in the Soviet Union.

4. Conclusion

When Deng Xiaoping and the new leadership emerged triumphant from the Third Plenum in December 1978, they promised the nation two things: economic modernization and political democratization. It is not an overstatement to say that their entire popular legitimacy depends upon the extent to which they fulfil these two promises.

How should the several years of liberalization and reform ushered in by the Third Plenum now be assessed? Undoubtedly, by comparison with the drabness, sterility and authoritarianism of the early and mid-1970s, this had been a period of great diversification and innovation in the fields of economic strategy, culture and intellectual endeavour. Indeed, efforts within all of these fields have already yielded quite considerable results. Economic liberalization has brought welcome material benefits to the population, and particularly important in this respect has been the shift in emphasis in economic planning away from accumulation and towards consumption. At the same time, certain problems have arisen. The erosion of collective production in the countryside, and the increased role given to market forces in the deployment of labour in both town and country, have led to a marked widening in income differentials between the better and less-well endowed areas and between one family and another, and this may prove to be socially divisive in the extreme. Also, much of the increase in output has been due to the utilization of slack productive capacity. In quantitative terms, the new economic strategy has so far proved most effective, and therefore very popular; but it remains to be seen whether it will continue to deliver the goods in the longer term. Certain of the more qualitative aspects of the economic reforms will be considered shortly.

Much attention has been given in the West (and, of course, in China itself) to what are undoubtedly the very considerable *social* benefits of the recent liberalization. Ordinary citizens now enjoy much greater freedom of choice in terms of material and cultural consumption. The downplaying of politics and ideology—and in particular the ending of the seemingly interminable 'mass campaigns' of the past two decades—has been received with unalloyed relief by the masses themselves. In intellectual life, the activities of the party inquisition have been greatly curtailed, there is far greater diversity in creative literature and in academic and social-scientific writing than ever before, and the new meritocratic criteria in educational and job advancement are widely perceived to be much fairer than the previous political ones. In general, the reduced encroachment by the state upon the sphere of personal privacy has freed millions from a large part of the intense anxiety and insecurity which they experienced as individuals living in Mao's China. People can now cultivate flowers and practise Beethoven sonatas without being denounced by politically vigilant neighbours or having their fingers smashed at public rallies.

It is essential, however, to draw a clear distinction between economic, social, intellectual and cultural liberalization on the one hand, and political liberalization—democracy—on the other.[44] Although the two have been inseparably linked by the party on the levels of theory and propaganda, there is little evidence to support the claim that China is now well on the path towards socialist democracy. *Intra-party* democracy is certainly greater than before, and although the charge can be made that this has been achieved only by the total organizational destruction of the Cultural Revolutionary left (which numbered many millions of party members), the fact remains that such a destruction was probably the main prerequisite

44. This is not, of course, to establish a *wall* between the two spheres: radical intellectual change, in particular, may indeed spill over into politics although such an outcome is by no means inevitable in the present instance.

for any kind of democratization of the party. But the attempts to extend democracy beyond the confines of the party, to transfer some modicum of political decision-making power down to the grass-roots of society, have either been half-heartedly and insincerely made by those at the top, or else have been rendered largely abortive as a result of direct interference by the middle and lower levels of the bureaucracy. The introduction in 1979 of direct elections to local People's Congresses was a step in the right direction, but the short shrift given to genuinely independent candidates is as clear an indicator as any of the character of the elections themselves. Centrally directed attempts ('rectifications)') to weed out corrupt and despotic local cadres who make citizens' lives a misery are paternalistic in conception, and can do little more than scratch the surface of a problem whose real solution requires a transformation of the politically powerless status of those who live and work at the grassroots.

At the factory and work-unit level—the vital social interface between political and economic democracy—the results of current reforms are slightly more encouraging. The labour unions have been urged to play a more independent role in representing the workforce, and, in some experimental instances, new 'workers congresses' have been given the power to elect the factory director, and to ratify or reject overall production plans, and so on. It remains to be seen whether these organs of worker representation will be allowed to act with any significant degree of independence of *de facto* party control. Furthermore, such developments have been accompanied by strict Taylorite management reforms (the 'worker responsibility system'), piece-rate payment, and a marked tightening-up of the technical division of labour. The overall effect has been not merely to raise productivity and economic output, but also to intensify competition between individual workers and to minimize the potential areas within which the workforce is actually *able* to exercise autonomy.

When we come to consider the present position of the Chinese intelligentsia, it is necessary to bear in mind the deeply ambivalent attitude to this layer always held by Mao and the left faction of the CPC. In the early and mid-1950s, their hope had been that the old intelligentsia could be coaxed, by means of persistent 'thought reform', into serving the socialist cause. Subsequently, the extensive opposition to the regime expressed by the intelligentsia during the

'Hundred Flowers' liberalization of 1957 had convinced Mao that the only way forward lay in the creation of an entirely new generation of intellectuals: an 'army of proletarian intellectuals'.[45] In the course of the next two decades, however, virtually all attempts in this direction were in practice marked by a pervasive anti-intellectualism, an attitude of mind which reached its apotheosis during the Cultural Revolution when *all* intellectuals (save the 'worker-peasant-soldier study personnel' inducted into colleges after 1970) were reviled as belonging to a 'stinking ninth category'.[46] Thus, the moves towards a Soviet-style fusion or integration of the political bureaucracy and the intelligentsia-technocracy which had taken place around the time of the 8th Party Congress in 1956 had been thrown violently into reverse. The overthrow of the 'Gang of Four' in 1976 meant, pre-eminently, liberation for the intelligentsia, and it is therefore this section of society which now identifies *most* strongly with the Deng Xiaoping leadership. The doors of the party have been thrown open to it, in a long-delayed 'historic compromise', signalling the progressive formation of a relatively unitary politico-intellectual elite whose purpose it is to serve the needs of the modernization programme[47]. This of course makes it all the more laudable that significant numbers of establishment writers and intellectuals have proven themselves still willing to publish ideas and material which frequently verge upon the dissident. Individual moral conscience is an evergreen quality.

But freedom from persecution nevertheless provided, unsurpris-

45. In China, the term 'intellectual' (*zhishi fenzi*) denotes virtually everyone whose education is that of an upper-middle school graduate or above.
46. The other eight categories in this hierarchy of social undesirables were: former landlords, former rich peasants, counter-revolutionaries, 'bad elements', 'rightists', renegades, spies and 'capitalist-roaders'.
47. The Hungarian dissidents Konrad and Szelenyi, in their *Intellectuals on the Road to Class Power* (1974), advanced the thesis that the social structure of the post-revolutionary state ultimately favours the ascendancy of the intelligentsia over all other strata, and at the expense (primarily) of the working class. One of the fringe participants in the debate on Chen Erjin's book, a young worker from South China named Wang Yifei, reached a similar conclusion in an article of June 1980 entitled 'New Class, New Society' (pub. in *Minzhu Zhonghua*, Hong Kong, 1982). In Wang's view, however, the rise of the intelligentsia marks the birth of a truly socialist society: *knowledge* is the first really 'communist commodity' since it is amenable to distribution on the basis of the principle 'from each according to their ability, to each according to their need'. He rounds off a startling article with the startling rallying-call: 'Intellectuals of the World—Unite!' (*quan shijie zhishizhe lianheqilai!*).

ingly, enough 'democracy' for the Chinese intelligentsia as a whole, and the social basis and dynamic for the unofficial Democracy Movement primarily came from a section of the working class with a high level of political consciousness. The distinctive 'mass-mobilizing' aspects of Maoism—by no means unique to its later and more radical form—have almost certainly been the main historical factor underlying this fundamental point of difference between Chinese and Soviet 'dissidence'. To be sure, as the official media never tired of pointing out, the Democracy Movement never comprised more than a 'tiny minority' of the population. But political history is almost invariably made by minorities—as the success of the Chinese Communist Party itself demonstrates. It goes without saying that for such political minorities to be successful, they have to be socially representative to a greater or lesser degree and to mobilize public opinion in support of their cause. Clearly, though, the political and organizational monopoly exercised by the party served to preclude, in the case of the Democracy Movement, all possibility of further development to the point where such indices of representativeness might actually have become manifest within society. One can therefore only speculate about what the long-term potential of the movement might have been.

In certain respects, the preclusion of this kind of possibility was vital to the success of the party effort. For the Democracy Movement was in the position of attempting, as a minority, to impart its own particular political vision to the members of society, and this brought it into unwilling confrontation with a party which is all too well aware of the power of propaganda in moulding public opinion. This was true despite the considerable convergence between official and unofficial conceptions of the requisite reforms—many of the proposals first raised at Peking's Democracy Wall now form part of official policy. But the real irony and tragedy is that even if the party had been correct in claiming that the Democracy Movement was 'anti-socialist', there would still have been no need for the movement to be silenced and suppressed: for the present leadership group is arguably more stable and secure, and enjoys more support from the population, than any since 1949.

The Democracy Movement was as insistent as the party in demanding economic growth and modernization. No one could seriously dispute the need to transform the conditions of grinding

poverty under which the Chinese masses still live. But the movement, in demanding as well the 'fifth modernization', was saying
something very important. Indeed, the centrality of the 'fifth
modernization' to a genuinely *socialist* programme for economic
development has been obliquely acknowledged by many in the party
leadership. According to the high-ranking official reformer Liao
Gailong, in a major speech of October 1980: 'Democracy is both a
means and an end; it is the means by which we attain political ends,
but at the same time it is itself our final aim. Let me put the question:
Do our people merely want a prosperous life and nothing else? We
also want freedom, we want extensive freedom, we want high-level
democracy.'[48] This, and a slightly earlier speech by Deng Xiaoping,
marked the high-point of the official democratic reform movement.
From the summer of 1980 onwards, it has been increasingly clear
that 'democracy', in the official conception, really means greater
freedom of thought and publication for the intelligentsia, and greater
economic and cultural freedom for the workers and peasants. It does
not mean greater *political* freedom: the structuring and distribution
of power within society has not, in my view at least, been noticeably
altered.

Two main arguments are often advanced, both inside and outside
China, to explain and justify this state of affairs. The first is that
China lacks any historical tradition of democracy, and that considerable time will therefore be needed for democratic ideas to take root.
There is much truth in this, but clearly a start must be made somewhere. After all, neither did China have a tradition of socialist
government until 1949. And as Wang Xizhe pointed out, in an
interview in December 1980: 'The democratic system is not some
lofty and unscalable peak, but something which itself provides a
training ground for acquisition of the necessary skills by the popular
masses. Television, for example, is something which the Chinese do
not understand, but this cannot be made into a pretext for claiming
that we don't need it. We can view the democratic system itself as
being a kind of consumer item, the consumption of which in turn
stimulates a certain need.'[49]

48. See 'Zhong-Gong "Geng Shen Gai Ge" Fang An', *Qishi Niandai* No. 134, March
1981, Hong Kong, p. 39.
49. 'Interview with Wang Xizhe', *New Left Review*, No. 131, January/February 1982,
pp. 65–66.

The second argument is that economic growth and modernization is an absolute priority to which all other goals must (temporarily at least) be subordinated: real democracy would only serve to disrupt 'stability and unity', and so would seriously endanger the modernization programme. Implicit in this argument is the view, shared by many orthodox Marxists, that democracy will 'grow outwards' from the development of the economy, and in particular from the introduction of market forces. To deal with the last point first: one has only to consider the experience of such countries as Brazil, Chile after 1973, or even Hungary to see that there is no necessary connection between economic growth and/or market forces on the one hand, and political democracy on the other, and this is especially true in the underdeveloped world to which China belongs. The argument proper is even more fraught with danger, for it gives insufficient attention to the fact that the modernization process itself has frequently been, to a greater or lesser extent, a brutalizing and alienating experience for populations throughout the under-developed world. Assuming that a 'non-capitalist path to development' is indeed possible, any notion of 'socialist modernization' must surely include the notion of political democracy. Wang Xizhe elucidates this point also: 'Four modernizations won't do, because they only cover the "material" aspect and not the "human" one . . . Material construction can also be achieved under fascism and despotism. The essence of socialism, is *democratization*. Production purely for production's sake . . . gives rise to a new form of alienation.'[50]

Even if one takes the conservative view that China, despite the rhetoric, is simply a 'modernizing' nation like any other, and so discounts the possibility of any recognizably socialist form of modernization, convincing arguments can still be found as to why the imperatives of modernization should not be allowed to overrule all other considerations. The question has been taken up in recent years by no less a body than the UN Commission on Human Rights, where, increasingly, the 'right to development' or economic modernization is legally defined as a 'right of states', and growing recognition is given to the fact that the practical exercise of this right of states may conflict with, or even militate against, the rights of individuals ('human rights'). The new concept of a 'human right to

---

50. This passage comes from the full transcript of the interview edited and published by New Left Review, op. cit.

development', which is gaining currency within such international bodies, has as its underlying rationale the principle that economic modernization and growth must at all times be 'people-centred'. Correspondingly, the concept of human rights has been expanded to include those *political* rights which are necessary for the relationship between state and individual to be suitably mediated during the modernization process: 'Participation of the people in the institutions and systems which govern their lives is a basic human right and also essential for realignment of political power in favour of disadvantaged groups and for their social and economic development.'[51]

Perhaps the strongest argument against the subordination of democracy to economic modernization in China, is that as long as the exercise of political power remains the exclusive prerogative of the party, there exists every danger of an eventual return to some form of authoritarian ultra-leftism. This would be especially likely to happen if the current economic reforms, upon whose success Deng Xiaoping has virtually staked his reputation within the party, were to run into serious difficulty. For the 'democratic-centralist' party functions primarily, in reality, as a machine for implementing the policy preferences of those at the top, and as the post-Mao changes have demonstrated, a high-level transfer of power followed by one or more brisk doses of rectification suffice to convert it to the loyal service of an entirely new policy orientation. To regard its present role in China as one of benignly guarding the economic modernization programme against possible disruption by over-zealous grassroots democrats would be either to miss, or to ignore, this profoundly *structural* dimension of the problem of democracy in China. Should the authoritarian left ever return to power, the second of Deng's promises to the nation—democratization, would be rendered quite worthless.[52]

51. This is part of a declaration enacted as the centrepiece resolution of the FAO-sponsored 'World Conference on Agrarian Reform and Rural Development', Rome 1979, and is taken here from an unpublished paper by James C. N. Paul entitled 'Developing a Human Right to Development'.
52. Such a possibility was graphically depicted in a short story by Su Ming entitled 'A Tragedy Likely to Occur in the Year 2000', published in the unofficial journal *Peking Spring* in May 1979: in 1998 the figure who has led the CPC for the past twenty years (meaning Deng Xiaoping) dies; in September 2000, at the 18th Party Congress, extensive criticism of the late leader and of his 'bourgeois headquarters' is launched; on 1 October, the new leader announces at Tiananmen the all-out restoration of ultra-leftist policies.

During the second half of 1983, a massive campaign of party rectification was launched to remove all residual 'ultra-leftists' from office. This looks set to be the most extensive organizational shake-up within the party since the Cultural Revolution (and possibly even, in a different sense, since 1942). It has been several years in the planning, and coincides both with a major crack-down on organized crime and economic corruption, and with a large-scale ideological drive against 'spiritual pollution'. This latter campaign is designed, in the main, to curb the growing influence of 'bourgeois' life-styles and ways of thinking which have resulted from China's increased contact with the West. For our present purposes, however, perhaps the most significant aspect of these various events is that influential sections of the party and army bureaucracies have apparently demanded a curtailment of 'rightist' tendencies within party ideology as the price for their compliance in the rectification campaign. In practice this has involved the reduction, almost to a whisper, of the criticism of Mao, and public condemnations of one of the most interesting and promising new developments within party ideological circles for many years: a Marxist-humanist debate on 'alienation' and its relevance for present society in China. This is greatly to be regretted, not least because several of the leading participants—high-ranking party ideologists such as Wang Ruoshui, Zhou Yang and Hu Jiwei—are precisely those whom the Democracy Movement regarded as leading members of the 'reform faction': the new force in Chinese politics in which it invested so many of its hopes. And, while this particular round of ideological criticism has not, in the event, been allowed to develop into a full-scale anti-rightist campaign, and the object of party rectification appears to have remained firmly the residual left, the incident as a whole provides a minor intimation of the underlying danger alluded to above.

Those of the Red Guard generation who later, during the Democracy Movement, re-emerged as members of the new 'thinking generation' had had bitter personal experience of the 'feudal fascism' of the Cultural Revolution. Perhaps the most far-reaching conclusions which that experience eventually led them to draw may be summarized as follows: first, that all talk about the 'superiority of the socialist system', if it is not to be mere apologetics, must be substantiated by reference to the real experience of those actually living under that system; and secondly, that despite the subjective good intentions of those who struggled so hard to found the New China, and despite its description as socialist, there is in fact nothing necessarily or immanently socialist about it. The attitude adopted by Chen Erjin, and those who subsequently discussed and developed his theory, was that present Chinese society must be considered and analysed from first principles, as a distinct social formation in its own right, in which elements of socialism might or might not be found to exist.

Particularly important in this respect was the analytical focus upon the discrepancy between form and substance in the relations of ownership, for this allowed a breach in the psychological barrier whereby the juridical existence of public ownership was seen as an immanent safeguard of socialist 'essence'. Chen's rudimentary theory of 'privilege–capital', together with his analytic focus upon the 'commodity nature' of labour-power and its 'absolute and unconditional subordination' within the existing labour process, laid the foundations for a critical materialist analysis of the social relations of production as a whole and of the labour process itself (although this was not in fact accomplished). It also led others to the conclusion that China is a system of state capitalism *potentially* in transition to socialism.

Chen Erjin and his friends may or may not have been right in what they wrote. Particularly in view of the current leadership's injunction to 'seek truth from facts', however, we are entitled to insist upon the absolute moral right of those in the Democracy Movement to pursue their theoretical inquiries to a logical conclusion, and to publish on their own account whatever truths, comforting or otherwise, they themselves may have reached in the course of studying the particular social facts before them. A system of democracy which denies individuals the right to be wrong can only be described as manipulative and disingenuous, and any who try to take it seriously do so at their peril. Certainly, those in the Democracy Movement took a conscious decision to challenge the party's monopoly on truth, and were well aware of the price they might eventually be called upon to pay. Valour of this order is unlikely to be diminished by the experience of prison, however harsh.

In conclusion, let us recall the words of Tan Tianrong, a leading representative and prominent casualty of the short-lived 'Hundred

Flowers Movement' of 1957: 'The fighters who have come to an awareness of historical necessity, and they who are trampled underfoot like leaves, must form themselves into a great army, and must carry out a democracy movement from below. Our heads may fall, and our blood may be spilt, but the will to freedom will remain.'[53] Twenty years were to elapse between then and the founding of Democracy Wall. We must hope that the next wave of unrestrained free expression and bold social analysis will not be so long in coming. When it does, we may well hear from Chen and his comrades again.

53. 'Jiaotiaozhuyi jiqi chanshengde lishi biranxing', in *Minzhu Zhonghua*, Hong Kong 1982, p. 2.

I. History

1
Revisionism

1. A Predatory New System of Exploitation

Today, it has become clear that the social systems of slavery, feudalism and capitalism are not the only systems of oppression and exploitation to have emerged in the course of human history. New historical conditions have given rise to the formation of a new kind of social system, one in which the oppression and exploitation of man by man proceeds in a manner more devious and rapacious, more sinister and diabolical than any previously known. Such, indeed, is the social system presently in force in the Soviet Union and other similar countries — namely, the system of revisionism.

2. The Characteristics of the Revisionist System

i) Ownership by a bureaucrat-monopoly privileged class

This new system of exploitation has evolved from within societies that have already undergone the transformation to public ownership of the means of production. Its primary characteristic is: the conversion of socialist public ownership of the means of production into pseudo-socialist ownership by a new class — the bureaucrat-monopoly privileged class. The means of production and overall wealth of society, nominally publicly owned by the working people and society as a whole, have in reality been converted in their entirety into the private property of this class; indeed, even the workers themselves have become mere instruments in its hands.

ii) Collective monopolization, and ownership in common

Ownership by the bureaucrat-monopoly privileged class appears not in the form of blatant private possession, but rather – concealed and dignified as 'public ownership' – in the form of collective monopoly, and possession by the class in common.

iii) The capitalization of privilege

Such ownership forms an immensely competitive system of capital accumulation, one whereby the bureaucrat-monopoly privileged class – in a fusion, or 'unicorporation',[1] of the political and the economic – draws within itself the twin powers of political leadership and economic control, and imposes a high degree of organization, concentration and monopoly upon the human and material resources of society as a whole. It is an enhanced, *privilegized* form of the private ownership system. For the bourgeoisie pools its capital for investment purposes, and derives profits in proportion to the amount of capital individually invested; exploitation is carried out through the capitalization of the means of production. But the bureaucrat-monopoly privileged class bands together for political purposes, and enriches itself through the sweat and toil of the people in proportion to the amount of *power* individually possessed; exploitation is carried out through the 'privilegization' of the concentration of power demanded by social production under public ownership, and through the subsequent capitalization of privilege.

iv) A cunning unity of means

The conjoint use of deceit and coercion forms the principal means of exploitation under this system of capital accumulation, a system at which even the capitalists themselves gaze in envy and wonderment. Under the signboard of 'socialism', the forces of revisionism bang the gongs and drums of narrow-minded patriotism and nationalism, advertise the ersatz wares of 'goulash' welfarism,[2] using all instruments and means at their disposal to construct an all-encompassing web of deceitful propaganda, and employing the paraphernalia of material incentives and bonuses to further propagate the sweat-and-blood wages system; thus is accomplished the inveiglement of labour. Simultaneously, under the banner of 'proletarian dictatorship', they reinforce the bureaucratic-military machine, pursue terroristic policies of fascist dictatorship, engage in external wars that

distract attention from the domestic scene, intensify general preparations for war, militarize the national economy, and employ such
coercive means as the continual raising of work quotas and production norms and an intensified search for management profits; thus is
labour enslaved, and the last possible ounce .of surplus value
extorted.

v) The sharp antagonism between labour and privilege

The revisionist social system is one whereby labour and privilege,
the working people and the bureaucrat-monopoly privileged class,
are placed in a day-to-day condition of intense mutual contradiction
and antagonism. A perpetual state of tension prevails within the
sphere of human relationships. The working people forfeit all means
of defence, and live in constant fear of falling victim to various forms
of personal and political disaster. They are, indeed, left with nothing
at all: for the entire system of revisionist production is founded upon
the worker being no longer able to sell his labour-power as a commodity, but having rather, like some slave, to submit to complete
domination by the new ruling class. Whereas under the capitalist
system labour-power is a commodity and hence may be freely sold,
under the revisionist system labour-power is reduced in status to
absolute and unconditional subordination. The bearer of labour-
power becomes indeed a mere slave, obliged to obey those in power,
the so-called 'organization', in all matters and all respects. Under
such pretexts as 'the establishment of a powerful, modern, socialist
state' and 'the preparation of an abundant material basis for the
realization of communism', the Soviet revisionist renegade clique
carries out unprecedented exploitation of the working people as a
whole, and, in the name of 'strengthening the dictatorship of the
proletariat', tyrannizes and oppresses them in a most savage and
destructive manner. The products of labour are not owned by the
workers themselves, but rather are appropriated by the real owners
of the means of production — the bureaucrat-monopoly privileged
class.

The cruelty of the latter towards the workers is revealed most
clearly in spiritual and ideological matters, and in matters concerning the basic rights of man. Whereas the slave-owners used to bury
their slaves physically to symbolize their eternal power of dominion,

the bureaucrat-monopoly privileged class buries the human dignity, freedom, sovereignty and creative spirit of the workers to symbolize its absolute power of possession. And, as the final indignity, the bureaucrat-monopoly privileged class also tries to force the working people to regard themselves as *existing* only through the good grace of their rulers, and even 'to recognize and acknowledge the fact that they are *dominated, ruled* and *possessed* as a *privilege from heaven!*'[3] In short: in order that the maximum benefit for the bureaucrat-monopoly privileged class may be secured, the workers are forced, on the one hand, to once again undergo separation *from* the means of production, and on the other to objectify themselves *as* means of production. Placed in the most desperate of plights, stripped of all human rights and security, the worker is thus expropriated anew, and this time to the very core.

vi) Social fascist politics

Politics, under revisionism, is a realm of intrigue and chicanery, an oligarchic, factional underworld dominated by a handful of party-military-financial warlords. It is a world devoid of truth, light or beauty. For the bureaucrat-monopoly privileged class conducts its political activities in much the same way as it pursues economic exploitation; that is, by dual recourse to mendacious propaganda on the one hand and fascist dictatorship on the other. The party is sanctified, the bureaucratic-military machine reinforced, and a policy of terror implemented in order to facilitate the stifling of criticism and the suppression of revolt; the class struggles of former times are highlighted in order to distract attention from those of the present, and the shortcomings of other systems are blown up as a way of prettifying an even worse domestic situation; the ugly revisionist essence is then shaded from view by a screen of socialist verbiage. Oligarchic and fraudulent in nature, this is clearly no more than the standard politics of fascism.

Under the capitalist system, ' . . . for exploitation, veiled by religious and political illusions [the bourgeoisie] has substituted naked, shameless, direct, brutal exploitation.'[4] But under the revisionist system, the reverse is the case. Behind the noble, glowing facade of the 'communist ideal', the bureaucrat-monopoly privileged class replaces the capitalist form of exploitation with one many times worse. However, the more brazenly the bureaucrat-monopoly privileged class attempts to identify the new order – the class enslavement and exploitation of working people by privilege – with the 'struggle for communism', the more contemptible, vile and hateful does that order actually appear in the eyes of the people. As Marx observed of such social phenomena: 'In themselves they are not *worthy of thought*: rather, they are *existences* as despicable as they are despised'.[5] Under revisionism all aspects of society become tinged with a false air of sanctity and virtue; yet still, the foul odour of privilege is everywhere apparent. Violence and mendacity are intrinsic to the system, and the substance of its politics is social fascism.[6]

vii) The grave challenge of periodic political crisis

No amount of fine clothing or attractive make-up can suffice to conceal the filth and blackness at the heart of such barren and reactionary politics. The various factions and cabals within the revisionist ruling clique are locked together in a perpetual state of bitter conflict and power-struggle. Furthermore, revisionist rule sits on a volcano of popular revolution. The subterranean energy unleashed by the irreconcilable and ever-sharpening contradictions within society, and the feelings of opposition and resistance engendered amongst the broad masses, are even now fusing together, and will one day erupt with a mighty force!

Under capitalism, economic crises occur periodically within the system as a result of its inability to resolve fundamental, irreconcilable contradictions within the mode of production. Likewise, the revisionist system too finds itself gravely challenged by the emergence of fundamental contradictions within its own mode of production, which it is similarly powerless to resolve. However, prior to the decisive eruption of a state of general crisis within the system, this challenge finds expression in the periodic occurrence, over an approximately ten year cycle, of major *political* crisis. At its sharpest and most concentrated, such crisis takes the form of a vicious, violent struggle within the highest levels of the ruling echelon over the question of the succession and redistribution of power.

viii) A special type of imperialism

The above comprise the characteristics of revisionism in its domestic political aspect. In its external aspect, the international relations of the revisionist system constitute a special variety of imperialism, namely social imperialism. (To emphasize the contrast with capital imperialism, this might also be termed 'privilege imperialism'.) Monopoly, the fundamental and essential *economic* characteristic of capital imperialism, is something quite intrinsic to the revisionist system. However, whereas monopoly under capital imperialism has its source in the concentration of production arising out of free competition, only emerging once that process of concentration has attained a certain stage of development, under the revisionist system of social imperialism both productive concentration and monopoly are attained directly, through the resources of political power. In the former case, monopoly is based upon the private-ownership system, but monopoly under social imperialism has a different basis. Only with the emergence of the revisionist system can the special *political* characteristic of imperialism – total reaction and the denial of all democracy – attain full expression and embodiment. Internally, ' . . . the yoke of a few monopolists on the rest of the population becomes a hundred times heavier, more burdensome and intolerable',[7] whilst externally, social imperialism not only rivals but actually surpasses the achievements of capital imperialism in those areas of activity most characteristic of the latter, namely the invasion, penetration, carving up, plundering and expansion of the natural resources, markets and colonies of the whole world. Moreover, wherever social imperialism perpetrates such base acts of self-enrichment at the expense of others, it invariably does so in the name of 'socialism' and 'internationalism', or under pretexts such as 'division of labour and mutual economic aid within the great family of socialism' and 'support for national liberation movements'. Clearly, the foreign policy of social imperialism comprises the same judicious combination of force and deception as applies within the field of domestic policy-making. This special variety of imperialism differs from capital imperialism in the following respects:

(a) it is based upon a highly organized, politico-economically 'unicorporate' form of private ownership – ownership by the bureaucrat-monopoly privileged class

(b) it is imperialism which masquerades as socialism

(c) it is thus even more highly monopolistic in nature than capital imperialism, has greater competitive strength, and is more rapacious, deceitful and dangerous.

3. The Present Meaning of Revisionism

As the emergence and characteristics of the revisionist system demonstrate, this is no longer simply 'revisionism' in the original sense in which that phenomenon appeared within the history of the development of Marxism and within the international communist movement.

During the period prior to the seizure of state power by the proletariat, in societies still under the system of private ownership, the split between Marxism and revisionism centred primarily on the issue of the path by which the proletariat would finally seize power. At that time, the concept of revisionism mainly denoted betrayal of the Marxist doctrine of violent revolution—a betrayal consisting also in the repudiation of proletarian dictatorship, advocacy of co-operation between classes and calling off the class struggle, and espousal of the notion that 'the final aim is unimportant, the movement is everything.' The class basis of this revisionism consisted mainly of the broad petty-bourgeois strata existing alongside the proletariat, together with the labour aristocracy and other degenerate turn-coat elements within the ranks of the proletariat accustomed to receiving the scraps and leftovers of the bourgeoisie. In essence, revisionism arose as a consequence both of the super-profits of monopoly capital and of the tactical twists and turns undertaken by the bourgeoisie, and was a trend of thought most damaging to the course of Marxist revolution.

However, the split between Marxism and revisionism which has arisen *since* the proletariat's seizure of state power, within societies under the system of public ownership, has mainly centred upon other issues: such as, how the proletariat is to consolidate its political power, and whether or not it shall, in the final analysis, proceed to the abolition of *all* systems of exploitation. In the present context, therefore, what the concept 'revisionism' mainly denotes is: betrayal of the Marxist doctrine of the state, and betrayal of the fundamental Marxist standpoint regarding the abolition of exploitation in general. Specifically, it consists in the invocation of 'class struggle' against the bourgeois exploitation of former days as a cloak for the perpetration, by the bureaucrat-monopoly privileged class, of oppression and exploitation in the present; the reinforcement under the pretext of 'persisting in violent revolution' of the bureaucratic-military machine; the imposition in the name of 'strengthening proletarian dictatorship' of a dictatorship *over* the proletariat, and out-and-out fascist dictatorship over the working people as a whole; and finally, the authoritative espousal (no longer just through words, but rather by force of the seal of office) of the notion that 'the final aim cannot be achieved, the interest of the bureaucrats is everything'. The social basis of this present-day revisionism lies mainly in the savage, power-holding bureaucrat-monopoly privileged class. In essence, present-day revisionism is the direct product both of the self-interest of this class, and of the internal laws of the mode of production wherein it exerts ownership. As an evolutionary product of societies which have already undergone the transformation to public ownership, it is a political entity which spells death for the cause of Marxist revolution, and leads to the emergence of a new and most predatory system of exploitation.

Struggle against the Soviet Union is thus by no means equivalent to a struggle against revisionism *per se*. Indeed, the surreptitious engenderment of nationalistic thinking forms the precondition for a wholesale perpetration of revisionism. We can therefore only be counted as genuinely and fully struggling against revisionism when we not only oppose the entire revisionist system propagated by Soviet social imperialism, but also strive to eradicate the actual source from which such a system derives.

4. The Parlous Outcome of Revisionism

The emergence of the revisionist system precipitated a grave crisis within marxism, led to a profound disintegration of the international communist movement, and gave rise to widespread feelings of doubt and scepticism concerning the validity of marxism itself. Revisionism arose as a reaction against scientific socialism, and has resulted in socialism sliding downwards once more into the utopia.

2
The Struggle Against Revisionism

1. The Great Significance of the Struggle

The task of struggling against revisionism which confronts us at the present critical conjuncture is one of grave historical significance.[1] History ordains that 'The socialist system will eventually replace the capitalist system; this is an objective law independent of man's will'.[2] Thus, the vain attempt to replace the socialist system with that of revisionism may be regarded as constituting a reaction against the historical process. The need to steadfastly repel this reactionary counter-current, resolutely restore and protect the fundamental principles and purity of Marxism, unflinchingly defend the owner-ship base and communist orientation of socialism, reinstate the subverted dictatorship of the proletariat and avert the descent of mankind as a whole into the dark abyss of enslavement — herein is constituted the great historical significance of the present struggle. It is now the sacred and bounden duty of Marxists everywhere, and of the world-wide army of labour as a whole, to strive boldly and unflinchingly in both theory and practice for total victory in the great struggle against revisionism. This is the primary historical mission of our time.

2. The Theoretical Tasks

'Marxism is not a lifeless dogma, not a completed, readymade, immutable doctrine, but a living guide to action'.[3] Hence, the sig-nificance of Marxist theory lies not in verbal repetition but in actual application. Equally, though, the defence of any theory in the field of

social science invariably requires and entails its own further development — and particularly so with the advent of key stages and links
in the course of historical evolution.

But the cycle of development appears often to return to the
previous point of departure. Only after Marx and Engels had
demonstrated the essence of the capitalist mode of production and
hence the inevitability of capitalism's destruction, only after they
had indicated the historical mission of the proletariat together with
the conditions and nature of its action, did the first form of utopian
socialism change into scientific socialism. Today, in order to bring
about the ascent from the second form of utopian socialism to the
great hall of scientific socialism, anti-revisionist theory must fulfil
the following two tasks:

1) the nature of the mode of production *engendering* the revisionist
system must be revealed; only after the root cause of a disorder has
been diagnosed can an appropriate cure be devised;

2) the conditions, form and route for the achievement of victory in
the struggle against revisionism must be specified.
These are tasks placed upon theory by the advent of a new era, a new
transformation, a new task and a new practice. History has now also
conferred upon us the objective conditions for their fulfilment.

'Without revolutionary theory, there can be no revolutionary
movement'.[4] There is profound truth in this. We must emphasize to
the full the importance of studying and propagating the theoretical
issues involved in the present struggle; for 'The role of vanguard
fighter can be fulfilled only by a party that is guided by the most
advanced theory'.[5]

3. China at the Front-line of the Struggle

The stricken Chinese nation experienced more than a hundred years
of pain and suffering in the course of searching for an answer to its
problems, before discovering the great truth of Marxism in the
aftermath of the salvoes of the October Revolution. The Chinese
people, led and educated by Chairman Mao, arrived at a profound
recognition and understanding of the truth that – given the vast size
of their country and the immense complexity and intensity of its
social contradictions – 'Only socialism can save China'.[6] The painful

historical fact of the turn to revisionism on the part of certain socialist countries (above all, that of the Soviet Union), taught the Chinese people a profound lesson, and provided them with a most clear warning. Both the external factor, in the form of the real threat posed by Soviet-revisionist social imperialism, and the internal one, in the form of the real danger of the ascendancy of revisionism here, made the Chinese people acutely and painfully aware of the pernicious and reactionary nature of revisionism as a political force. The onerous dual task of combating existing revisionism and forestalling its further emergence has thus fallen upon their shoulders.

The great polemic with the Soviet Union, presided over and directed by Chairman Mao, and the Great Proletarian Cultural Revolution, an unprecedented undertaking initiated and led by him, amounted to the turning of the first page in the history of the struggle to oppose the revisionist system and prevent it from enslaving mankind. The overall course of events since the start of the Great Proletarian Cultural Revolution – from the first cries of warning against revisionism, to the ensuing practice aimed at preventing China changing its political colour and the red flag falling to the ground, the repeated process of struggle, criticism and transformation which ran throughout the movement, and the awesome political struggles which accompanied it and became increasingly cut-throat and severe as the movement progressed – all this has made a profound impact upon the minds and lives of the Chinese people. Chairman Mao sounded the warning: 'We must be vigilant against the emergence of revisionism, and especially against the emergence of revisionism within the Central Committee',[7] and henceforth the revolutionary millions began to awaken to this danger. The Great Proletarian Cultural Revolution performed an immensely important role in mobilizing, educating and tempering the Chinese people. It allowed them, through individual participation in the struggle against revisionism, to accumulate concrete political experience and learn concrete political lessons, and it led to the formation of a broad contingent of theoreticians dedicated to the cause of struggle against revisionism. It released the Chinese people to a considerable extent from their general condition of ideological bondage, dispelling their superstitious faith in things and returning them to the path of real experience. The Great Proletarian Cultural Revolution smashed the pack-ice and pointed the way forward, bringing the Chinese proletarian revolution into the front-line of the struggle against revisionism within the international communist movement, and establishing it as the focal point of contemporary socialist revolution. If the May 4th Movement was the prelude to New Democratic Revolution[8] in China, then the Great Proletarian Cultural Revolution may likewise be the prelude to World Proletarian-Democratic Revolution. In all, it has supplied an enormous impetus to the forward march of history. As Hegel once said: 'China awaits and expects a conjoining of certain elements which will induce its most vigorous progress.'[9] That day, it would seem, is finally upon us. China has now shouldered the great and historic task of countering revisionism, and will, provided a genuine Marxist line is followed, go on to perform immense services to the common cause of mankind.

II. Necessity

1. Wherein Lies the Root Cause of the Revisionist System?

Class struggle is, unquestionably, the motive force of historical development. However, if in searching for the root cause of major change within the social system, we were merely to tackle the issue of class struggle then we could not be said to be applying the Marxist, materialist, monistic view of history in a thorough-going way. For we must consider not only the existence and consequences of class struggle, but also such questions as the way in which classes are produced, and why a given epoch produces certain classes and not others. As Engels pointed out: ' . . . Production and, next to production, the exchange of things produced, is the basis of every social order; . . . in every society that has appeared in history, the distribution of wealth and with it the division of society into classes or estates are dependent upon what is produced, how it is produced, and how the products are exchanged. Accordingly, the ultimate causes of all social changes and political revolutions are to be sought, not in men's brains, not in their growing insight into eternal truth and justice, but in changes in the modes of production and exchange. They are to be sought, not in the philosophy, but in the economics of each particular epoch'.[1]

Clearly, the emergence of the revisionist system in societies where public ownership has been established cannot simply be attributed to 'capitalist restoration'. Here, indeed, since the modes of exploitation of revisionism and capitalism are actually quite different, so-called 'capitalist restoration' can be no more than a symbolic figure of speech. It is true that in the period following the completion of the New Democratic Revolution and prior to the establishment of public ownership there did exist a real danger of the restoration and further growth of capitalism. However, the successful establishment of public ownership, the development of social production, and the progress made in terms of general awareness, are all factors which now militate against any simple repetition of the capitalist modes of production and exchange based on private ownership. In fact, the achievements of the revisionist mode of oppression and exploitation already far exceed those of the capitalist mode. Thus, we see that the root cause of the revisionist system lies not in the domestic influence of the vestigial forces of capitalism, nor in the imposition of pressure and encirclement by international capital, although both these factors do indeed perform a certain role. The root cause of its formation is located rather in the internal characteristics of the new mode of production generated by the transformation to public ownership, and in the exacerbation of contradictions among these.

2. Socialist Society at the Crossroads

What then forms the true nature of a society subsequent to its conversion to public ownership? May such a society indeed be characterized as socialist? These questions will be more fully considered and analysed presently; here, suffice it to say that the actual occurrence of a shift to revisionism on the part of the 'socialist' Soviet Union, and the present danger of China itself following suit, both indicate that a society which has undergone the transformation to public ownership is but a society possessed of a twofold-transitional nature. That is to say: while manifesting a transition to socialism, it also (and to a greater extent) manifests a transition towards revisionism. In itself, therefore, such a society cannot really be described as socialist. However, if in deference to custom we must refer to it as such, then for our present purposes we shall coin and employ the more qualified term of 'socialist society at the crossroads'.

To regard the immense contradictions which emerge throughout society at this time, and the attendant disturbances, general unrest and uncertainty, as in some sense 'labour pains' heralding the birth of a genuinely, fully socialist society, would be wrong in two senses: first, because these phenomena express, rather, the protracted agonies of parturition itself, and second, because the birth in question is merely that of the infant socialist society as it emerges from the womb of the old society.

To ensure the survival of 'crossroads socialism' and prevent its possession in infancy by the incubus of revisionism, it is first and foremost necessary to ascertain clearly the nature of the basic contradiction specific to its mode of production.

3. The Basic Contradiction in Crossroads Socialist Society

The capitalist mode of production is characterized by the existence of a fundamental contradiction between the *socialization of production* on the one hand, and *ownership by private individuals* on the other. In the case of crossroads socialist society, the basic contradiction in the mode of production resides in the following: the incompatibility between, on the one hand, *highly organized and politico-economically unicorporate social production under public ownership*,★ and on the other, *coercive monopolization of power by the minority*.

★*Translator's Note:* This lengthy formulation of the first aspect of the basic contradiction (*gaodu zuzhide zheng-jing yitihua gongyouzhi shehuí shengchan*) has in most subsequent instances been abbreviated, in the present edition, to the term '*unicorporate publisocial production*' – its repetition in full being overly burdensome to the English language, and hence disruptive to a proper comprehension of Chen's actual line of argument. The new, shortened coinage should be understood, as the full form suggests, as denoting the following: a form of socialized production which proceeds under a system of public ownership, and is characterized by a fusion, into a single and highly-organized whole, of the formerly distinct spheres of the political and the economic.

4
Unicorporate Publisocial Production

1. The Transformation to Public Ownership of the Means of Production.

The transformation to public ownership was a crucial step forward in the socialist revolution and was accomplished on the direct basis of victory in the New Democratic Revolution. This latter revolution was bourgeois-democratic in nature, the protection of the national bourgeoisie and the distribution of the land amongst individual peasants both falling within its scope. But it was, in the last analysis, a bourgeois-democratic revolution led by the vanguard of the proletariat — the Communist Party. This factor determined that the New Democratic Revolution would be no more than a necessary preparation for socialist revolution. After the victory of the New Democratic Revolution, social production assumed five economic forms. Despite the dominance of the state-run sector of the economy at this time, production based on private ownership continued to contend with state-run enterprises for possession of raw material and markets, and to present, objectively speaking, a relatively powerful competitive force with respect to the state-run sector. At the same time, the flood of capitalism forced the weak petty producers and individual peasants to the brink of bankruptcy and accelerated the growth of the gap between rich and poor — above all in a new process of rural class division. All this prepared the ground for socialist revolution, the latter now becoming a real requirement which the broad masses were both willing and able to accept. Socialist revolution became a necessary outcome of the New Democratic Revolution, and Chairman Mao then placed upon the political agenda the fundamental task of the Marxist proletarian revolutionary movement — the transformation of the means of production to public ownership. Under the leadership of the Chinese Communist Party, assisted by the immense coercive power resources of the state, and spurred forward by the great reserves of popular enthusiams for socialism, China embarked upon the road of collectivization. In a series of stages, from the time of the joint state-private running of enterprise to the establishment of completely state-run enterprise, the means of production were eventually placed entirely under either collective ownership or ownership by the whole people. By 1956, the eighth year after Liberation, China had in the main completed this process of transformation. The main characteristic of the process (and one which distinguishes it from the more developmental process of capitalism, whereby free competition gives rise to concentration and concentration then gives rise to monopoly) was: its imposition, simultaneous with the change-over (through state power) from private to public ownership, of organization, concentration and monopoly throughout the entirety of social production.

2. High-Level Organization and Politico-Economic Unicorporation

Capitalist production is *socialized* production. Socialist production does not entail any destruction of the socialized production created by capitalism; rather, through the dual agency of state power and public ownership, it imposes upon this social production a still greater degree of concentration and monopoly, generates a high level of organization, unites and integrates the powers of political leadership and economic control, and thus leads to the formation of more formidable productive forces than before. In the immediate aftermath of the transformation to public ownership, industry in China underwent a process of concentration and integration culminating in state monopoly. In agriculture too, the development from cooperatives to People's Communes entailed a combining of governmental administration with commune management. The state-monopoly network of financial credit and its mechanism of commercial sale and purchase were extended to every town and village in the country, controlling the arteries of circulation and exchange throughout the economy. And this was not all – for not only was production organized, but also daily life as a whole, and the overall sphere of ideology. The party organization and the various mass and political organizations under its leadership – such as the Communist Youth League, the labour unions, the Women's Federation, residential street committees, the United Front and all kinds of study groups, not to mention the household registration system and the rationing system for grain, cotton cloth and other daily necessities – all of these have penetrated into every inhabited corner of the land, into every workplace and every corner of society. Above all, the engenderment of this form of social production entailed: a drawing together of the entire human and material resources of society into a most tightly organized network, and the exercise of a unicorporate mode of leadership whereby political power proceeded to perform a controlling and managerial function with respect to production, distribution and exchange throughout the national economy. Here, 'political power' signifies in essence the power of the party.

3. The Superiority of the Form

Unicorporate publisocial production, with its high degree of organization, concentration and monopoly, stands as a necessary outcome of historical development and has progressive significance. It has the capacity to mobilize efficiently the resources of society as a whole, to organize the overall wealth of society by establishing the total means of production in society and engaging them within a planned and proportionate process of production. And, of paramount importance, it forms itself as the *socialist organism* of the new society. As long as a Marxist line prevails, and proletarian-democratic revolution – namely, the revolutionary transformation of the superstructure necessitated by previous change within the economic base – is carried out at an appropriate time determined by objective laws of development, then unicorporate publisocial production will retain its socialist character, and provide the basis for an eventual transition to communism. This will require of us: steadfast adherence to the principle of permanent revolution,* faithful obser-

* See Translator's Note, p.201

vance of the sovereign rights, creativity and personal dignity of the worker, eradication of bureaucratic privilege, and restriction and gradual elimination of the old relations of legal right. Lastly, insofar as its inherent capacity to accomplish the liberation of each and every worker is indeed realized, unicorporate publisocial production will itself undergo a process of profound self-redemption, and display a rate of expansion far higher than that of any previous form of production. This is one aspect of the matter; there is, however, a further aspect.

4. The Public-Ownership System itself Displays, at this time, State-Capitalist Attributes

Collective ownership and ownership by the whole people, while negating the overall pattern of private ownership of the means of production, remain nonetheless subject to the form of management characteristic of private ownership. Socialized production under capitalism requires the capitalist to exercise a centralized management function. But in the case of highly organized, unicorporate social production, the manager is at the same time the 'organizer', and the system requires him to exercise his function with a still *higher* degree of power centralization than in capitalist management. Moreover, this management function is, like that of capitalism 'in form . . . purely despotic'.[1] Like capitalist management, the management of production under public ownership is exercised neither by the workers themselves directly, nor even by elected representatives of the workers; rather, it is exercised by professional managerial staff appointed by organs of power over which the people have no control. Thus, the twofold nature of capitalist management persists within social production under public ownership, manifesting itself as: ' . . . not only a special function arising from the nature of the social labour process, and peculiar to that process, but . . . at the same time a function of the exploitation of a social labour process'.[2] The question therefore arises: does the wealth created through social production under public ownership actually *belong* to the working people and to the Marxists; is the *power* of ownership really theirs? While bourgeois right confers 'real control more valuable than official position', the new bureaucratic privilege is such that, 'officials may burn bonfires but commoners may not even light candles'! Bureaucratic privilege expands continuously, seeking an ever-greater position of control over the spheres of production, exchange and (above all) distribution. Numerous remnants of the private-ownership system and of small-scale production have found fresh sanctuary within the new division of labour. Not only is there no prospect of the disappearance either of the commodity system or of the exchange of currency, but on the contrary, through the relationship between state, collective and individual these have become ever more thriving and developed — as the flooding of the market with grain coupons, cotton cloth coupons, and coupons for non-staple foods and items of everyday use serves to illustrate. With this, the black market runs riot, and capitalist commercial speculation is reliably guaranteed. And since management of the planned economy is highly imperfect, it often becomes necessary to carry out, in the name of 'coordination', a form of free adjustment resulting in the persistence of a trading market typically monopoly-capitalist in nature — to say nothing of the free market in agricultural produce. As Lenin pointed out: '. . . Between capitalism and communism there lies a definite transition period' – socialist society – 'which must combine the features and properties of both these forms of social economy.'[3] Within the *socialist organism* of crossroads socialism, therefore, there lies the *stone of state-monopoly capitalism*.

5. A Dualistic Monopolization of Political Power, Extending to the Whole of Social Production

Where capitalist production relies upon adjustment carried out through the market, socialist production relies upon control exercised through political power (in essence, the power of the party). In unicorporate publisocial production, the content of production is laid down politically through the plan, the manner of production is organized under the political leadership, and, in the sphere of exchange, unified allocation occurs under the same political direction. In short, the monopolization of power allows a monopoly to be exerted over all spheres. But just as the public-ownership system itself exhibits a twofold nature (socialist organism and state-capitalist stone), so too does this highly organized unicorporate type of production. That is to say, it may either, under the dominance of the political power, undergo a rapid development along the path of socialism in the direction of communism, or else, again under political direction, relinquish its socialist nature, change orientation, and slide rapidly downwards in the direction of revisionism. For the extension of the political monopoly to all other spheres causes production to become extremely dependent upon power, and induces a condition of allergic response within the reciprocal relationship between economic base and superstructure, such that mere *fluctuations* within the political line cause major *upheavals* throughout social production as a whole. The nature, orientation and efficiency of production are all subject to changes arising from change in the political line. Furthermore, the nature of the political power (determined by the correctness or otherwise of the political line) will at all times in a class- and class-producing society exhibit a certain duality. This duality manifests itself, not in the transfer of homogeneous political power, as entailed in the necessary reselection and replacement of leadership personnel, but rather in the potentiality for an alienation of the essential *nature* of political power. Chairman Mao's repeated warnings to us to maintain vigilance against the possible emergence of revisionism, particularly within the Central Committee, point to this duality most clearly: 'If revisionism were to appear in the Central Committee, what could you do about it? It is quite possible that it will appear, it represents the greatest of dangers.'[4]

6. The Crucial Role Performed by the Division of Labour in the Exercise of Power

As all this demonstrates, political power forms the dominant and controlling resource in the sphere of unicorporate publisocial production. But power requires, as common sense informs us, not merely a specific structure for its embodiment, but also specific people, for its execution and implementation. The more the nature of power becomes dependent upon the ideological and political line, the more crucial becomes the human factor — that is, the question of who participates in fixing and implementing the line. Hence, the question of who wields power and how they wield it decisively influences the orientation, nature and efficiency of social production itself. *The division of labour in the exercise of power thus forms the crux of the course taken by unicorporate publisocial production.*

'The line is the basis, and leadership the key link'. These words have profound meaning and derive from hard experience. A division of labour in the exercise of power made from the standpoint of the revolutionary Marxist line would, without any doubt, impart immense dynamism to the total sphere of production and send it speeding along the socialist path towards communism. Conversely, one made from the standpoint of the counter-revolutionary revisionist line would inevitably generate fear and resistance and induce within the total sphere of production an ever greater inertia, driving it downwards along the path of state-monopoly capitalism and into the bleak depths of revisionism. But the question of the correctness or otherwise of any given division of labour in the exercise of power is decided not only by the nature of the particular line and standpoint adopted; it is decided also by the nature of the particular *ways and means* by which that division is established. The real question in this crucial regard, therefore, is this: *are the working people, the creators of history, to be relied upon to choose their own leaders, or are leaders simply to be forced upon them?*

5
Coercive Monopolization of Power by the Minority

1. The Origin of the Fixed Monopoly of Leadership Power

'In all these movements [the Communists] bring to the front, as the leading question in each, the property question, no matter what its degree of development at the time.'[1] These words from the battle manifesto of Communists fighting for the transformation from traditional private ownership to public ownership. Upon its assumption of power, after leading the country to victory in the New Democratic Revolution, the Communist Party constituted the sole agency capable of promoting the socialist revolution. More-over, that which made possible its assumption of power at this time was the *historical necessity* of capitalism's replacement by socialism. It was precisely by grasping and acting in accordance with this his-torical necessity, in the course of a long period of bitter struggle, bloodshed and sacrifice during which it awakened the consciousness and expressed the interests and aspirations of the masses, that the Communist Party won the people's trust, love and support, and so managed to unite and mobilize their energies and lead them in overthrowing the forces of reaction.

The assumption of political power by the Communist Party was no mere change of dynasty; it was a great revolution that trans-formed the nature of society, the social system, and the direction of historical development. A revolution of this nature found itself confronted by resistance not only from the old ruling classes, but also from the traditional relations and concepts of ownership, and from the sheer force of custom within the old society as a whole. Hence, and most especially at a time prior to the advent of a high-tide in the world-wide socialist revolution, at a time when the revolution had only erupted in partial areas of the globe, the vanguard of the proletariat – the Communist Party – had no alternative but to take power by forcible means. Its mobilization of the broad masses, its use of revolutionary force as a means of smashing reactionary force, demonstrated clearly that 'political power grows out of the barrel of a gun'. Practice had shown that the Communist Party could not possibly obtain political power at that time by any alternative path, and, equally, that 'Without the Communist Party, there would be no New China.' Simultaneous with its accomplishment of the New Democratic Revolution, the Communist Party took the first steps towards accomplishing a fixed monopoly of power.

2. During the First Stage of Socialist Revolution – the Form Assumed by the Development of the Productive Forces

After the conquest of power and the carrying out of land reform, the primary historical task facing the Communist Party was the transformation of the means of production from private to public ownership. In other words, New Democratic Revolution turned into socialist revolution. We refer to this transformation of the economic base as the first stage of the socialist revolution. The Communist Party mobilized, organized and led the people in carrying out this task, and, in the process, imposed a fixed and comprehensive organizational monopoly over all the various levels of state power. This too was a historically necessary development, and formed, as such, an irreproachably progressive act. Indeed, without it, successful completion of the transformation to public ownership would not have been possible. For the new society was at this time confronted with immense political and economic pressure: encirclement by international capital, the danger of aggression and subversion by the imperialist reactionaries, the last-ditch struggles and rabid resistance of the overthrown exploiting classes, and (most of all) the powerful instinctual tendency towards capitalism on the part of a vast sea of petty producers. The Communist Party in power therefore had no alternative but to rely on the iron hand of dictatorship, to back itself with force and create the so-called 'autocracy'. Moreover, the Communist Party at this time stood poised on the brink of an era of flourishing ascendancy and youthful vitality; the glorious prospect of wielding political power and actually implementing its ideals lay before it, and it showed, as yet, no sign or symptom of the deadly process of corruption and fragmentation arising from a position of such power. Now during the period in question, the public ownership base remained unstable, petty production remained strong, and the restoration of capitalist relations of production remained a constant real danger. It was thus not yet possible for proletarian dictatorship to be realized in the form of an enjoyment of democracy by the overwhelming majority of the population. Rather, it had to be embodied through the agency of the Communist Party, and through the political power at its disposal. Given, moreover, an international economic structure characterized by high concentration of capital and unprecedentedly fierce competition, and China's need to confront the economic challenge of imperialism and survive encirclement by international capital, both socialist principle and the national predicament dictated that a progressive, revolutionary concentration and monopoly be built up in order to counter the reactionary, counter-revolutionary concentration and monopoly.

For all these reasons, then, the Communist Party imposed a fixed monopoly of political power, and, what is more, proceeded therewith to monopolize both the power of *management* over social production as a whole and the power of *control* over society's total wealth. This was in complete accord with the development of the productive forces, and with the requirements of socialist revolution in the relations of production. In fact, this fixed monopoly in itself served as the fundamental guarantee for socialist revolution in the economic base, as the expression of the new relations of production. It thus promoted a great expansion in production and an extensive liberation of the social productive forces — and herein lay the reason for the swift and universal improvement in the living standards of the Chinese people around the time of the transformation to public ownership. The Communists who established this fixed monopoly of political power were, of course, only a social minority; but at this time they fully represented the interests, reflected the aspirations and satisfied the demands of the great majority of the people. In their own actions they performed as genuine models of wholehearted service in the interests of the people, and so won the sincere love, esteem and support of the great majority. *At this time*, therefore, during the first stage of socialist revolution, the imposition of a fixed monopoly of power by the minority formed a necessary and rational requirement for social change. Though backed by force, it was not however *coercively* imposed upon society. It represented, not a fetter upon the productive forces, but rather the form assumed by their development.

3. The Transfiguration of Power

Power, however, *corrupts*. From the outset, this fixed monopoly began to exert an extremely corrosive influence upon the minority concerned. As we earlier observed, power originates as a require- ment of the social labour process, as simply the function of conduct- ing and administering the public affairs of society. But the holder of power, in actually exercising such a function, is at the same time given scope to exploit the social labour process. And power not only confers, inevitably, particular interests upon he who holds it, but also in itself provides conditions most favourable to the enhancement and furtherance of those interests. As Engels well said: 'Society gives rise to certain common functions which it cannot dispense with. The persons appointed for this purpose form a new branch of the division of labour *within society*. This gives them particular interests, distinct, too, from the interests of those who empowered them; they make themselves independent of the latter . . . '[2] What the term 'indepen- dent' signifies here is the actuality whereby, in exercising the func- tions and powers of management, the power-holder frees himself from supervision by the broad mass of producers and arrogates particular powers to himself. 'So long as the effective working population were so much occupied with their necessary labour that they had no time left for looking after the common affairs of society . . . the concomitant existence of a special class freed from actual labour to manage these affairs was always necessary; by this means it never failed to saddle the working masses with a greater and greater burden of labour to its own advantage.'[3] '. . . . The ruling class, once in the saddle, has never failed to strengthen its domi- nation at the cost of the working class and to convert its direction of society into exploitation of the masses.'[4] This, to the present day, has been the consistent common attribute of all organs of power. For the very deficiencies which make power necessary, lead also to its inevitable abuse. The need for power creates the peril of power. The power of administering public affairs may become: the privilege of oppressing and exploiting the social public, the labouring majority. Power exhibits, generally speaking, a necessary tendency to swell into privilege.

Clearly, society subsequent to the transformation to public ownership has not only failed to eliminate this necessary general tendency, but has on the contrary actually accentuated it. Unicorporate publisocial production confers a new particular position upon the holder of power, a position which strengthens his particular interests, and raises them to a still higher level. It is this, an immense material force, which causes ordinary power to swell into privilege. In other words, this transformation – whereby the concentrated power function necessary to the publisocial labour process turns into privilege, the capacity to extensively appropriate unpaid labour and exploit the social labour process – is determined, in substance, by none other than the characteristic feature of the crossroads socialist mode of production itself (coercive monopolization of power by the minority, in the context of highly organized unicorporate production under public ownership). In form, this transformation is accomplished through *the system of appointment to office, the hierarchical order, the autonomization of the state organs* and *the sanctification of the party.* A truly alarming level of correspondence between form and substance has now been attained. Consequently, power itself has become intensely, unprecedentedly corrosive. Where previously it corroded with the force of mere vitriol, power now corrodes with all the ferocity of concentrated H_2SO_4—and the minority which coercively monopolizes power has jumped into a vat thereof!

4. The System of Appointment to Office

Throughout history, under the successive despotisms of the slave-owning, landlord and capitalist classes, the system of appointing people to office has been used as a talisman for securing the preservation of the bureaucratic-military machine. For, 'The magistrate could not usurp any illegitimate power, without giving distinction to the creatures with whom he must share it';[5] and what is more, those engaged in toadying and currying favour from others in the pursuit of wealth and office '. . . submit to slavery, that they may in turn enslave others.'[6] To be sure, during the initial stages of social change, before the newly-emergent forces have imposed and con-solidated their rule, the system of official appointment performs a certain positive role. Once rule is consolidated, however, because of the resultant change in contradictions, and as a result of the corrosive nature of power itself, an unmistakable general tendency sets in. The system comes invariably to serve the interests of the exploiters, allowing them to band together for personal gain, engage in corrup-tion and malpractice and perpetrate terror and despotism. For this reason, even the democratic republican parties of the bourgeoisie have long since despised its use. Britain, France, Germany, Japan, Canada, Australia and most notably America have all consigned it to the dungheap, and any evidence of it is preserved purely for purposes of museum display. Naturally, certain offices are still filled by way of appointment in these countries, but this merely represents a form of indirect election operating within the context of a parliamentary system of universal suffrage.

In the words of Chairman Mao: 'Who was it that gave us our power? It was the working class, the poor and lower-middle peasants, the broad mass of working people amounting to more than ninety per cent of the population.'[7] The system of official appoint-ment totally obliterates this point, making the acquisition of power a favour to be received through the patronage of one's superiors, and thanked with one's tears. Those aspiring to high office and a fat salary jostle for position, wag their tails, strive assiduously and in all possible ways to secure the favour of 'the leadership', offering it their unprincipled obedience and submission, and flattering and toadying in the most base and shameful way, in order that they may one day secure the coveted appointment or promotion. And the high bureau-crats themselves, more often than not, are concerned merely with defending their own vested interests, preserving the wealth, fame and honours they already have, and maintaining the stability of the old order. A conservative and reactionary line in political matters means a similarly conservative and reactionary line in matters of personnel selection — the outcome being generalized nepotism and a vast network of running dogs and flunkeys. 'The adherents and dependents of the authorities concerned, if not stupid and ignorant of the impending calamity, must be corrupt and mind no wickedness.'[8] Thus, the power-holding stratum sinks ever deeper into rot, impotence and reaction.

In relations of production whereby power is coercively monopolized by the minority, the system of official appointment results in those in power holding themselves responsible not to the masses under their leadership, but simply to the trappings of office and to the patron who promoted them. It intensifies the conservative and reactionary nature of the political power, reinforces the despotic and imperious rule of the bureaucrats, and fosters an utterly shameless servility. It provokes the degeneration of political morals to a most squalid and contemptible level, induces a state of generalized sectarian warfare within the nexus of political power, and, in the end, leads to a total expropriation of the sovereignty of the workers and broad masses.

In short: the system of official appointment is an obstacle to continuing the revolution, and amounts to a total shackling of the people's democracy!

The system serves as the *political key* unlocking a process whereby proletarian dictatorship degenerates into revisionist, social-fascist dictatorship by the bureaucrat-monopoly privileged class, and socialist public ownership is gradually usurped by that class![9]

'But don't they also hold *elections* under Soviet revisionism?', some will enquire. Indeed; but what sort of elections? The candidates are decided upon internally by 'the leadership', who choose only those whom they desire to see appointed as their own personal 'successors'. The outcome of the election is thus a foregone conclusion. Indeed, the whole thing is a pure farce and deception. The 'electoral conference' functions as a mere voting machine, and the 'electoral process' is just one great puppet-show. In performances of this genre, thêre is no way that a puppet can raise its left hand if, on the contrary, those pulling the strings desire that it should raise its right hand. Such elections are merely, then: for power itself — an exercise in self-appreciation; for the power-holders — a puppet-show aimed at 'securing a phony popular sanction for the political power';[10] and for the people—an out-and-out deception, manipulation, debasement and humiliation of themselves by others. The people's right to vote and their right to stand for election have been flagrantly snatched away!

5. The Hierarchical Order

Whereas the system of official appointment is the talisman which maintains the bureaucratic-military machine, that which actually symbolizes this machine is its hierarchical structure. 'In the earlier epochs of history, we find almost everywhere a complicated arrangement of society into various orders, a manifold gradation of social rank'.[11] The collusion between the hierarchical order and the system of appointment to office is such that the political power of the state comes to be vested in a stratum of people who, in the course of their upward climb on the promotion ladder, have been seriously contaminated by bureaucratism – 'a trained caste – state parasites, richly paid sycophants and sinecurists in the higher posts'.[12]

Oppressors and exploiters have always, throughout history, used the hierarchical order as a means of imposing their own pyramid of rule upon society. The only factors valued under such a structure are seniority, age, rank, status and family influence. The hierarchical order is eminently suited to the purposes of the reactionary ruling classes, as regards both their general conservatism, and their need to enslave the people. The only kind of leadership it is capable of mustering is that by decrepit and senescent half-wits; all sense of revolutionary creativity is stifled, and any evidence of youthful vitality, enthusiasm, flexibility or sensitivity is interpreted as a sign of weakness! Times may change and situations may alter, but the hierarchical order allows for no real change of leadership to occur; it is dominated by the representatives of a single era and embodies the rule of one generation over the subsequent generation. Indeed, so far above them are the rulers placed in this order that the people must gaze far upwards in order to discern even the soles of their masters' feet.

Crossroads socialism, far from having brought about the destruction of this utterly inequitable hierarchical order, has on the contrary brought about, by artificial means, its further intensification and elaboration, and has caused it to become more profoundly ossified than was the case even in bourgeois society. The hierarchy in cross-roads socialist society is no ordinary one — it is densely and rigidly constructed. The hierarchical arrangement of persons exists not merely on the political level – as for example in the scale of more than twenty grades for political cadres – but also on the economic level, with more than eight grades within the single category of 'worker'. Furthermore, this is not simply a question of a hierarchical distinction in wages, but also of a hierarchical distinction in the real value of money. A meal which could scarcely be bought by working people for as much as twenty *yuan* may be written off on expense account or paid for with a mere twenty *fen* by certain individuals.[13] Again, the cost of the same one-pound piece of meat will vary, depending upon whether one is paying the price set by the state or that set by the black market. That differences in social status should generate a hierarchical discrepancy of this order even in the purchasing power of money is truly remarkable. Yet even this pales in significance compared to the quite intolerable state of affairs whereby hierarchical divisions are applied also within the sphere of knowledge, news, and cultural and spiritual life. Access to certain books, documents, films and news-items is made available only to specific levels of the hierarchy, while those at other levels are excluded from viewing, reading, assimilating, or even knowing of the existence of such material. Little wonder, therefore, that in such an order people concern themselves solely with the scramble for power, position and profit. In the context of unicorporate publisocial production, the use of the hierarchy as a means of consolidating relations of production whereby power is coercively monopolized by the minority amounts to a restoration of private ownership in disguised form, and to a clear and unequivocal re-differentiation of classes.

The art of leadership in the hierarchical order does not require creativity, merely a witless facility for straight-forward, mechanical transmission. Talent is not called for, just servility. A member of the leadership may be nothing more than an incompetent, know-nothing charlatan devoid of the slightest enthusiasm either for his work or for the revolution as a whole, and yet he will still be able – by virtue of the 'secret' documents disseminated down to his particular level of the hierarchy, and through privileged access to speeches by and information about the members of the ruling clique – to put himself forward as a 'real somebody'. The 'reports' which he delivers with so much gusto and animation before his assembled underlings invariably amount to little more than the regurgitated drivel of his own superiors, and betray not a glimmer of ideological originality or creativity on the part of the speaker himself — indeed, this absence forms a prerequisite for the job. Alternatively, he may simply, without acknowledgement or compensation, exploit the labour of others by reading out in mindless and pompous fashion a script written on his behalf by some secretary or subordinate. The hierarchical order does not require the presence of either ability or integrity on the part of those engaged in politics, and talent is attacked and suppressed right across the board.

The hierarchical order hatches forth the class of bureaucrats, hastens the corruption and moral degeneration of those in power, and deepens the sense of estrangement and antagonism between the power-holders and the great mass of the people. It places the working people at the lowest level of the social pyramid, where it is their lot to endure exploitation, oppression and manipulation.

In short: the hierarchical order is a catalyst promoting an ever greater degree of confusion and corruption within the sphere of bureaucratic politics, and weighs down upon the people's democracy like a great boulder!

The hierarchical order provides the *political mainstay* of the process whereby proletarian dictatorship degenerates into revisionist, social-fascist dictatorship by the bureaucrat-monopoly privileged class, and socialist public ownership is usurped by that class!

6. The Autonomization of the State Organs

The coordination between the system of appointment and the hierarchical order allows the organs of the state to acquire complete autonomy. This autonomization of the state organs means: a situation in which the people are left without the right, the means, or the power to exercise supervision over the power-holders, and the latter are left entirely free to indulge in the issuing of orders and decrees on the basis of their own interests, will and aspirations. It allows those in power to suppress and expropriate the sovereignty of the people, and gives them the necessary material resources and organizational wherewithal to persecute and wreak vengeance upon any who dare criticize them. The working people are able neither to elect the functionaries of the state organs, nor to dismiss and replace them, and have no right of access to the actual workings of the administration. The mass of producers are powerless even to participate in, let alone control, the various processes of discussion, investigation

and decision-making on matters directly relating to production —
for example, the formulation of production costs, the state of financial income and expenditure and the circulation of money within the
production process, and (above all) the use of production profits and
the distribution of the produce. Instead, the organs of the state
dispose of that which has been produced exactly as they see fit, while
those who have actually done the producing are expected not to
concern themselves with such matters.

In any case, the producers are in no position to do so even if they
try. As Marx said: 'The capital-relation presupposes a complete
separation between the workers and the ownership of the conditions
for the realization of their labour . . . The process, therefore, which
creates the capital-relation can be nothing other than the process
which divorces the worker from the ownership of the conditions of
his own labour; it is a process which operates two transformations,
whereby the social means of subsistence and production are turned
into capital, and the immediate producers are turned into wage-
labourers. So-called primitive accumulation, therefore, is nothing
else than the historical process of divorcing the producer from the
means of production'.[14] Quite clearly, the process whereby, in unicorporate publisocial production, the minority coercively monopolizes power and effects an autonomization of the state organs, constitutes none other than a new kind of primitive accumulation of
capital, one proceeding under the revisionist ownership-system of
the bureaucrat-monopoly privileged class: a process, that is to say, of
the *primitive accumulation of privilege-capital*.

Capital, under capitalism, is money which generates more
money; but under crossroads socialism, such money-capital transforms itself into privilege-capital. Now, the primitive accumulation
of money-capital, while separating the producer from the means of
production, at the same time also turned him into a free worker. But
the primitive accumulation of privilege-capital, in separating the
worker from his proprietary rights over the conditions of work,
reduces him to the status of a 'talking tool', and consigns him
directly to the category of means of production *per se*. Hence, the
autonomization of the state organs causes '. . . the state political
power, in pursuit of its own particular interest, to become the master
rather than the servant of society.'[15] Herein lies the crux of the
process of autonomization: it transforms the organs of state, whose

proper role is one of serving the people, into a bureaucratic-military machinery of rule located high above them. Thus, the bureaucrat class acquires the freedom wantonly to usurp the people's wealth and vital energies!

In short: the autonomization of the state organs gives sanctuary to vermin who render the socialist economy no longer worthy of the name, and places a straitjacket upon the people's democracy!

The autonomization of the state organs forms the *political bastion* for the process whereby proletarian dictatorship degenerates into revisionist, social-fascist dictatorship by the bureaucrat-monopoly privileged class, and socialist public ownership is usurped by that class!

7. The Sanctification of the Party

The factor which causes the system of appointment, the hierarchical order and the autonomization of the state organs to develop in such a pernicious direction is: the sanctification of the party. What this term signifies is a situation whereby the people are expected to prostrate themselves in adulation before the party as if it were some kind of buddha or god. First of all, it is the party leader who is canonized and idolized, and then eventually each level and each individual member of the party organization. Opposition towards individual members, work-groups, committees or branch organizations of the party is regarded as representing opposition towards the party as a whole: 'Since I have been sent by the party, to oppose me is to oppose the party'; 'It is anti-party, anti-socialist and counter-revolutionary to voice criticisms of the party leader'; and so forth. The sanctification of the party means the prohibition of any opinion expressing even slight dissent – let alone outright opposition – towards the viewpoints, policies and practices of the party. One is obliged to show the party respect, gratitude, deference and obedience at all times. Minor infringement of this precept is stamped upon and earns imprisonment for the perpetrator, while major infringement is treated as unpardonable wickedness meriting not merely the execution of the perpetrator, but also the wreaking of vengeance upon relatives and friends, and even upon later generations of his descendants.

Most assuredly, however, the party is not made up of gods or buddhas sent down to us from paradise, but, on the contrary, of real live people, people who need food and clothing, people capable of both action and change. Real live people such as this are contained within classes, their class nature being determined by their economic position and, moreover, liable to change in accordance with any change in the latter; it is certainly not something acquired in the mother's womb, and it is certainly not immutable either. Generally speaking, people are at their most revolutionary when they do not have enough food to fill their bellies or enough clothes to keep themselves warm, when their very existence is insecure; once life begins to treat them more favourably, and they feel snug and well-fed, they become somewhat less revolutionary; and once they have attained high status and prosperity and got hold of certain privileges, they most often become still less so.

The sanctification of the party, however, denies the people the right to take an objective attitude towards such change and development. And further, for it not only precludes the adoption of an objective view of the party by the people, but also prevents the party from taking an objective look at its own situation.

But as the words of Rousseau reveal, the phenomenon of sanctification is nothing new; historically speaking, it has long been with us: '. . . the frightful maxims of those accursed and barbarous men, of whom history furnishes us with more than one example; who, in order to support the pretended rights of God, that is to say their own interests, have been so much the less greedy of human blood, as they were more hopeful their own in particular would be always respected.'[16]

The sanctification of the party is no more than a repeat performance of that cunning old trick whereby the church clergy used to promise the people eternal happiness in heaven while proceeding to deprive them of happiness in the present. So thoroughly anti-Marxist is the process as a whole, that Marxism itself is turned into a sterile new religion, and the party of revolution is transformed into a new and savagely corrupt clerical fraternity.

The revolutionary character of the Communist Party becomes so gravely undermined by the latter's own self-image of 'innate genius', and by the rest of the metaphysical clap-trap perpetrated through the sanctificatory process, that the party ends up being communist in name alone. In reality, it turns into a party of slave-driving, paternalistic bureaucrats, a 'tiger whose backside no-one dare slap', a revisionist, fascist party of tyranny, deception and counter-revolution. Such sanctification serves to accelerate the destruction wrought upon the revolutionary character of the party by the corrosive force of the system of official appointment, the hierarchical order and the autonomization of the state organs.

In short: the sanctification of the party lies at the very root of the party's eventual shift to revisionism and the nation's change of political colour, and is an ideological monstrosity engulfing the forces of people's democracy!

The sanctification of the party is the *political foundation* of the process whereby proletarian dictatorship degenerates into revisionist social-fascist dictatorship by the bureaucrat-monopoly privileged class, and socialist public ownership is usurped by that class!

Taken as a whole, the above four factors account for the immensely and peculiarly corrosive nature of the coercive monopolization of power which occurs within socialist society at the crossroads. And quite evidently, the object of this intensely corrosive combination of forces is none other than that minority which plays about, in a 'unified but unrestricted style', with the greater political and economic powers now concentrated in its own person, that minority which has already 'jumped into the acid' — namely, the Communist Party in government.

8. With the Advent of the Second Stage of Socialist Revolution – A Fetter upon the Productive Forces

'In no sphere can one undergo a development without negating one's previous mode of existence'.[17] The authority of the dialectic asserts itself throughout. Boldly and unexpectedly, the dialectic plunges even that which is considered 'sacred' into a process of ceaseless flux and development. So intrepidly, indeed, that: 'For it, nothing is final, absolute, sacred. It reveals the transitory character of everything and in everything; nothing can endure before it except the uninterrupted process of becoming and of passing away, of endless ascendancy from the lower to the higher'.[18] In sum: coercive monopolization of power by the minority – accomplished via the four factors described – forms, in the context of publisocial production, a superstructure in disharmony with the socialist economic base. If left to the tender mercies of this governing superstructure, the socialist revolution will inevitably exhaust itself in mid-course. For ultimately, such a superstructure comes to exert upon the public-ownership base a reaction so pernicious as to begin to transform its very nature.

Thereupon is inaugurated the second stage of socialist revolution. During this stage, that necessary fixed monopoly of power which had hitherto been the form assumed by the development of the productive forces now becomes their fetter, a reactionary superstructure inhibiting further social change. Once a rational requirement of social change, it turns into an obstructive force coercively imposed upon society, and blocks the course of social revolution. This transformation operates in accordance with certain laws, and likewise represents a developmental necessity.

'The facts are before us, indisputable and incontrovertible.'[19] This proposition, that coercive monopolization of power by the minority imposes, during the second stage of socialist revolution, a fetter upon the productive forces, will be further substantiated in the following chapters.

6
The Rise of the Bureaucrat-Monopoly Privileged Class

1. Change In the Communist Party

(i) The drug takers

The Communist Party has undergone, as described above, a change in its position. Having rebelled against the former state it has become the ruler over the new. Once persecuted and suppressed by political power, it now becomes simultaneously protected and corroded by that power. The crossroads socialist mode of production – unicorporate publisocial production, and coercive monopolization of power by the minority – operates in such a way that the Communist Party in government finds itself not only in possession of an immense power of dominion over society, but also under threat of external attack and internal corrosion by the combined forces of evil, new and old, of the society as a whole. Its own particular position and vested interest in the fixed monopoly of power immerses the Communist Party in the intensely corrosive combination of the system of official appointment, the hierarchical order, the autonomization of the state organs and the sanctification of the party. This situation leads, inevitably, to 'perhaps even a considerable majority' of those who are in such a position and who have such an interest being struck down by 'sugar-coated bullets'. And, most serious of all, these latter issue not so much from the enemy as from within the party's own ranks; they arrive not as a gift from others, but in consequence of the party's own requirements. All in all, the Communist Party's change in status exposes it to the danger of suffering a fate similar to that of a poor but vigorous young lad, who, after growing up to become a man of wealth and means, falls foul of the opium habit and is destroyed by it.

(ii) The stepping stone to success

A miasma of careerism envelops the party. Under the circumstances described, the conditions necessary for an independent existence on the part of capital cease to exist. Henceforth, it is only as an appendage to privilege, and through privilege, that capital is able to reproduce itself. In other words, the form of capital changes from that of money-capital to that of privilege-capital. In private-ownership society, capital is money capable of generating more money. In public-ownership society, however, capital takes the form of privilege — a function able to derive large amounts of money from zero expenditure. In unicorporate publisocial production, the extension of the political monopoly to all other spheres means that all the blood-sucking vermin in society have to strive to the utmost to worm their way into the ranks of the party. Because of the party's fixed monopoly of power, it is impossible to hold official position or exercise authority without having first acquired party membership. For all the various opportunist elements and parasitical careerists in society, therefore, party membership comes to represent the stepping stone towards official position, wealth and fame. Slavishly supporting and noisily eulogizing the party, pandering to the tastes of their local party organization and decking themselves out in a variety of suitable garbs, they crowd into the Communist Party in droves. Confronted by this, an enraged Lenin once bluntly declared: 'Now that the party has secured victory, we should say that we do not require any new party members. We are perfectly clear about the fact that as capitalist society becomes increasingly undermined, many bad elements are bound to attempt to worm their way into the party.'[1]

Once the bitter and arduous revolution in which party members had to risk their very lives in the struggle for truth and light has passed into history, and the party has established itself in a stable and long-term position of government, it is perhaps unsurprising that it should become enveloped in this miasma of careerism. Indeed, '. . . It was absolutely inevitable that adventurers and other pernicious elements should hitch themselves to the ruling party.'[2] The trouble is, 'birds of a feather flock together', and, once into the party, 'those who are only "out for" the benefits accruing to membership of a government party and do not want to bear the burden of devoted work on behalf of communism'[3] then proceed, in accordance with their own interests, to seek out and cultivate further 'new comrades' for admission to the party. Co-option and infiltration can then no longer be checked, while '. . . the genuinely enlightened, those who can be totally relied upon to spurn flattery and remain true to their own consciences',[4] namely the progressive elements willing to work selflessly for the cause of communism, are more often than not denied admission to the party. As a result, the danger arises of the party in government becoming a veritable sink of iniquity, and undergoing a quantitative change which in turn produces qualitative change.

iii) The cancer cell

'Capitalist-roaders' denotes the emergence of a power-holding faction taking the revisionist road.[5] The danger referred to above, stemming from a mutual interaction of internal and external factors, no longer represents merely a 'possible eventuality'; it has now become a 'real existence'. The appearance within the party of a power-holding faction taking the 'capitalist road' is proof of this. Actually, though, the road taken by these so-called 'capitalist-roaders' is not really that of capitalism, but that of revisionism. To ascertain the truth of this, one need only look at the refusal of these 'capitalist-roaders' to allow peasants to clear a modicum of uncultivated land for themselves, or workers to produce privately a few items beyond the norms of the production plan; or at the much-vaunted sense of 'bitter suffering and deep hatred' with which they mobilize and organize the masses to struggle against the children and grand-children of former capitalists, landlords and rich peasants. Above all, one need only observe how completely dependent upon and inextricably bound up with privilege are the new methods by which these 'capitalist-roaders' proceed to oppress and exploit, scheme for private gain, subvert the sphere of public ownership and engage in bribery, corruption, theft and speculation. This shows plainly that the road they are taking is not in fact that of capitalism, but that of out-and-out revisionism. What they are endeavouring to do is, not to drag publisocial production backwards to capitalism and private ownership, but quite the opposite. Imposing through politico-economic unicorporation a high degree of organization and concentration upon production, and permanently hegemonizing the power of leadership and bequeathing it to their own descendants, they steer society towards revisionism. From the outset, this power-holding faction taking the revisionist road displays, in its unrivalled avarice and hypocrisy, the intrinsic characteristics of the bureaucrat-monopoly privileged class. Having once experienced the taste of human flesh it can be satisfied with nothing less. The emergence of this faction complements the interaction between the two above-mentioned changes within the party in such a way that the overall tendency of this faction's development is not decline, but daily and even hourly increase. This situation is now seriously undermining the fighting strength of the Communist Party in government and seriously threatening its political purity as a revolutionary body. This then is the 'cancer cell' lurking deep in the body of the Communist Party in government, which may one day cause it to undergo a qualitative change and become a revisionist, fascist party.

2. Change In the Workers

(i) A desire for autonomy

The first change (apart from initial economic liberation) to occur within the workers as a result of the establishment of public ownership was their initial liberation from the traditional enslaving ideology of the exploiting classes. Hitherto, the proletarian workers had possessed nothing at all but their own labour-power; deprived of the means of production they were unable to produce any material goods — other than, of course, cold and hunger for themselves. As Marx, quoting William Petty, declared: 'Labour is the father of material wealth, the earth is its mother.'[6] Hence, the workers were forced to sell their labour-power by hiring themselves out to those who held the proprietary rights to the means of production, namely the landlords and capitalists. In the case of socialist society at the crossroads, however, private ownership of the means of production has already been replaced by public ownership, and the two different manifestations of the latter (namely collective ownership and ownership by the whole people) now represent the basic form of the state economic structure. The workers have thus been liberated from their previous economic enslavement, and corresponding to this liberation there has arisen, on the part of the workers, an increasingly general acceptance of Marxist socialist theory and the ideals of communism. The ideological enslavement of the workers by the exploiting classes has, for the first time in many thousands of years, now been broken. The great transformation in the ownership of the means of production, together with the stormy political movements accompanying this process – land reform, cooperativization, sustained socialist education, the 'four clean-ups' movement, the Great Proletarian Cultural Revolution, and the Movement to Criticize Lin Biao and Confucius – has made the workers increasingly aware of their natural position of mastery within the overall structure of the national economy, and ever more conscious of their responsibility and role within the overall history of mankind: 'Toilers from shops and fields united, the union we of all who work — the earth belongs to us the workers, no room here for those who shirk!'[7]

As this idea from the *Internationale* takes root in the souls of the workers, their superstitious belief in saviours and immortal rulers falls to one side, and their consciousness becomes increasingly firmly established as that of subject. The workers become ever more dissatisfied with their own position of powerlessness in the organization of production, and so they demand the right to participate directly in management; they become ever more discontented with relations of production whereby power is coercively monopolized by the minority, and demand their transformation. The workers wish to be masters in their own house: they desire the right to vote, and the right to stand for election.

(ii) A contradictory aggregate

Formerly only a commodity, labour-power now assumes a contradictory-aggregate nature as at once commodity, subject, and absolute and unconditional subordinate; this constitutes the second change within the workers. Hitherto, the workers had sold their labour-power to the capitalist as a commodity in exchange for a subsistence wage. Their ideological recognition of this act accorded with their actual performance of it, so practice and ideology did not then come into contradiction. Now, however, both general theory and the socialist education continuously propagated by the party inform the workers that public-ownership has, first and foremost, negated the commodity nature of labour-power. It is sought to make the workers appreciate that when they employ their labour-power and participate in productive activity, they are doing so for themselves and not for others. They are given a clear ideological sense of their responsibility and duty as masters of society. However, this establishment of their *consciousness* as subject is by no means equivalent to the genuine realization and consolidation of their *position* as subject. For all that wage labour is held to be non-existent in law and propaganda, nonetheless the state-capitalist attributes of the public-ownership system function in such a way as to make labour-power retain its commodity nature. The wage system manifests the fact that labour-power is still a commodity — unless they go to work, the workers get no wages.

Of particular importance is the matter of the workers' position within the organization of production. Hitherto, the workers had lived in a society characterized by relatively lax organization, and thus had a degree of free choice as to where they sold their labour-power and where they lived. Labour-power appeared as free labour, and the proprietary rights to labour-power rested with the workers themselves. At that time, therefore, the workers were, as Marx said, 'free workers'.[8] Now, however, the workers live in a highly organized and politico-economically unicorporate society under public ownership, and are no longer free workers but 'workers-within-organization'. The proprietary rights to labour-power no longer rest with the workers themselves, but with the politico-economically unicorporate organization, with society. The workers thus forfeit their free and independent nature. The place at which they are to employ their labour-power is determined for them by 'the organization', and as mere ordinary workers they must submit to such arrangements. On no account may they change jobs or move from one place to another on the basis of their own personal wishes, but only if 'the organization' arranges for or permits them to do so as part of its allocation of the division of labour. Indeed, they must submit to control by the higher leadership, those who hold the power and embody 'the organization', in all matters relating to the content, place and time of production.

Clearly, therefore, the position of the workers within the organization of production is one of absolute and unconditional subordination. This position of the workers within the organization of production is in contradiction both with their consciousness as subjects in the sphere of ideology, and with their role as commodities in the sphere of distribution. Thus, in socialist society at the crossroads, the basic contradiction in the mode of production functions through the workers, by causing the two-fold nature of labour-power to express itself in the form not only of use-value and exchange-value, but also of voluntary labour and constrained labour. Labour-power thus becomes an aggregate of contradictions. Herein lies the secret to all the problems arising within crossroads socialist society. In the words of Marx: 'All understanding of the facts depends upon this';[9] 'This is, in fact, the whole secret of the critical conception.'[10]

(iii) The enslavement of labour gives rise to an ever greater sense of despondency

The workers' lack of freedom to choose for themselves the place at which their labour-power is employed engenders within them the demand to be allowed actively to *assert* their subjective sense of mastery, through an intervention on their own behalf in the public matter of the determination of place of work and living environment. This demand stems not only from the workers' overall search for the means by which to assert the sense of mastery now present within their own thinking and ideology, but also from a degree of entrenchment within the social division of labour such that the workers' place of work and living environment become factors bearing directly and intimately upon their own interests, and even upon those of their descendants, for the whole of their respective lives. However, practice has shown that, under relations of production whereby power is coercively monopolized by the minority, not only is such intervention generally quite futile, but it also generally brings disaster, and bitter persecution from the powers that be. Consciously or otherwise, each and every worker experiences the utmost sense of inner contradiction and adversity because of this. Inevitably, the lesson of negative experience sinks in: each should get by as best he can by simply flowing with the tide, and by concerning himself with wider matters as little as possible. All talk of the workers being masters in their own house, and of working creatively, comes to seem just too far divorced from their actual condition of total impotence. Dominated by the reality of their existence – enslaved labour – the workers succumb to an ever greater sense of despondency.

The influence exerted upon social production as a whole by this change within the workers is truly immense. As Lenin correctly pointed out: 'The primary productive force of human society as a whole is the workers, the working people.'[11] The degree of development of the productive forces is, in any era, primarily determined by the extent to which the initiative of the workers can be released. And the universal suppression and destruction of the socialist initiative, sense of mastery, and spontaneous zeal for labour on the part of the workforce in society — this serves eloquently to indicate the point at which coercive monopolization of power by the minority has turned into a fetter upon the publisocial productive forces.

3. Change in Class Relations

(i) Times change and circumstances alter

During the first stage of the socialist revolution, class relations remained fundamentally the same as in the period of New Democratic Revolution. Chairman Mao, in his historic writing 'An Analysis of the Classes in Chinese Society',[12] made an extremely clear and precise dissection of these class relations: this article served as a powerful tool for ascertaining class relations during the entire period of New Democratic Revolution and during the first stage of the socialist revolution, and for distinguishing between genuine friend and enemy during those periods. Apart from the correctness of Chairman Mao's practical application of the method of Marxist class analysis, the main reason for this having been so is that the major problem of social existence and the basic target of revolution during both these periods remained the private ownership of the means of production.

However, once this problem had been solved, and the transformation to public ownership achieved, could the previous class relations be said to have persisted unchanged? Only a lunatic or else someone wishing to distort public perceptions would claim this to be the case. Any sane person would rather maintain that when change occurs in the relations of ownership – that is, in the base, – then of course, since class relations are dependent upon the nature of the relations of ownership and the mode of production, changes in class relations must (and in this case indeed did) inevitably follow.

(ii) Roots of the change in class relations

How are classes produced? Marx and Engels considered class divisions as being, primarily, '. . . determined by the division of labour'[13]— '. . . the law of the division of labour lies at the root of the division into classes.'[14]

It is quite true to say that the emergence of class divisions occurred after the emergence of the system of private ownership. But how then did private ownership first arise? Actually, private ownership arose in the first instance from the division of labour. As primitive society came to acquire a surplus produce by virtue of the development of the productive forces, and as those assigned under the division of labour to administer this surplus produce began to turn their administrative function into an exploitative one — then it was that private ownership first emerged. As Marx and Engels explicitly pointed out: 'Division of labour and private property are, moreover, identical expressions; in the one the same thing is affirmed with reference to activity as is affirmed in the other with reference to the product of the activity.'[15] Evidently, the division of labour forms not only the necessary condition for the existence of commodity production but, furthermore, the precondition for the emergence of private ownership and (hence) for the division of society into classes.

Indeed: 'The thing is easiest to grasp from the point of view of the division of labour'.[16] From the point of view of the division of labour, the crossroads socialist society arising out of the transformation to public ownership bears a considerable resemblance to the situation that prevailed during the later period of primitive communism. The transformation to public ownership of the means of production accomplished during the first stage of socialist revolution constitutes a transformation of private ownership only with respect to that which Marx referred to as 'the product of activity', and is still far from having abolished private ownership with respect to that which he referred to as 'the activity' itself. Thus, the precondition for the emergence of private ownership – and hence the precondition for division into classes – goes on existing within socialist society at the crossroads. Change within class relations occurs as a necessary outcome of the movement of contradictions in the existing mode of production. From the point of view of the division of labour, the system propagated by the crossroads socialist mode of production within the crucial sphere of the division of labour in the exercise of power – coercive monopolization of power by the minority – constitutes a grave and potentially fatal disorder. This same disorder lies at the very root of the new polarization of class relations.

(iii) On the definition of class

As Lenin pointed out: 'Classes are large groups of people differing from each other by the place they occupy in a historically determined system of social production, by their relation (in most cases fixed and formulated in law) to the means of production, by their role in the social organization of labour, and, consequently, by the dimensions of the share of social wealth of which they dispose and the mode of acquiring it. Classes are groups of people one of which can appropriate the labour of another owing to the different places they occupy in a definite system of social economy.'[17]

(iv) The new class relations

I. A new class antagonism in place of the old

Unicorporate publisocial production serves to reduce the broad and diverse membership of society as a whole to two simple categories: administrators and producers. It remains the aim of Marxism to accomplish, in the full course of socialist revolution, the breaking down of the line of demarcation between these two categories of people and, thence, '. . . the transition to the *abolition of all classes* and to a *classless society*'.[18]

However, coercive monopolization of power by the minority, and the corresponding entrenchment of the social division of labour, serves on the contrary to make this simple division again much more complex. What this diversification means, in effect, is that the crossroads socialist society which has arisen in the wake of the destruction of capitalist, or semi-feudal/semi-colonial society, '. . . has not done away with class antagonisms. It has but established new classes, new conditions of oppression, new forms of struggle in place of the old ones.'[19]★

★*Translator's Note:* The remainder of this section, and subsequent sections II-VIII, were deleted from Chen's manuscript in the *April 5th Forum* edition.

7
The Crisis

1. The Irreconcilability of the Basic Contradiction

The foregoing analysis allows us now clearly to ascertain that the basic contradiction in the crossroads socialist mode of production – that between unicorporate publisocial production and coercive monopolization of power by the minority – is in nature quite *irreconcilable*. This irreconcilability is prominently expressed in the three major changes occurring, respectively, inside the Communist Party, among the workers, and in class relations, and is reflected above all in a sharply antagonistic class struggle between the bureaucrat class and the mass of the working population. And precisely because the contradiction displays this irreconcilable nature, society as a whole must confront the following choice:

Either, to smash the fetter of coercive monopolization of power by the minority, while preserving unicorporate publisocial production, and then to carry out (by reliance upon the mass of the people, through proletarian–democratic revolution) the reform of all aspects of the superstructure not in harmony with the socialist economic base, and the readjustment of all constituents of the economy not in accordance with socialist principles, thereby leading public-ownership society in the direction of true socialism, and accelerating the transition to communism. This, clearly, would constitute the Marxist revolutionary line.

Or, to reinforce relations of production whereby power is coercively monopolized by the minority, changing the essential nature of publisocial production, and then to further strengthen those aspects of the superstructure not in harmony with the socialist economic base (namely, the system of official appointment, the hierarchical order, the autonomization of the state organs and the sanctification of the party), thereby altering the economic base in such a way that highly organized and politico-economically unicorporate production becomes production under the exclusive ownership of the bureaucrat-monopoly privileged class — and so completing the social evolution towards revisionism. This, clearly, would constitute the revisionist counter-revolutionary line.

One way or another, this is the choice which must be made. The basic internal contradiction of the mode of production causes socialism to vacillate at this crossroads. At such a time, the least slip could spell disaster.

2. Reformism is No Solution

(i) The reason

There exists, however, another line — the *reformist* line. The proponents of such a line seek to uphold unicorporate publisocial production, but remain fearful of confronting the relations of power which fetter its productive forces, preferring instead to effect a series of minor reforms and alterations in response to mere derivative problems. But such a line is doomed to failure from the outset, the reason being quite simply that the basic contradiction in crossroads socialist society is, as we have seen, an antagonistic one, an irreconcilable one. The reformist line seeks not the destruction of the bureaucratic-military machine, but merely its passage from the control of one group of individuals to that of another group of individuals; the evolutionist theory of the young inevitably triumphing over the old is masqueraded as dialectics and substituted for class theory; voluntarism, with its excessive emphasis upon the spiritual turning into the material, is masqueraded as materialism and substituted for the principle that being determines consciousness; and lastly, metaphysical methods of struggle are substituted for revolutionary, dialectical methods of struggle. Reformist methods merely address the symptoms of the problem — rather like taking aspirins for heart disease, or trying to scratch an itchy foot from the outside of one's boot. Such methods do no more than delay the total collapse by ushering in an alternative process of gradual erosion. In view of the structural complexity and stubborn resistance to change displayed by the class rule of the bureaucrats, and in view of the unprecedentedly sharp and intense nature of the class struggle, reformism can look forward to no other future than either capitulation or total liquidation.

(ii) The reformists

This reformist line originates from within the left wing of the ruling clique, proceeds from the 'revolutionary' standpoint of the petty-bourgeoisie, is prompted by the actual class struggle, and reflects the wavering and vacillation at the crossroads experienced by socialist society at this stage. The majority of reformists are people with vested interests, but they differ from the die-hards within the ruling circle in so far as they do at least perceive the ineluctable nature of the pressure for change. 'Change' for them, however, means nothing more than minor inconsequential reform aimed at the maintenance of old-style stability and the old ruling order. They also recognize that defects have arisen within the apparatus of rule, and may even acknowledge the existence of major dysfunction. But what about the source of the problem? They remain either incapable of fathoming this, or – having once done so – fearful of actually confronting it. In short, their methods of cure mistake symptom for cause, and are hence quite inadequate. Restricted by their own vested interests, they are incapable of escaping from the general sphere of vested interests.

One cannot cure an illness simply by treating the part of the body that happens to be hurting. Equally, in the case of a patient requiring urgent surgery, emergency injections prove effective for only a limited period of time, and postponement of surgery will eventually prove fatal. Of course, we should not preclude the use of reform as a revolutionary *tactic*: injections and painkillers are sometimes indispensable. However, it is sheer quackery to treat illness solely by such means — and a great many people have come to grief at the hands of quacks. Emerging with their so-called panaceas during times of dramatic social change, the reformists are of precisely this ilk. They seek to excise the 'cancer cell' while understanding neither the source of its production nor the laws governing its activity.

The reformist critique of revisionism is similar to the utopian socialist critique of capitalism – indeed, the blue-print for 'continuing the revolution' which they have devised bears fair comparison with the *phalanstères* of Fourier! Reformists of this variety possess all the characteristics of the petty-bourgeoisie, *the most prominent of which is the pernicious tenacity of small-scale production*. On the one hand, they possess revolutionary fanaticism, and on the other they may easily turn to the right ideologically. They are strongly swayed by considerations of personal gain or loss, and either remain subject to restriction by the interests of the bureaucrat class, or else drool at the prospect of acquiring those vested interests themselves. While they were capable of sacrificing their past for the sake of the present, they dare not sacrifice their present situation for the sake of the future. The position in which they find themselves – economically, politically and in terms of class – renders them unable to 'carry the class struggle through to the end', and incapable of daring to 'brave any danger whatsoever' or to 'strive for the most important things'. On the contrary, the slogans best describing the struggles in which they engage are: 'totally without strategy' and 'making rebellion on one's knees'. They fail to understand that 'the restriction of bourgeois right', when carried out under the overall control of the bureaucrat class, can amount to nothing more than an empty phrase. They are placed in an extremely perilous situation, being not only divorced from the mass of the people, but at the same time hated by the bureaucrat class as a whole. At the decisive juncture, the bureaucrat class will assuredly drown them in their own blood.

As Lenin pointed out: 'The Marxists recognise struggle for reforms, i.e., measures that improve the workers' conditions without destroying the power of the ruling class. But the Marxists wage a most resolute struggle against the reformists who, directly or indirectly, confine the aims and activities of the working class to the winning of reforms. Reformism is deception of the workers by the bourgeoisie, for as long as there is the domination of capital, the workers are condemned to remain wage slaves, notwithstanding individual improvements.'[1] Following the liquidation of the reformist line, divisions are bound to emerge within the ranks of the reformists, with a majority taking a leftward turn and adopting the standpoint of proletarian-democratic revolution, a certain number simply deserting the struggle, and a tiny minority taking a rightward turn and becoming capitulationists and instruments of the reaction.

(iii) The objective effects of reformism

The main objective effect of reformism is: the stripping away of the veil covering the bureaucrat class, and the creation, moreover, of a situation wherein '. . . the *"lower classes"* do not want to live in the old way and the "upper classes" *cannot carry on in the old way.'*[2] However, once the contradiction between forces and relations of production has become so acute '. . . that the approaching collapse of this mode of production is, so to speak, palpable; that the new productive forces themselves can only be maintained and further developed by the introduction of a new mode of production corresponding to their present stage of development',[3] once this has become a task of the utmost urgency — it is then that the inherent insufficiency of reformism is revealed. For rather than engaging in this task, reformism proceeds on the one hand to emphasize the workers' sense of mastery — thereby in effect negating the rule of privilege; but on the other to reinforce 'unified leadership' by the bureaucrat class — thereby in effect reinforcing the workers' slavelike position of unconditional subordination. The workers are thus thrown into an even more acute state of contradiction than before, and the whole of social production consigned to a state of utter chaos.

Inevitably, all this merely accelerates the fall of the entire national economy into stagnation and imminent collapse. As Engels pointed out: 'The reaction of the state power upon economic development can be of three kinds: it can run in the same direction, and then development is more rapid; it can oppose the line of development, in which case nowadays it will go to pieces in the long run in every great people; or it can prevent the economic development from proceeding along certain lines, and prescribe other lines. This case ultimately reduces itself to one of the two previous ones. But it is obvious that in cases two and three the political power can do great damage to the economic development and cause a great squandering of energy and material'.[4] The reformists have failed to locate the basic internal contradiction of the mode of production of crossroads socialist society, and hence are incapable of resolving that contradiction in a way that would confirm the orientation towards socialism. While wishing the economy to develop towards socialism, reformism is nonetheless unable effectively to abolish the governing and controlling function exerted upon the public-ownership economy by the revisionist superstructure. Should production fail to rise in a capitalist enterprise, then the enterprise may declare itself bankrupt, but should the same situation occur in an enterprise in 'socialist society', not only can the enterprise not be dissolved, but the state is even obliged to support it instead, so that all may have an 'iron rice-bowl' and 'eat from the communal pot'.

'Accumulation, the most important progressive function of society, is taken from society'.[5] The workers' sense of being their own masters, or labouring voluntarily, becomes gradually more and more fallacious. Or rather, positive intervention on their part is driven towards its own opposite, becoming – as in the case of machinery-smashing by workers during the early period of *laissez-faire* capitalism – either conscious or unconscious negative resistance. The workers engage in a disguised form of strike action: universal slow-down at work. In such circumstances, the whole of social production suffers disruption. This disruption brings in its wake a shortage of consumer items and items of daily necessity, adverse effects upon the state plan and the people's livelihood, an inability of supply to keep up with demand in the sphere of material life, a further dramatization of social contradictions, a universal increase in popular discontent, and, inevitably, a placing in jeopardy of the stability of the political power. Reformism, although having served to place certain obstacles in the forward path of revisionism and, also, to spur revolutionaries towards further efforts in the quest for truth, nonetheless remains in the last analysis powerless to arrest a process of social evolution controlled by the internal characteristics of the existing mode of production.

3. Revisionism: Favourable Present Conjuncture – Parlous Future Outcome

(i) An opportune moment for revisionism to gain the ascendant

The fall of the national economy into stagnation and imminent collapse is due, in essence, to the disruption inflicted upon the productive forces by the workers in response to coercive relations of power and production which have caused each one of them to become a contradictory aggregate and, through the enslavement of labour, to succumb to an ever greater sense of despondency. Superficially, however, the problem appears to stem from a so-called 'incorrect line', a situation which the bureaucrats are able to take advantage of in order to shift the blame elsewhere, deluding not only other people but even themselves in the process. This, then, provides initial grounds for fearing that revisionism may indeed now gain the ascendant.

The collapse of the national economy and the squandering of resources and general exploitation carried out by the bureaucrat class, serve continually to aggravate the burden borne by the great mass of people in the course of their daily lives. The combined effect of the unending and perniciously deceitful propaganda carried out by the bureaucrats, the myopia of small-scale production and the constraints of the small family, is such that a considerable number of people become more concerned about achieving an improvement in their present condition of material poverty than about securing their fundamental and long-term interests. The bureaucrat class can avail itself of this fact, and proceeds to pander to their general psychology. By unfurling the banner of developing production and satisfying the people's material requirements in clothing, food, housing and travel, the bureaucrat class provides itself with plausible, indeed 'perfectly justifiable' grounds for snuffing out the revolutionary movement, the struggle against revisionism. This is the second reason why revisionism now poses a real threat.

As a contradictory aggregate, each worker is continuously searching, consciously or otherwise, for a way of resolving his state of internal contradiction. In the course of their own practical experience of the ruling order, the working masses come to ascertain that they are masters of society in name alone, and that in their actual existence they are mere slaves. For many, consequently, the fervent desire to act genuinely as master in their own house gives way to the minimal demand for a mere increase in wages, as a means of solving some real-life problems. Catering to this mentality, the bureaucrat class proceeds to take advantage of the still-existent commodity attributes of the workers themselves as a means of stimulating anew the latter's zeal for labour. This is the third reason why revisionism now poses a real threat.

As a result of their common failure to grasp the basic contradiction, the critiques of revisionism and the bureaucrat class offered, respectively, by the proponents of reform under a revolutionary strategy and by the proponents of revolution under a reformist strategy are both lacking in rigour and thoroughness. Neither tackles the serious (indeed potentially fatal) disorder engendered by the coercive monopolization of power, and neither have succeeded in finding at all viable alternatives to the system of appointment, the hierarchical order, the autonomization of the state organs or the sanctification of the party — those fertile hotbeds for the growth of revisionism. The establishment of a superstructure in harmony with the socialist economic base is still a long way off. This is the fourth reason why revisionism now poses a real threat.

The bureaucrat class represents the principal basis through which the system of revisionism may acquire actual existence. Not only have the foundations of the bureaucrat class never been disturbed, but, on the contrary, shaded from view by the great red parasol of 'strengthening unified leadership', its system has become firmly rooted in every corner of society. The firm dependence upon power which so distinguishes unicorporate publisocial production means that although the bureaucrat class is numerically small, its strength is nonetheless immense. The bureaucrat class wields great power, occupies the commanding position, and holds the initiative. This is the fifth reason why revisionism now poses a real threat.

The entire superstructure and political configuration has become an instrument of dictatorship highly responsive to the needs of the bureaucrat class; the system of official appointment, the hierarchical order, the autonomization of the state organs and the sanctification of the party are all essentially in the service of revisionism, and instinctively tend in that direction. The reaction exerted upon the economic base by such a superstructure is one of a purely revisionist nature. This is the sixth reason why revisionism now poses a real threat.

The superstructure and political configuration long ago imposed, in fact, a *separation* of the masses from the sphere of politics. The broad mass of people are completely without the right, power, or means with which to gain access to or intervene effectively in the sphere of politics. Even the general membership of the Communist Party itself is incapable of either gaining access to or intervening in the inner workings of the political struggle; the membership has no power to express an opinion while events are taking place, its role being merely that of awaiting notification of the outcome of events. Conditions do not exist even for the open expression and discussion of views opposed to those of the power holders, let alone for the testing of such views in practice. The colossal scale of the instruments of violence is such that an outbreak of disturbances from below comes to form a less likely eventuality than the occurrence of a crisis of rule as a result of internal rivalries at the centre of power. The monopolistic nature of power, the secretive nature of the power-struggle, and the bureaucratic class nature of the revisionist-roaders within the party all serve not only to make it inevitable that conspiratorial elements will engage in extensive plotting and intriguing, but also, at the same time, to create 'legal' safeguards for such activities. This is the seventh reason why revisionism now poses a real threat.

Khruschev carried out his conspiratorial intrigues in collusion with Zhukov, the wielder of bureaucratic-military force. Together, by exploiting the sanctification of the party and the force of the state apparatus as a whole, they succeeded in carrying out a peaceful counter-revolutionary armed coup, usurping supreme party and state power. This pattern of events represents the primary and most dangerous form in which crossroads socialist society may be alienated 'at a stroke', and transformed into revisionist society. The most propitious time for such a pattern of events to manifest itself would seem always to be during the period around the death of the supreme party or state leader. The necessary conditions, both formal and temporal, for the use of such methods are daily coming closer to fruition. The birth of revisionism will very likely take place 'at a stroke', through either a bloody or a bloodless palace coup. This is the eighth reason why revisionism now poses a real threat.

'Therefore, if people like Lin Biao come to power, it will be quite easy for them to rig up the capitalist system'.[6] This was the verdict reached by Chairman Mao in late 1974, on the night of his eighty-first birthday. It is a conclusion which points, clearly and un-equivocally, to the real danger of revisionism gaining the ascendant!

(ii) The doom awaiting revisionism in China today

I. The profound and far-reaching influence of the Great Pro-letarian Cultural Revolution

For the whole range of present and historical reasons discussed above, China now stands in the forefront of the struggle against revisionism. China, under the impetus and leadership of the Chinese Communist Party headed by Chairman Mao, has built a steel wall of defence against revisionism. Even if revisionism should gain the ascendant for a while, its rule would be destined to be both unstable and brief. As Chairman Mao declared, at the start of the Cultural Revolution, '. . . I am sure they will know no peace . . . and their rule will most probably be short-lived.'[7] This applies with still greater validity now, after the Chinese people have been tried and tempered for a whole decade in the raging flames of the Great Proletarian Cultural Revolution. They have acquired an 'infallible eye' for revisionism, and personal experience of politics and every-day life has made them aware of the changes occurring within class relations, and heightened their consciousness of the new class struggle. The Chinese people's vigilance against revisionism, their resentment of bureaucrats, and the fighting spirit and revolutionary will which has been fostered within them by Marxism and Mao Zedong-Thought represent both a spiritual resource and an immense material force in the struggle against revisionism. Revisionism would be hard put even to circumvent – let alone nullify – the profound, far-reaching and soul-inspiring influence of the Great Proletarian Cultural Revolution. The discourses of Chairman Mao on the struggle against revisionism and on continuing the revolu-tion, are like so many Golden Hoops[8] restricting the activities of the bureaucrat class. These are all factors which Khruschev never had to contend with in the Soviet Union, and together form a first, fatal problem confronting revisionism in China today.

II. A population of one billion: coerced production, voluntary consumption

China's population is increasing by leaps and bounds, and now totals nearly one billion. The great problem of providing items of daily necessity, clothing, food, employment and housing for such a huge population is an ever-present one. Clearly, this problem may only be solved by expanding production. However, under circumstances not of free competition but rather of unicorporate-monopoly pro-duction characterized by a strong dependence upon power, the main prerequisite conditions for such an expansion of production are, quite clearly: an overall state of political calm, and relations of production which both fully arouse the workers' zeal for labour and fully liberate their powers of creativity. Equally obvious, is the fact that this same creativity and zeal for labour are snuffed out in the vast majority of people under the revisionist system. No expansion of production or liberation of the productive forces can possibly occur so long as the bureaucrat class continues, through its monopolization of power, despotically to suppress the labour enthusiasm and creativity of the great mass of workers. Even supposing the bureaucrats were indeed able, by applying their judicious combination of deceit and coercion, to provide a temporary stimulus to production, the effect would be merely a limited and transient one. The whole system of material incentives, *when controlled by the bureaucrats*, can only exacerbate social contradictions and serve as a revisionist device for squeezing more out of the workers. Such a system was repudiated by Chairman Mao precisely because it had been proven in practice during the 1950's and 1960's that material incentives were neither appropriate nor conducive to socialist production in China. Furthermore, as a result of the ongoing critique of such matters over the past decade, the workers have now lost any apathy they may once have had, and have become acutely aware of the evil consequences arising from material incentives.

The bureaucrat-monopoly privileged class has, by its virtually complete deprivation of the workers' sovereignty, cancelled the responsibility which the workers should by rights be shouldering. The bureaucrats are more than capable of crudely and arbitrarily suppressing the creativity and labour enthusiasm of the mass of the working population; what they cannot do, however, is to stem the demands of the latter for daily consumer items, clothing, food, employment and housing. The privileged class is more than capable of riding roughshod over the longing for democracy and freedom of the mass of the working population; what it cannot do, however, is to restrain its own rapacious desire to suck out, to the very last drop, their vital energies and resources. For that class to maintain the rule of revisionism in China on a permanent basis would be most problematical: 'because it is incompetent to assure an existence to its slave within his slavery, because it cannot help letting him sink into such a state that it has to feed him, instead of being fed by him.'[9] The problems endured by one billion people in the course of their daily lives, and the severe class contradiction and struggle which these provoke, exert enormous pressures of a kind that the Khruschevites never had to contend with in the Soviet Union. This forms a second fatal problem confronting revisionism in China today.

III. The ossification of domestic politics allows pressures to accumulate to an explosive level

The social structure of China is not quite the same as that of the Soviet Union. The Soviet Union is a semi-European nation, social control is less strict there than in China, and so the contradictions in society allow a certain room for manoeuvre. There are written laws, political prisoners are not simply slaughtered, and there is a certain degree of freedom of speech and freedom of publication, with dissidents such as Sakharov and Solzhenitsyn being able to express oppositional viewpoints, hold press conferences and the like. The educational system, to a certain extent, gives people opportunities to further their studies on the basis of their own abilities; rather than striving for academic uniformity, it tries to provide conditions which both permit and encourage the development of free discussion and creative invention. Such an approach offers definite prospects and career outlets to those with talent and ability in society. But by the same token it also gives them a vested interest in the system. The revolutionary movement is thus deprived of potentially outstanding leaders, people who would otherwise be willing to sacrifice everything for the cause.

In China, the situation is different. The bureaucrat class operates within a feudal despotism rather than within a modern system of law. Policy is highly changeable, being based upon the likes, dislikes and general whim of the bureaucrat class – representing 'unified leadership' – and varying in accordance with the exigencies of the short-term situation. There is basically no freedom of speech, assembly, association, or publication. The fate of so-called counter-revolutionaries is either summary execution or lengthy imprisonment. In the educational system and the field of science and research, what counts is not ability, but rather personal connections and influence. The strict degree of social control maintained by the privileged class results in a conspicuous lack of room for manoeuvre within social contradictions. Dissatisfaction and resentment fuel a longing for change, and countless fine individuals feel compelled to stand forth and be counted, to search for a way forward regardless of the dangers involved. The longer such feelings accumulate, the greater becomes the likelihood that they will surface in a sudden manner; the more deeply oppressed that people become, the more uncompromising will be the resistance they finally offer. At the same time, the bureaucrat-monopoly privileged class becomes, in the course of its long-term, coercive monopolization of power, increasingly ossified and increasingly bereft of the moral resources with which to maintain its own authority in the eyes of the people. 'He who finds the proper course has many to assist him; he who loses the proper course has few to assist him.'[10] The increasing ossification of the leadership clique engenders a similar process of ossification within society as a whole, and thereby sows the seeds of a total collapse of the system. These factors form a further fatal problem confronting revisionism in China today.

IV. The real threat of regional rebellion

The course of Chinese history for the past few thousand years is filled with examples of the waging of separatist warfare by feudal nobles, military governors and warlords. The operation of the new mode of production has allowed the formation within Chinese society of a dominant elite of new feudal nobles, new military governors and new warlords. While such a state of affairs may have constituted the cause of social upheaval in previous eras, it may, in fact, now turn into a *positive* factor, and contribute to the destruction of revisionist conspiracies and intrigues aimed at the usurpation of party and state power. For with Chairman Mao having raised the call for supervision to be exercised over the Centre by the regions, and for the regions to rebel if revisionism should appear within the Centre, each area of territory equipped with its own integrated political, economic and cultural structures may be regarded as a ready-made potential revolutionary base area. This, then, poses a latent, underlying threat to the future of revisionism in China today.

V. Exposure to the world-wide wave of democracy as a result of contact with other countries

With development of the productive forces being sabotaged and disrupted by the relations of production, a large portion of the extensive amounts of foreign exchange which could no doubt, under revisionism, be procured through the sale of China's natural resources and industrial raw materials, would nonetheless, in order to secure the maintenance of the political power, have to be spent within the sphere of consumption. Thus only limited funds would remain for investment in re-production. The Chinese people would refuse to countenance a situation whereby China – through the sale of its natural resources by the bureaucrat class – would degenerate once more into being a mere semi-colonial appendage of the industrialized nations. Furthermore, such a situation would inevitably lead to changes in the internal structure of the country. In the contemporary world, democracy forms the main-stream while anti-democracy forms a mere counter-current. Even today, the human rights movement which has surfaced in the Soviet Union and the Eastern European nations provides an omen of the flood-tide to come. The expansion of contact with other countries is broadening the horizons of the people day by day; as a result of the widespread dissemination of culture, science and technology, they are becoming ever more perceptive, and their thinking ever more developed. Inevitably, the international tide of democracy will evoke the most ardent response in those parts of the world which are the least democratic. This constitutes a further challenge facing revisionism in China today.

VI. The people's forbearance will assuredly come to an end

The primary, most intrinsic reason for revisionism being doomed to failure in contemporary China lies in the reactionary and anti-popular nature of the revisionist line itself. The revisionist line, far from achieving a triumphant resolution of the basic contradiction in the crossroads socialist mode of production, instead exacerbates it most insidiously. The revisionist line thus continues to be inescapably dominated and increasingly undermined by this basic contradiction. Under the revisionist line, social production under public ownership is transformed into production under ownership by the bureaucrat-monopoly privileged class; the tyrannical order of privilege is forcibly imposed, the commodity attributes still possessed by labour-power are exploited, and a form of 'goulash' welfarism encouraged involving the bestowal of alms and minor favours upon the people in order to induce their cooperation and '. . . break their revolutionary strength by temporarily rendering their situation tolerable.'[11] In essence, the revisionist line serves to reinforce the workers' slave-like position of absolute and unconditional subordination. Indeed, its aim in thus restoring the vitality of the commodity nature of labour-power, is to throw the workers still deeper into the abyss of absolute and unconditional subordination to

134

the bureaucrat, to a point where they turn into steady, submissive slaves. The revisionist line seeks nothing less than the decisive obliteration both of the worker's consciousness as subject and of his actual position as subject. However, because of its anti-popular and reactionary nature, the revisionist line inevitably encounters conscious opposition and determined resistance from the entire people, who have been forearmed with consciousness in the struggle against revisionism. Of this there need be no doubt.

VII. The swan song of exploitation

In sum: no form of deception can endure indefinitely. Revisionism does not have a happy future ahead of it in China today; indeed it is doomed to failure. Even if it were in fact to gain the ascendant, it would not succeed in holding sway for long, for the victory of revisionism 'at a stroke' would merely foretoken its inevitable and equally rapid downfall. The ignorant and benighted have blind faith in the present, but the wise and perspicacious look to the future. The system of revisionism is nothing more than the swan song of the entire exploitative class system. Its mode of operation in China today is somewhat like that of feudal socialism, and its fate will also be that of feudal socialism: 'The aristocracy, in order to rally the people to them, waved the proletarian alms-bag in front for a banner. But the people, so often as it joined them, saw on their hindquarters the old feudal coats of arms, and deserted with loud and irreverent laughter.'[12] As we quoted earlier from Chairman Mao: '. . . I am sure they will know no peace . . . and their rule will most probably be short-lived, because it will not be tolerated by the revolutionaries, who represent the interests of the people making up more than 90 per cent of the population.'[13]

4. The Life and Death Struggle Between the Two Lines at the Critical Juncture

(i) The nature of labour-power betokens the nature of society as a whole

Labour-power, the sum of the physical and mental energies of man, is the basic factor of production in any society. In the absence of the participation of labour-power there can be no productive activity whatever. Of equal significance is the fact that change in the nature of labour-power reflects, in a striking and sensitive manner, change in the nature of society. Under capitalism, labour-power is turned into a commodity; if this were not the case, that mode of exploitation and oppression could not exist. 'The whole system of capitalist production is based on the worker's sale of his labour-power as a commodity.'[14] Under revisionism, the workers are stripped of the proprietary right to their own labour-power, and labour-power is subordinated, absolutely and unconditionally, to the will of the bureaucrat – in other words, enslaved. Without such unconditional subordination of labour-power to the will of the bureaucrat, the establishment of a system of super-enslavement and super-exploitation under the revisionist fascist tyranny of privilege would not be possible. Production under the revisionist system is production under slavery. And, in the slave system of production, 'the forced labour of the slaves formed the basis on which the super-structure of all society was reared.'[15] Under communism, by contrast, 'in place of the old bourgeois society, with its classes and class antagonisms, we shall have an association, in which the free development of each is the condition for the free development of all.'[16]

It is thus evident that the nature of labour-power betokens the nature of society as a whole. Comprehension of this principle is vital to an understanding of the essence of line struggle during the period of socialism.

ii) The unfolding of two-line struggle around the question of liberation versus enslavement of labour-power (– concerning the basic economic law of socialism)

The contradictory-aggregate nature of labour-power in crossroads socialist society offers a clear indication of the transitional nature of socialist society. Labour-power, matching the vacillation at the crossroads experienced by socialism itself, is continuously searching – consciously or otherwise – for a way of resolving its own internal contradiction. It is around precisely this point that there unfolds a struggle between two political lines. In the last analysis, is the contradictory nature of labour-power to undergo a process of purification whereby labour-power is raised to the status of subject, or is it to be further exacerbated, until labour-power is driven into a state of enslavement? Is society to be steered in the direction of genuine and complete socialism, and thence into the transition to the promised shores of communism; or is it to be pitched into the dark abyss of revisionism? These questions contain the essence of the two-line struggle. Since a straightforward restoration of private ownership of the means of production would be most problematical, and because of the high degree of organization to which social production has been subjected, retrogression to a state of affairs whereby labour-power would re-assume the nature of pure commodity has now become most unlikely. The instinct of labour-power is to demand vehemently the establishment of its position as subject and the resolution of its present plight as contradictory aggregate. The ruling class – the bureaucrat class together with the superstructure under its control – strives, however, in accordance with its own interests and inertial nature, to reduce labour-power to a state of total enslavement.

Herein lies the class basis of the two-line struggle. From the standpoint of the working people, everything which, by patterning itself upon their fundamental interests, serves earnestly and honestly to bring about the establishment and enhancement of the position of labour-power as subject (not merely in terms of ideology but also with respect to production, distribution and society as a whole) represents a firm realization of the line of Marxist revolution. That is, a line calling for adherence to the principles of 'proletarian politics in command' and 'distribution according to labour', for continuous improvement in mutual relations between individuals, and for the liberation of the worker. The implementation of such a line would lead ultimately to the abolition of the commodity attributes of labour-power. During the stage of socialism, however, the commodity nature of labour-power would still be recognised: it would neither be simply repudiated on the one hand nor magnified on the other, but would instead be subject to restriction. Such a line would result in a decisive and fundamental negation of the slave-like nature previously displayed by labour-power in circumstances of its subordination to the bureaucrat. Herein lies the revolutionary, popular nature of this line.

If, guided by the terms of reference of the latter, we were to formulate *a basic economic law of socialism*, the formulation we should arrive at *would not merely be* 'The securing of the maximum satisfaction of the constantly rising material and cultural requirements of the whole society through the continuous expansion and perfection of socialist production on the basis of higher techniques'[17] [Stalin], for this focuses only upon the instruments of production. Our formulation would focus upon a *still more vital factor*, namely the worker himself, he who wields the instruments of production and represents the primary element within the productive forces, and would be as follows:

The replacement of labour performed on a constrained and coercive basis by labour which is freely and enthusiastically given, the liberation of the productive forces via the liberation of the worker, and the active transformation of the worker into the true master of society, state, means of production and activity of production; that is to say, the vigorous development of socialist production and the creation of an abundant social material base genuinely owned by the working people themselves, by means of democratic self-government on the part of the worker, and through the continuous realization of a higher degree of organization of social labour, the continuous adoption of new and higher modes of social production, the continuous discovery and utilization of new, scientific techniques of production, the continuous augmentation of a scientific synthesis between the state-planned economy and the socially autonomous market economy; and, lastly, the continuous inducement of the worker into further participation in the sphere of politics so as to perfect distributition according to labour and make management increasingly scientific.

Diametrically opposed to this stands the counter-revolutionary line of revisionism. We have earlier expounded at some length upon revisionism and its basic economic laws, and will dwell no further upon it at this point except to make one necessary observation: the contradictory – aggregate nature of labour-power constitutes the *source* of the struggle waged in socialist society between the Marxist line and the line of revisionism—so long as the contradictory – aggregate nature of labour-power continues to exist, the struggle between the Marxist line and the revisionist line will not abate for a single moment. This two-line struggle will run, from start to finish, throughout the entire historical period of socialism.

iii) The form assumed by the struggle is unfavourable to the revolution

The line struggle, however, finds concentrated expression in the struggle for power. The special characteristics of unicorporate publi-social production cause the power struggle to assume a role of major significance, for the extension of the political monopoly to all other spheres means that whoever holds power also holds the power of initiative in the struggle. Since the extensive concentration of the larger state powers (military, political, financial and cultural) is located entirely within the Communist Party and placed under its monopoly, and since all possibility of other political organizations competing legally for power with it (or even existing at all) has long since been eliminated, the struggle itself also comes, inevitably, to be concentrated within the governing Communist Party. The communist cause, 'The development of the proletariat, proceeds everywhere through internal struggles'.[18] This applies prior to the Communist Party having obtained political power, but it applies still more once the Communist Party has enjoyed a long-term, consolidated monopoly of government. The weightier the power, and the greater the gains and losses concerned, the more acute is the struggle for the possession of power. As we have seen, the class resources of the Marxist line are to be found in the mass of the working population headed by the proletariat, while those of the revisionist line are to be found in the power-holding bureaucrat class. However, the outcome of the power struggle within the Communist Party is actually determined, not by the views of the people, but by the subversive manoeuvres going on within its own upper echelons.

To be sure, the Communist Party believes in revolutionary theory, reveres Marxism and has its own past inheritance of revolution; and it is certainly possible for the Marxist revolutionary forces within the party – particularly if the party is still *led* by a Marxist – to offer resolute resistance to revisionism and the bureaucrat class. However, long-term, coercive monopolization of power by the minority has already brought about change, both within the party and in class relations as a whole. Those in charge of the party are subject to the highly corrosive effects of power, and some of them, succumbing to this, have degenerated into bureaucrats. This bureaucrat class lives in clover, neither working nor studying, and engaging in neither research nor social investigation. Standing high and mighty, divorced from the people and from reality as a whole, it sets itself up as master and overlord. 'It is not the consciousness of men that determines their being, but, on the contrary, their social being that determines their consciousness'.[19] The particular position and vested interests of the bureaucrat class have long since caused it to betray Marxism. The bureaucrats idolize power, worshipping it exclusively and superstitiously in a kind of power fetishism; power is their religion. In their class nature, the bureaucrats display an unparalleled degree of viciousness, treachery and rapacity. Their general outlook is myopic, benighted and entirely lacking in any sense of history. They are capable of performing any base and shameful act and of stooping to all manner of conspiracy and intrigue in order to usurp power. Thus, the power struggle assumes an abnormally high degree of deviousness and brutality.

Precisely because of this state of affairs within the party; because of the instinctual tendency towards revisionism displayed by the entire superstructure and relations of production whereby power is coercively monopolized by the minority; because of the fall of the national economy into stagnation and imminent collapse; because revisionism is afforded an opportunity to gain the ascendant; because the mass of the working population has been deprived of both the power and the means to participate in the sphere of politics; because of the absence of open expression, of discussion and the testing out of differing viewpoints; and lastly, because accumulated quantitative change leads inevitably to qualitative change — for all these reasons, the forces of revolution will assuredly find themselves in a position of inferiority within the party power-struggle when the moment arrives for socialism's final, decisive step at the crossroads. The form assumed by the struggle is extremely unfavourable to the revolution. Quite clearly, unless direct appeal is made to the people at this critical juncture, and unless they immediately and resolutely resort to proletarian-democratic revolution, then a crisis will occur within socialism, and the ascendancy of revisionism will become inevitable.

8
Proletarian-Democratic Revolution as a Necessary Tendency of Historical Development

1. The Two Stages of Socialist Revolution

To sum up — 'It is the interaction of two unequal forces: on the one hand, the economic movement, on the other, the new political power, which strives for as much independence as possible, and which, having once been established, is endowed with a movement of its own. On the whole, the economic movement gets its way, but it has also to suffer reactions from the political movement which it itself established and endowed with relative independence, from the movement of the state power, on the one hand, and of the opposition simultaneously engendered, on the other.'[1] Such action and reaction between economic base and superstructure, and between forces and relations of production, forms the basic contradiction in the mode of production, and determines the two stages through which the socialist revolution must necessarily pass. The first stage is that of change within the economic base, namely the transformation to public ownership of the means of production. The second stage is that of the transformation of the superstructure, namely the stage of proletarian-democratic revolution. As regards periodization in the instance of China, the first stage spanned, in general terms, the period from 1953 to 1963, and encompassed the movements to promote mutual aid teams, co-operativization, and the joint state-private running of enterprise, together with the founding of the People's Communes and the struggle for their consolidation. The second stage was then inaugurated by the great polemic with the Soviet Union, and its unfolding was symbolized by the outbreak, in 1966, of the Great Proletarian Cultural Revolutionary Movement.

2. The Origin of the Great Proletarian Cultural Revolution

The question of the struggle against revisionism is, essentially, one of carrying the socialist revolutionary movement through to the end, one of steadfastly continuing it on the basis of victory in the first stage of socialist revolution. For only by its deliverance from this *partial* victory over the private ownership system can the proletariat secure a total liberation from the shackles of private ownership. Following the transformation from private to public ownership of the means of production, those aspects of the superstructure not in conformity with the socialist economic base must also be reformed. 'With the change of the economic foundation the entire immense superstructure is more or less rapidly transformed.'[2] From this perspective, we see that the outbreak of the Great Proletarian Cultural Revolution in 1966 was by no means the result of a momentary impulse on the part of particular individuals, but was, rather, a necessary development following the transformation in 1956 to public ownership of the means of production; and that it represented the beginning rather than the conclusion of that process whereby the entire immense superstructure is more or less rapidly transformed.

3. The Limitations of the Great Proletarian Cultural Revolution

We have already, earlier in our discussion, amply affirmed the mighty historical achievements of the Great Proletarian Cultural Revolution (see, for example, 'China at the Frontline of the Struggle Against Revisionism'). However, as the beginning of that process whereby the entire superstructure is transformed, the Great Proletarian Cultural Revolution also displayed the unavoidable limitations of any such 'beginning'.

These limitations derived, in the main, from two aspects. *First*, our guiding ideology offered insufficient insight into the basic contradiction in the new mode of production formed during the first stage of socialist revolution. While it was realized on the basis of general Marxist principles that the basic contradiction of socialist society remained that between economic base and superstructure, and between forces and relations of production, there was nonetheless no specific indication given regarding the particularity of the present economic base and superstructure, and of those forces and relations of production which were held to be in contradiction. This task was, however, one which we could scarcely afford to neglect at that time. *Second*, there was merely the search for change within a conventional framework of existing forms, and no pursuit of transformation, no break with this conventional framework.

The Great Proletarian Cultural Revolution failed to confront the primary, most fundamental, and most deadly disorder of the superstructure, namely coercive monopolization of power by the minority. Or rather, it confronted the symptoms and not the root of this disorder, being directed merely at the 'capitalist-roaders' themselves, rather than at the real, fundamental causes underlying their emergence. Just as before, 'its critics* had hitherto attacked its evil consequences rather than the process as such.'[3] The 'revolution in the arts', the 'revolution in health-care', the 'revolution in education', the 'reform of the state organs', the 'Shanghai January Storm', and the 'restriction of bourgeois right' were all carried out entirely under the dominance of coercive monopolization of power by the minority.

These limitations determined the ultimate incapacity of the Great Proletarian Cultural Revolution — for all its expression of the democratic demands of the proletariat and the mass of the working population, and for all its intimations of a socialist superstructure (for example, the driving of emperors and high officials from the theatrical stage, and the scaling of the superstructure by the working class) — to accomplish the task of reforming all those aspects of the superstructure not in harmony with the socialist economic base.

These limitations meant that the Great Proletarian Cultural Revolution served merely to express the impulse towards, the demand for, a transformation of the superstructure, and remained fundamentally insufficient to the task of actually satisfying this demand. Still more serious than this insufficiency in the face of fundamental issues was the fact that the Great Proletarian Cultural Revolution, in the course of its various 'revolutions', 'reforms', 'restrictions' and so forth, gave rise to such widespread malpractices that favourable conditions were created for the rebirth of the old in new form.

Take the case, for example, of the 'revolution in education', the

* i.e. the critics of capitalism

policy of 'recommendation and selection of workers, peasants and soldiers to attend university' — a policy which had proceeded from a correct and revolutionary desire to break the ubiquitous rule of the exploiting classes. Yet under the dominant influence of monopolization of power by the minority, it was reduced to a means of enabling the new exploiting class – the bureaucrat class – to engage in graft and malpractice, and gain access to university 'through the back door'. This new form of student recommendation and selection allowed the bureaucrat class to make free play of its privileges, and thus came to be invested with the same old content as before. 'When the ignorant are promoted to high positions of learning, and when those declared to be filial and honest drive away their own fathers, then the poor and stainless are made corrupt as the mire, and high officials and noble generals are made timid as chickens.'

Again, in the case of the 'revolution in health', policies which were supposed to achieve the revolutionary aim of transforming health departments in such a way that they would no longer simply serve the interests of the urban elite, resulted, by virtue of the power-minority's leadership, in these same health departments turning into veritable quagmires of concerted, self-seeking graft and malpractice by those at all levels of both the urban and the rural elite. Controlled by the bureaucrat class, much of co-operative medicine in fact operated in the service of officialdom, whether in terms of access to medical treatment and supplies, or in terms of the selection of personnel to be trained as 'barefoot doctors'. Co-operative medicine degenerated into a form of 'hospital commerce' facilitating the legal pursuit of private ends. Accounts were not made public, and phenomena such as the private appropriation of resources, and hoarding, speculation and profiteering in medicines became rife.

Any reform which fails to strike at the real roots of a problem will remain at the level of meaningless talk, for that which has become obsolete will not only strive for rebirth in a new form, but may even find that the new form provides it with the most agreeable of conditions under which to continue its existence.

4. Conclusions on the Great Proletarian Cultural Revolution

However, because the Great Proletarian Cultural Revolution was in the last analysis revolutionary in essence, because it was a large-scale mass movement which involved the enthusiastic participation of countless numbers of the masses, and because of the series of tortuous, convoluted, and soul-stirring struggles which it entailed, and which steadily deepened over the course of an entire decade, the Great Proletarian Cultural Revolution nevertheless succeeded both in exposing the basic contradiction in the existing mode of production, and in broadly unfolding the future scenario of proletarian-democratic revolution. It shattered the sanctification of the party, tore aside the veil of phoney socialism, accentuated the contradiction between forces and relations of production, and provided a forceful vindication of Marx's thesis: 'At a certain stage of their development, the material productive forces of society come in conflict with the existing relations of production, or – what is but a legal expression for the same thing – with the property relations within which they have been at work hitherto. From forms of development of the productive forces these relations turn into their fetters. Then begins an epoch of social revolution.'[4]

Coercive monopolization of power by the minority results in the despotic form of management characteristic of private ownership being taken over, further intensified, and imposed upon social production under public ownership as a new and ultra-despotic means of exploitation, through the function of privilege. Such a situation obstructs the expansion of the productive forces, and intensifies the contradiction between forces and relations of production, to the point where: '. . . society cannot free itself unless each individual is freed. The old mode of production must therefore be revolutionized from the bottom up, and above all the old division of labour must disappear.'[5] The issue of top priority facing societies under public ownership is the need to remedy, with all haste, the grave disorder existing within the crucial sphere of the division of labour in the exercise of power. It is essential that this particular division of labour be determined by the vast majority, by the working people in its entirety. For in order to secure the liberation of the social productive forces as a whole, it is first of all necessary to strive for the liberation of each social unit of labour-power. 'The political rule of the producer cannot coexist with the perpetuation of his social slavery.'[6]

A particularly important aspect of the Great Proletarian Cultural Revolution was that it revealed, in quite unequivocal terms, the necessity of smashing the previously existing bureaucratic-military machine: the 'legitimate functions [of the old governmental power] were to be wrested from an authority usurping pre-eminence over society itself, and restored to the responsible agents of society . . . ';[7] — '. . . no longer, as before, to transfer the bureaucratic military machine from one hand to another . . . '.[8] No longer, as before, should the bureaucratic-military machine simply be transferred from the hands of those walking along the capitalist road to the hands of those *running* along the capitalist road! Coercive monopolization of power by the minority must now be brought to a halt, for it has given rise to a new and most inhumane process of class division, to a new and most avaricious, cunning and treacherous exploiting class, to a new and most sinister, barbarous and iniquitous system of exploitation!

'*No* form of bondage can be broken without breaking *all* forms of bondage.'[9] The conclusion which should therefore be drawn from the experience of the Great Proletarian Cultural Revolution is as follows: the form assumed by the development of the productive forces during the first stage of socialist revolution has now, with the advent of the second stage of socialist revolution, turned into their fetter. It now becomes necessary – in order to accomplish the transformation of these relations of production and achieve the establishment of a socialist superstructure – to smash the bureaucratic-military machine together with the overall system of coercive monopolization of power by the minority; to shatter thoroughly the sanctification of the party and transform it in such a way that it no longer performs the role of slave-driver but instead serves as an instrument in the hands of the slaves themselves; to 'afford the rational medium in which that class struggle can run through its different phases in the most rational and humane way';[10] and lastly, to strengthen and perfect the legal system and carry out the reinstatement of human rights. Proletarian-democratic revolution is now urgently required, and must therefore vigorously be carried out!

5. The Completion of Preparations for Proletarian-Democratic Revolution

i) General preparations

'Mankind always sets itself only such tasks as it can solve; since, looking at the matter more closely, it will always be found that the task itself arises only when the material conditions for its solution already exist or are at least in the process of formation.'[11]

The establishment, in the course of the first stage of the socialist revolution, of social production under public ownership, has laid the economic basis for proletarian–democratic revolution. Highly organized and politico–economically unicorporate social production has effected the organizational preparations for proletarian–democratic revolution. The evil consequences and intensification of contradictions resulting from the coercive monopolization of power by the minority, have provided both the target and the motive force of proletarian–democratic revolution. Lastly, the expansion of production and the popularization of scientific and technical education have established that threshold level of culture which forms a prerequisite for the carrying out of proletarian–democratic revolution.

The lessons which have been learned from historical experience, both of proletarian revolution in the course of the century and more since publication of *The Manifesto of the Communist Party*, and of proletarian dictatorship in the course of almost six decades since the October revolution, have served greatly to enrich the treasure-house of Marxism. This is particularly true with respect, on the one hand, to the bitter experience of the shift to revisionism within the Soviet Union, and, on the other, to the valuable experience, both positive and negative, gained in China during the Great Proletarian Cultural Revolution. These experiences have supplied the abundance of factual data and the foundational strength required for the building of a correct understanding of the laws of socialist society, and for the development of the theory of proletarian dictatorship and the struggle against revisionism.

ii) The active element

What is of particular importance is that all these factors have served greatly to heighten the level of the proletariat's understanding of Marxism. Victory in the New Democratic Revolution and the establishment of public ownership brought about the liberation of the proletariat from enslavement to the means of production and filled it with great hopes for the achievement of socialism. The unfolding of the Great Proletarian Cultural Revolution then brought about a further liberation of the proletariat by releasing it from the bonds of old ideas. This further liberation engendered within the proletariat the firm conviction that it must carry the socialist revolution through to the end, and brought it to an increasingly clear recognition of the essential differences between scientific socialism on the one hand, and feudal socialism, petty-bourgeois socialism, and all other shades and varieties of phoney socialism on the other. Moreover, this further liberation brought the proletariat to a progressively greater understanding of the major historic significance of the struggle between Marxism and revisionism, and to an intense and immediate awareness of the new exploiting class and the new system of exploitation. The pain one feels through senses which have been numbed and dulled is as nothing compared to the pain one experiences in a state of full awareness. Only scars remain from the sufferings of the past, but those of the present jab at every nerve. The total and long-term forfeiture of its own interests has made the proletariat realize that it now stands more thoroughly expropriated than before; it is thus preparing to carry out an equally thorough expropriation of the expropriators. The heart of the proletariat is burning with hatred, ablaze with anger! The proletariat sees quite clearly that the target of the new and still more turbulent settling of accounts that lies ahead is no longer simply the exploitation of the past, but rather that of the present. Hitherto, the proletariat drew inspiration from mere surface perception and propaganda; now, however, through its own experience in political practice, it has attained a secure understanding of the truth: 'It is our interest and our task to make the revolution permanent . . . Our concern cannot simply be to modify private property, but to abolish it, not to hush up class antagonisms but to abolish classes, not to improve the existing society but to found a new one.'[12]

iii) All social systems now in existence are coming to a dead end

Immense changes have now occurred in the world situation and in the sphere of international relations. Just as the sprouts of socialism are beginning to grow and burst forth within the capitalist world, and within the semi-colonial/semi-capitalist – or semi-colonial/semi-feudal – countries, the socialist revolution has been prematurely snuffed out in the great majority of 'socialist' countries. The capitalist world, for its part, despite its much-vaunted values of 'democracy and freedom', is presented with a merciless challenge from the theory of surplus value and from people's revolution. And in the revisionist countries, whilst great play is being made of the 'superiority of socialism', the human rights movement nevertheless fully reveals the cruelty and darkness of the system, and the existence of sharp antagonisms between the system and the people. Behind the joyous strains of 'socialism is marching to victory everywhere', there drifts upwards the banshee wail of revisionism. Under the dominance of their own internal disorders, all social systems now in existence throughout the world are heading down blind alleys and dead-end roads. The entire world longingly awaits the advent of new life — indeed, is itself pregnant with new life. The spectre of war has, moreover, imparted still greater urgency to this sense of longing and expectation, and serves to hasten the day when the new will be born. The thaw in Sino-American relations has, undoubtedly, created intense popular interest in China within the USA, but it must be remembered that what this thaw has meant for China is the throwing open of a window on the outside world. While the startling events which have taken place in China are now, one by one, being revealed to the eyes of the world, it should not be forgotten that the Chinese, for their part, have taken great interest in events such as the resignations of President Nixon of the US and Prime Minister Tanaka of Japan . . . .

iv) The passive element

All this, however, still does not amount to the totality of preparations necessary for proletarian-democratic revolution. Revolution requires the active element, but it also requires the passive element. Where circumstances are such that there exists, as compared to any previous period, '. . . a more variegated mixture of elements, more high-flown phrases, yet more actual uncertainty and awkwardness; more enthusiastic striving for innovation, yet a more fundamental retention of the old routine; a greater appearance of harmony throughout the whole society, yet a more profound alienation between its constituent parts . . .',[13] then the proletariat may only arrive at a recognition of the true path to liberation by way of a series of exploratory attempts ending in defeat. Moreover: 'What was overcome in these defeats was not the revolution. It was the pre-revolutionary, traditional appendages, the products of social relationships which had not yet developed to the point of sharp class antagonisms.'[14] What were overcome in these defeats were the persons, illusions, ideas and projects from which labour-power, seeking to escape its plight as a contradictory aggregate, had hitherto, before the raising of the banner of proletarian–democratic revolution, failed to free itself. Only when the proletariat has made the necessary break with such things will it become capable of rallying under the banner of proletarian–democratic revolution. It is only through practice, however, through a series of defeats, that the proletariat can in fact succeed in freeing itself from such things. Similarly, the proletarian–democratic revolution will have fulfilled its own preparations: 'not by its immediate, tragicomic achievements, but, on the contrary, by creating a powerful and united counter-revolution; only in combat with this opponent did the insurrectionary party mature into a real party of revolution.'[15]

Once the people have reached the point where they are no longer willing to endure the wantonly deceitful propaganda and the policy of unbridled terror perpetrated under revisionism; once they have generally recognized 'what a poor chance stands a political party whose entire stock-in-trade consists in a knowledge of the solitary fact that Citizen So-and-so is not to be trusted';[16] once the ascendancy of revisionism is no longer a secret as far as the broad membership of the governing communist party is concerned; once 'waving the red flag' has produced the severe constraints necessarily resulting therefrom, and the productive forces have been thrown into irredeemably deeper contradiction; once a definite section of the ruling clique has become so disgusted by the despotic nature of the overall system – a system with neither laws nor regulations, '. . . in which a single person directs every thing by his own will and caprice'[17] – that they are willing to accept it no longer; once the farcical redistribution of key government posts has culminated in a major dramatization of internal dissension within the ruling circle; and once the power of leadership in the revolution has passed from the reformists to the Marxists: then will the preparations for proletarian–democratic revolution have been completed in their entirety!

v) The necessary becomes the actual

To summarize: Proletarian–democratic revolution is conditioned by the existing mode of production under socialism, and constitutes a necessary tendency of historical development; it forms a necessary and ineluctable requirement, both for the path of national reconstruction and modernization, and for the struggle against revisionism; it represents, moreover, the necessary development of the Great Proletarian Cultural Revolution. And the necessary becomes, in the end, the real. *'A new revolution is only possible as a result of a new crisis; but it will come, just as surely as the crisis itself.'*[18] Any attempt to obstruct the advent of proletarian–democratic revolution would be not only reactionary but also quite futile. The creatures of reaction, no matter how great the physical and intellectual resources at their disposal, stand exposed in all their bankruptcy before the wheel of history; should they attempt to obstruct its forward progress, they will be mercilessly ground to dust! Of this there can be no doubt. 'The times of that superstition which attributed revolutions to the ill–will of a few agitators, have long passed away. Everyone knows nowadays, that wherever there is a revolutionary convulsion, there must be some social want in the background, which is prevented by outworn institutions from satisfying itself. The want may not yet be felt as strongly, as generally, as might ensure immediate success, but every attempt at forcible repression will only bring it forth stronger and stronger, until it bursts its fetters.'[19] — The necessary nature of events can be expressed no more clearly than in this passage from Engles! Let it firmly be borne in mind: *every attempt at forcible repression of the social want*, the historical necessity, expressed by proletarian–democratic revolution *will only bring it forth stronger and stronger, until it bursts its fetters!* The matter stands precisely thus. Proletarian–democratic revolution constitutes a necessary tendency of historical development, and that which is a necessity will, in the end, become a reality!

III. Actuality

Guiding Principles

1. The Task of Proletarian-Democratic Revolution

The task of proletarian-democratic revolution consists in the complete smashing of that which fetters the unicorporate publisocial productive forces — namely, the relations of production whereby power is coercively monopolized by the minority. This task will mean: converting the conclusions drawn from the Great Proletarian Cultural Revolution into the practice of millions of revolutionaries, in a political movement and social revolution of an unprecedented kind. Into that movement will be drawn both the entire working people at society's grass-root level, and the entire ruling clique at the top. It will mean carrying the great struggle against revisionism through to its conclusion, sweeping away the illusions of reformism and unfolding within the realm of the superstructure, in an all-inclusive and vigorous manner, a truly socialist revolution aimed at the consolidation of an authentic proletarian dictatorship and at the protection and development of a genuine socialist economic base. This would, on the one hand, lead to an unprecedented liberation of the workers and the social productive forces, along with a rapid expansion of socialist production; on the other, it would effectively cancel out the real danger of revisionism gaining the ascendant, and allow the winning of world-wide victory in the socialist revolution and – hence – the laying of a comprehensive and secure foundation for the realization of the great ideal of communism.

2. The Immediate Aim in Proletarian-Democratic Revolution

The immediate aim in proletarian-democratic revolution is to uphold the Marxist theory of the state and the Marxist dialectical-materialist conception of history, and establish a system of proletarian socialist democracy.

This system of proletarian democracy will combine public ownership of the means of production with 'government of the people by the people',[1] *and will thus constitute a socialist system of an entirely new type.*

The proletarian–democratic system will bring about the decisive overthrow of the bureaucrat class, and destroy the privilege-dominated relations of production which allow the minority to exercise coercive dictatorship over the majority; it will once and for all consign the system of appointment, the hierarchical order, the autonomization of the state organs and the sanctification of the party to the rubbish heap of history where they belong; it will bring about the clear establishment and gradual perfection of a system of Marxist legality, the implementation of universal suffrage, and the conversion of the party from an organization of slave-overseers to an instrument in the hands of the slaves themselves; it will found and reinforce a state form conducive to socialist economic development, and will provide, amongst other things, a decisive guarantee for human rights.

The proletarian–democratic system must and will ensure the ability of the working people genuinely to hold power. Under the proletarian–democratic system, each and every worker would enjoy true autonomy, human dignity would be given the respect it deserves, and talent and intelligence would be nurtured, tempered and made use of in a proper manner. A leader would only lead by consent of the majority of the led, and one of the led could in an open and aboveboard fashion become forthwith a leader, if the majority of workers so required. Conversely, if a leader happened to fall out of favour with the majority of workers, he would be able to return quite calmly to a normal life as one of the led, free of the crushing fear of suddenly standing exposed and defenceless before the vengeful machinations of his enemies. The great mass of people, under the proletarian–democratic system, would enjoy actual (rather than merely nominal) freedom of speech, publication, assembly, association, and so forth. The system would offer a secure protection for the people and the revolution; it would provide a firm safeguard for all viewpoints and activities of a creative and revolutionary nature, and would assist the people to break free from ideological bondage.

It would liberate the boundless creativity of the people, and thus provide the basis both for a comprehensive fulfilment of the task of proletarian–democratic revolution, and for a continuous perfection of the form of socialist revolution. This would lead society towards a speedy abolition of classes, exploitation and oppression; the development of science and the conquest of nature would quickly become the main focus of mankind's attention; people would soon achieve the freedom to choose their profession in accordance with their own interests and preferences. The establishment of such a system would provide the majority of people with excellent future prospects and opportunities; it would arouse anew their longing and their efforts in pursuit of a better life, and would rekindle their ardour in the struggle to achieve the lofty ideals of communism.

In short, the proletarian–democratic system represents the only effective weapon by means of which the state may be prevented, once it has undergone the transformation to public ownership of the means of production, from evolving into a state of the revisionist type. Such a system would effectively guarantee that the division of labour in the exercise of power rests with the people, and that, in terms of the actual exercise of power, the power-holders and organs of power exceed neither the bounds of Marxist legality nor the scope of the powers conferred upon them by the people. It is a form necessary to the achievement of modernization.

3. The Three Sources of the Proletarian-Democratic System

i) The means of eliminating the disorder may be drawn from the facts of the period since the October Revolution, and particularly from the facts of the Great Proletarian Cultural Revolution

As Engels points out: 'The growing recognition that existing social institutions are irrational and unjust, that reason has become unreason, and kindness a scourge, is only a sign that changes in the modes of production and exchange have silently been taking place with which the social order adapted to earlier economic conditions is no longer in keeping. From this it also follows that the means of eliminating the abuses that have been brought to light must also be present, in a more or less developed condition, within the changed relations of production themselves. These means are not to be *in-*

vented out of one's brain, but *discovered* by the brain in the existing material facts of production.'[2] This represents a precept of the greatest importance, and on its basis we may proceed to discover the means of eliminating the disorder which we have now located, by examining the historical experience and lessons of proletarian dictatorship over the past six decades, from the time of Russia's October Revolution until the end of China's Great Proletarian Cultural Revolution.

On the eve of his death, five years after the seizure of power, Lenin wrote the following: '[Our first task is to] reorganize our machinery of state, which is utterly useless, and which we took over in its entirety from the preceding epoch.'[3] 'The problem presented by our state apparatus and the task of improving it is very difficult, . . . it is far from being solved, and is an extremely urgent one.'[4] 'Our state apparatus is so deplorable, not to say wretched, that we must first think very carefully how to combat its defects . . .'[5] 'It is time we did something about it. We must show sound scepticism for too rapid progress, for boastfulness, etc. We must give thought to testing the steps forwards we proclaim every hour, take every minute and then prove every second that they are flimsy, superficial and misunderstood.'[6]

Turning to the Great Proletarian Cultural Revolution, initiated and led by Chairman Mao himself, we identify the following: a practice aimed at the reform of those aspects of the superstructure not in harmony with the socialist economic base, revolutions in the arts, in education and in health-care, reform of the state organs, and such phenomena as the Angang Charter.[7] In particular, we identify the ideas put forward by Chairman Mao: the doctrine that the bourgeoisie are to be found within the Communist Party and that the main antagonists of the socialist revolution are the capitalist-roaders within the party; the doctrine that a new change in class relations has occurred, that classes, class contradiction, class struggle and the two different types of contradiction should all be correctly understood and correctly handled; and the doctrine that revisionism represents the greatest danger confronting us at present. Also, we identify 'new-born things' such as the revolutionary committee,[8] and even such things as the problems of factionalism and armed struggle which arose in the course of the Cultural Revolution. All these factors – from the writings of Lenin to the events and ideas of the Cultural Revolution – reveal the nature of the contradiction and the nature of the disorder. They all, to a greater or lesser degree, show us the means of resolving the contradiction and eliminating the disorder. They all more or less exhibit the broad outline of the proletarian–democratic revolution. They form, therefore, the first source of the proletarian–democratic system.

ii) Uphold the principles of the Paris Commune

As Marx proclaimed, the Paris Commune was 'the dawn of the great social revolution which will for ever free the human race from class rule.'[9] 'Its true secret was this. It was essentially a working-class government, the produce of the struggle of the producing against the appropriating class, the political form at last discovered under which to work out the economical emancipation of labour.'[10]

Lenin affirmed the Paris Commune as: 'The political form "at last discovered" by which the smashed state machine can and must be *replaced*,'[11] and he explained also that this political form entailed certain measures 'which were specified in detail by Marx and Engels: — (1) not only election but also recall at any time; — (2) pay not to exceed that of a workman; — (3) immediate introduction of control and supervision by *all*, so that all may become "bureaucrats" for a time and that, therefore, *nobody* may be able to become a "bureaucrat".'[12] As Engels said: 'Look at the Paris Commune. That was the Dictatorship of the Proletariat.'[13] Thus, the principles of the Paris Commune form the second source of the proletarian-democratic system.

iii) Assimilation of the good features of the Euro-American social system

As Lenin once said: 'We must at all costs . . . adopt everything that is truly valuable in European and American science.'[14] 'We ought to send several qualified and conscientious people to Germany, or to Britain, to collect literature and to study this question.'[15] 'The same weapon as the bourgeoisie employs in the struggle must also be used by the proletariat, of course, with entirely different aims. You cannot assert that this is not the case, and if you want to challenge it, you will have thereby to erase the experience of all the revolutionary developments of the world.'[16]

Even more explicit is the following passage from Engels' *Critique of the Draft Social-Democratic Programme of 1891*, as cited and discussed by Lenin in *Marxism and the State* and *The State and Revolution*:

> '. . . complete self-government on the American model . . . is what we too must have. How self-government is to be organized and how we can manage without a bureaucracy has been shown to us by America and the First French Republic, and is being shown even today by Australia, Canada and other English colonies. And a provincial and communal self-government of this type is far freer than, for instance, Swiss federalism, under which, it is true, the canton is very independent in relation to the federation, but is also independent in relation to the district and the commune. The cantonal governments appoint the district governors and prefects, which is unknown in English-speaking countries and which we want to abolish here as resolutely in the future as the Prussian *Landräte* and *Regierungsräte* [committee members, provincial chiefs, county chiefs and all higher appointed officials. (Chen)] . . . "complete self-government in the provinces, districts and communes through officials elected by universal suffrage; the abolition of all local and provincial authorities appointed by the state".'[17]

Crucially, Lenin refers to this passage from Engels as: 'carrying forward the *programme views* of Marxism *on the state*'.[18]

How, then, in the USA and other examples of the Euro-American bourgeois social system, is local self-government organized, and how has the bureaucratic system been dispensed with there? There would appear to be two main points to this, the first of which may be drawn from the 'American Declaration of Independence':

> '. . . when a long train of abuses and usurpations pursuing invariably the same object evinces a design to reduce [the people] under absolute despotism, it is their right, it is their duty, to throw off such government, and to provide new guards for their future security.'[19] '[Governments] derive their just powers from the consent of the governed, — that whenever any form of government becomes destructive of these ends, it is the right of the people to alter or abolish it, and to institute new government, laying its foundations on such principles and organizing its powers in such form as to them shall seem most likely to effect

their safety and happiness.'[20]

Especially noteworthy here is the fact that, in America, the act of overthrowing the old government and organizing a new one has come, on the foundation of these same principles, to be sanctioned by law and regarded as fully rational as far as the bourgeoisie is concerned. What this replacement of old government by new ulti- mately reveals – even though it is true to say that there exists no fundamental difference in essence between the two – is the presence of a *form* allowing continuous change and renewal to take place. And the form itself provides a clear indication of the existence of class democracy within the ruling class, a class democracy which enhances its class resources. America, by means of its written con- stitution, has abolished the system of official appointment, imple- mented universal suffrage, a two–party system and regular elections, imposed a limitation upon the period of office of the president, placed the armed forces under civilian authority, and so forth. Most importantly, through a reliance upon such basic rights of the people as freedom of speech, publication, association and assembly, America has managed to institute local self-government and to dispense with the bureaucratic system.

The second point may be drawn from the following passage by Montesquieu:

'In every government there are three sorts of power: the legis- lative; the executive in respect to things dependent on the law of nations; and the executive in regard to things that depend on the civil laws . . . When the legislative and executive powers are united in the same person, or in the same body of magistracy, there can be then no liberty; because apprehensions may arise, lest the same monarch or senate should enact tyrannical laws, to execute them in a tyrannical manner. Again, there is no liberty, if the power of judging be not separated from the legislative and executive powers. Were it joined with the legislative, the life and liberty of the subject would be exposed to arbitrary control; for the judge would be then the legislator. Were it joined to the executive power, the judge might behave with all the violence of an oppressor. Miserable indeed would be the case, were the same man, or the same body whether of the nobles or of the people, to exercise those three powers, that of enacting laws, that of executing the public resolutions, and that of judging the crimes or differences of individuals.'[21]

America, precisely by means of this tripartite separation of the powers of the legislative, executive and judiciary, has achieved a mutual conditioning, balancing and limitation of power, with power governing power, and this has in turn enabled it to realize local self-government and dispense with the bureaucratic system. Practice has proven that the tripartite separation of powers, local self-government, the two-party system, regular elections and so forth, constitute, in a democratic republic, a truly effective means for dispensing with the bureaucratic system. It is, surely, not impossible that there might be here a certain rational element that the proletariat could usefully assimilate to its own ends – form, after all, invariably serves content. Here, let us again recall the words of Engels: 'The highest form of the state, the democratic republic, which under our modern conditions of society is more and more becoming an inevitable necessity, and is the form of state in which alone the last decisive struggle between proletariat and bourgeoisie can be fought out — the democratic republic officially knows nothing any more of property distinctions.'[22] And, according to Marx: '. . . it is precisely in this last form of state of bourgeois society that the class struggle has to be fought out to a conclusion.'[23]

To ascertain how, precisely, we should interpret these various passages from Marx, Engels and Lenin, we can do no better than turn again to these same authors. As Lenin says: 'To develop democracy to the *utmost,* to find the *forms* for this development, to test them *by practice*, and so forth — all this is one of the component tasks of the struggle for the social revolution.'[24] And, again according to Marx: 'Communism is for us not a *state of affairs* which is to be established, an *ideal* to which reality will have to adjust itself. We call communism the *real* movement which abolishes the present state of things.'[25] 'I assert, therefore', said Engels 'that modern democracy is communism; and is it not clear that I am correct in this?'[26]

A revolutionary sublation★ of the Euro-American social system, a process which would 'absorb whatever experience is useful to us',[27] is thus entirely appropriate. Hence, the good features of this system provide us with the third source of the proletarian-democratic system.

★ On this concept, see final chapter, p.251

4. Passages from the Marxist Classics on the Question of Form

i) Form is always neglected at first for content

As Engels points out: 'We have all, I think, neglected [this aspect of the matter] more than it deserves. It is the old story: form is always neglected at first for content. As I say, I have done that too and the mistake has always struck me only later.'[28]

ii) The principal reason for the bankruptcy of Kautsky and his ilk

As Lenin points out: 'The principal reason for the bankruptcy [of Kautsky, Otto Bauer and others] was that they were hypnotised by a definite form of growth of the working-class movement and socialism, forgot all about the one-sidedness of that form, were afraid to see the break-up which objective conditions made inevitable, and continued to repeat simple and, at first glance, incontestable axioms that had been learned by rote, like: "three is more than two". But politics is more like algebra than arithmetic, and still more like higher than elementary mathematics.'[29]

iii) The duty of Communists

As Lenin, again, points out:

'. . . it is enough to take one little step farther – a step that might seem to be in the same direction – and truth turns into error. We have only to say, as the German and British Left Communists do, that we recognise only one road, only the direct road, and that we will not permit tacking, conciliatory manoeuvres, or compromising — and it will be a mistake which may cause, and in part has already caused and is causing, very grave prejudice to communism. Right doctrinairism persisted in recognising only the old forms, and became utterly bankrupt, for it did not notice the new content. Left doctrinairism persists in the unconditional repudiation of certain old forms, failing to see that the new content is forcing its way through all and sundry forms, that it is our duty as Communists to master all forms, to learn how, with the maximum rapidity, to supplement one form with another, to substitute one for another, and to adapt our tactics to any such change that does not come from our class or from our efforts.'[30]

iv) Two very important practical conclusions

As Lenin says:

'History as a whole, and the history of revolutions in particular, is always richer in content, more varied, more multiform, more lively and ingenious than is imagined by even the best parties, the most class-conscious vanguards of the most advanced classes. This can readily be understood, because even the finest of vanguards express the class-consciousness, will, passion and imagination of tens of thousands, whereas at moments of great upsurge and the exertion of all human capacities, revolutions are made by the class-consciousness, will, passion and imagination of tens of millions, spurred on by a most acute struggle of classes. Two very important practical conclusions follow from this: first, that in order to accomplish its task the revolutionary class must be able to master *all* forms or aspects of social activity without exception (completing after the capture of political power – sometimes at great risk and with very great danger – what it did not complete before the capture of power); second, that the revolutionary class must be prepared for the most rapid and brusque replacement of one form by another.'[31]

v) A point which applies to politics even more than to the art of war

'. . . any army which does not train to use all the weapons, all the means and methods of warfare that the enemy possesses, or may possess, is behaving in an unwise or even criminal manner. This applies to politics even more than it does to the art of war.'[32]

vi) In order to solve the problem, we need to find a new form

As Chairman Mao, during the Great Proletarian Cultural Revolution, declared: 'In the past we waged struggles in rural areas, in factories, in the cultural field, and we carried out the socialist education movement. But all this failed to solve the problem because we did not find a form, a method, to arouse the broad masses to expose our dark aspect openly, in an all-round way and from below.'[33]

vii) The emergence of a new form of struggle is inevitable

Chairman Mao further pointed out: 'The next 50 to 100 years or so, beginning from now, will be a great era of radical change in the social system throughout the world, an earth-shaking era without equal in any previous historical period. Living in such an era, we must be prepared to engage in great struggles which will have many features different in form from those of the past.'[34]

10
The Proletarian-Democratic System

1. Supreme State Leadership under the Proletarian-Democratic System

i) The crisis of confidence in the party

In the political systems of the contemporary socialist world, state leadership is exercised by the single, unique communist party organization within each state. However, given the painful historical fact that some communist parties, in the Soviet Union and elsewhere, have lapsed into revisionism, the question inevitably arises: can socialist states afford to *retain*, and should the proletariat and the mass of the working population continue to *assent* to the leadership of such communist parties?

For, in fundamental terms, leadership by a party that is nominally communist but in reality revisionist ceases to be either Marxist or revolutionary in nature, and becomes, instead, vicious and counter-revolutionary domination by traitors to the Marxist cause. It ushers in a form of exploitation and oppression unprecedented in its inhumanity: the regime of the bureaucrat-monopoly privileged class. The only direction in which such communist parties are capable of 'leading', is down from the red heights of socialism and into the dark vale of revisionism. Thus, the indispensable first step in ensuring that socialist states remain so is to break away from and overthrow such communist party leadership.

But what such party would ever voluntarily repudiate the name 'communist' and admit itself to be revisionist? This has never happened in the past and will not occur in the future. On the contrary, a party which has become revisionist will go all out to proclaim itself as a model to other communist parties, as not merely revolutionary, but as the most revolutionary of all – as not merely Marxist, but as embodying the purest and most orthodox form of Marxism possible! Furthermore, none of the existing socialist states has been able to circumvent the practice of a mode of production comprising unicorporate publisocial production and coercive monopolization of power by the minority. Under the dominance of this mode of production, great changes must occur – and have already occurred – within the governing communist party and within class relations as a whole. Observing such change, people inevitably begin to wonder: what actually do we have here – Marxism or revisionism? Thus, with ruthless inexorability, history produces a crisis of confidence in the leadership of the communist party organization.

ii) Party leadership is indispensable

If the socialist cause were to be bereft of the leadership of the kind of communist party envisaged in the *Manifesto*, if it were to be bereft of Marxist leadership, then it could not possibly succeed. And, unquestionably: 'The force at the core leading our cause forward is the Chinese Communist Party. The theoretical basis guiding our thinking is Marxism-Leninism.'[1] The problem is, how may we ensure that the leadership of the Communist Party remains permanently grounded on a Marxist theoretical basis, that it does not betray that basis and sink into revisionism? Confronted by the reality of the main enemy of the revolution being located within a power-holding faction of the Communist Party, and as a consequence the present rapid proliferation of that faction, it now behoves us to consider in which form party leadership might best be embodied in order to make it accord with reality, with science, with development, with the overall orientation of the socialist economic base, and with Marxism in general.

iii) Organizational leadership is not the most fundamental aspect

Prior to the Great Proletarian Cultural Revolution, party leadership was regarded as consisting in leadership by individual party members, that is to say in leadership by work-groups appointed by the various branches, committees and organizations of the party, in leadership delegated to individuals by the party organization. As a result, party leadership fell for a period into a condition of extreme absurdity and reaction. It was precisely in the course of the defence of this putative party leadership that the counter-revolutionary revisionist line developed to a most alarming degree! That is, the inversion of right and wrong, the blurring of truth and falsehood, the encirclement and suppression of the revolutionary faction, the fostering of the ambitions of the bureaucrat class and the destruction of the power and prestige of the proletariat and working people as a whole. The tempests of the Great Proletarian Cultural Revolution and the intensity and acuteness of the actual class struggle dispelled this shameful confusion. At the same time, the evolution, disclosure and development of the situation as a whole, together with the series of directives from Chairman Mao indicating the presence of the bourgeoisie within the Communist Party itself and identifying the capitalist-roaders within the party as being the key target of the revolution, served to shatter the sanctification of the party. The Chinese people, tempered in the Great Proletarian Cultural Revolution, now possess a correct understanding of the concept of party leadership. The revolutionary masses have now understood that only when it is inspired by Marxism itself is 'communist party leadership' worthy of the description. Under Chairman Mao's leadership, the Communist Party itself has specifically laid down the principle: 'In the unified leadership of the party, correct ideology and a correct political line are fundamental.'[2]

This change and development in terms of the concept of 'party leadership' is a reflection of objective laws independent of man's subjective will, a product of the contemporary class struggle, and represents the summation of experiences painfully acquired in the course of revolutionary practice by millions of people. It substantiates, also, the following thesis: during the first stage of socialist revolution, under the White Terror, the party organizational leadership was, by and large, entirely at one with the revolutionary project of Marxism; but during the second stage, the structural system whereby power was coercively monopolized by the minority served to induce immense changes within the party, and in class relations as a whole, and these changes then gradually – and inevitably – began to render the party organization (that is, the power-holding clique within the party) more often than not an *obstacle* to the achievement of the Marxist revolutionary project. Hence, organizational leadership cannot be said to represent the most fundamental aspect of party leadership.

iv) The supremacy of the written Marxist constitution

Quite clearly, real party leadership can consist only in the leadership provided by Marxism itself. However, Marxism is a vast and expansive doctrine, and one which forms moreover (as the founders of Marxism frequently and explicitly pointed out) not a dead dogma but rather a living guide to action. How best then might we fashion out of it a 'steering wheel' enabling society as a whole to direct its own course towards a secure grasp and application of the spirit and essence of Marxism? How best might we prevent this living guide to action being, intentionally or otherwise, misrepresented and turned into a dead dogma? What is in fact required here, is that the basic principles of Marxism be summarized and condensed, and handed over to the people in clear and concise legal form.

Hence, under the proletarian–democratic system, the supreme leadership of the state would be vested in a written Marxist constitution. All would be equal before the constitution, and all, no matter who, would be obliged to respect, obey and be restricted by the terms of the constitution. Anyone infringing the constitution would incur the full penalties and sanctions of the law.

2. Political Parties under the Proletarian-Democratic System

i) The two-party system

In order to guarantee the supreme authority of the written Marxist constitution, so that the latter truly functions as the highest arbiter in the state, the communist party must be turned into an instrument for its faithful implementation, and must be prevented from becoming a means for its arbitrary and paternalistic manipulation or distortion. To this end, first and foremost, the single communist party system must be discarded, and replaced by a *dual* communist party system.

Under the proletarian–democratic system, the organizational leadership of the two parties would be principally embodied in their publications (books, newspapers, magazines and so forth). To facilitate the dissolution of factional prejudice, neither party would have a fixed membership. People would be entirely free to leave one party and join the other in accordance with their degree of support for the policies of either party, and would not thereby incur reproach of any kind. The newspaper editorial department of each of the two parties would serve as its principal standing body; the expenses of each party would be met on an equitable basis by the state, and the state would also supervise the use of such monies. Both parties would have the responsibility of providing their own candidates for formal administrative leadership posts so that the people would be presented with a choice in the matter. Political power would then fall to the party which had been shown by a general election to enjoy the support of a majority in the country.

Under the proletariat–democratic system, any organization or faction which did not believe in, respect and obey the written Marxist constitution would be resolutely proscribed. However, such a proscription would arise naturally out of the rational environment which would obtain once the irrefutable truth of Marxism had come to attain full sway. The glow-worm's feeble beam cannot compete with the brilliance of full sunlight.

ii) The advantages of the two-party system

'Marxism can develop only through struggle, and this is not only true of the past and the present, it is necessarily true of the future as well. What is correct invariably develops in the course of struggle with what is wrong. The true, the good and the beautiful always exist by contrast with the false, the evil and the ugly, and grow in struggle with them.'[3]

The two-party system would provide a rational form for the containment of such contrast and struggle. It would supply the requisite conditions and platform for the public expression, discussion and testing of opinions, views and policies contrary to those of the ruling party. The written Marxist constitution would, in turn, allow the opinions, views and policies of the ruling party to be integrated on a correct basis and orientation with those of the party in opposition. The presence of such democracy and legality would result in falsehood being driven into the open and deprived of all sanctuary. Controversy would be resolved by the people, by the constitution, and by appeal to reason, rather than by resort to sheer might; controversy would thus become, not a source of error and falsehood, but rather a means of establishing the truth. The two-party system would therefore legitimize the revolution, bring about a reverence for the truth, and remove all trace of the monstrous and shameless conspiratorial intrigues generated by the struggle for power under the one-party system. The establishment of a two-party system would provide an effective means for supervising the government's exercise of authority and for stopping those in power abusing that power, and would facilitate a rapid and smooth correction of mistakes in the political line; it would be a most forceful measure in the direction of preventing the governing communist party degenerating into a paternalistic, slave-driving organ controlled by the bureaucrat-monopoly privileged class.

iii) The historical origins of the two-party system

As has been eloquently proven by history, the two-party system of bourgeois democracy provides the bourgeoisie with an extremely effective means of consolidating its own rule. The Watergate Affair over Nixon in the USA has made people reflect deeply upon certain questions: What is it that prevents the American president from abusing his power of office? What is it that forces a bourgeois president to pledge his loyalty to the public office he holds, and makes it impossible for him to flout the law for private ends? What is it that left such a powerful president as Nixon with no other option but resignation? Is it not, precisely, the existence of bourgeois democracy and legality; and is it not, precisely, the implementation under such democracy and legality of a two-party system in which the political party, rather than being able to dictate to the bourgeoisie, can instead only serve as its instrument? Again, we need only enquire thus far to ascertain why, for example, the development of Japan has been so rapid, and why Tanaka was forced to resign close upon the heels of his American counterpart Nixon. The bourgeois two-party form represents the cumulative outcome of a historical process; it has the capacity to bring about an effective mobilization of the resources of the entire ruling class, it permits the operation of a mutual restriction and supervision within the ruling class itself, and thereby militates against the expansion of privilege and the bureaucratization of those in public office. It is thus conducive to the preservation of the rule of the ruling class, to the mitigation of contradictions both within the ruling class and between the latter and the classes over which it rules, and to the promotion of a healthy replacement of the old by the new within the organs of state. Form assists content, while content determines form. If the proletariat can copy *in toto* the army, police, prisons and so forth of the bourgeois dictatorship, why then should it not also be able to put the two-party system to its own use?

iv) The theoretical basis of the two-party system

The authors of the Marxist classics all fully affirmed the revolutionary role of the proletarian political party, but none of them said that the proletariat could have only one political party. The world has never witnessed a bird able to fly only with one wing, or a man or beast able to run on one leg alone. In searching for some theoretical proof that the proletariat is also quite capable of operating a two-party system, it is hardly necessary to invoke the dialectical principles of 'one dividing into two' and 'the unity of opposites', nor to cite numerous quotations; it is sufficient to point out the single fact that, in their famous work *The Manifesto of the Communist Party*, Marx and Engels explicitly state: 'The Communists do not form a separate party opposed to other working-class parties.'[4] We trust that this will be accepted as being a sufficiently authoritative and clear pronouncement upon the matter.

Why should the proletariat have only one political party? Why must we '. . . stir everything into one nondescript brew, which, at the moment it is left to settle, throws up the differences again but in much sharper contrast because they will then be all in one pot . . . For this reason, the biggest sectarians and the biggest brawlers and rogues,' – and none more than the political swindlers who specialize in conspiratorial intrigue and whose goal is revisionism – 'at times shout loudest for unity. Nobody in our lifetime has given us more trouble and been more treacherous than the shouters for unity.' . . . 'One must not allow oneself to be misled by the cry for "unity".'[5]

The attitude adopted by Marx and Engels towards the First International offers us a fine example of how to deal with a party which has hitherto played a major role and performed immense contributions to the cause. The First International, founded by Marx and directed by Marx and Engels, '. . . laid the foundation for an international organization of workers, and allowed the latter to prepare for a revolutionary offensive against capital.'[6] The time would come, however, when Engels could write of the First International that 'in its old form it has outlived its usefulness,'[7] and – without a trace of sentimentality – that '. . . the *old* International is anyhow entirely wound up and at an end. And that is well.'[8]

Engels also wrote the following concerning the International:

'Naturally every party leadership wants to see successes, and this is quite a good thing. But there are circumstances in which one must have the courage to sacrifice *momentary* success for more important things. Especially for a party like ours, whose ultimate success is so absolutely certain, and which has developed so enormously in our own lifetime and before our own eyes, momentary success is by no means always and absolutely necessary. Take the International for instance. After the Commune it had a colossal success. The bourgeois, struck all of a heap, ascribed omnipotence to it. The great mass of the membership believed things would stay like that for all eternity. We knew very well that the bubble *must* burst. All the riff-raff attached themselves to it. The sectarians within it became arrogant and misused the International in the hope that the meanest and most stupid actions would be permitted them. We did not allow that. Knowing well that the bubble must burst some time, our concern was not to delay the catastrophe but to take care that the International emerged from it pure and unadulterated. The bubble burst at the Hague . . . . Moreover, old man Hegel said long ago: A party proves itself victorious by *splitting* and being able to stand the split. The movement of the proletariat necessarily passes through different stages of development; at every stage part of the people get stuck and do not join in the further advance; and this alone explains why it is that actually the "solidarity of the proletariat" is everywhere being realised in different party groupings . . .'[9]

v) *Existing portents of the two-party system*

The first indicator of the emergence of a dual communist party system is, that in many places where public ownership has not yet been established, there has emerged alongside the main communist party – and especially since the time of the great polemic between China and the Soviet Union – one or even several new communist party organizations taking the postfix 'Marxist-Leninist'.

The second such indicator is that in all those countries where public ownership has already been established, major factional struggles have taken place from top to bottom within each of the communist parties in government. These struggles have, moreover, only become more intense with the passage of time, to the point

where there are now signs of the disintegration of the parties concerned. Throughout the course of the immense divisions and mortal
struggles that have occurred within the Chinese Communist Party
during the past decade, there have existed not merely two separate
headquarters, but also, from top to bottom and at all levels, two
distinct major factions. The sharp antagonisms of the actual class
struggle, the immense influence exerted by Marxism, and the actual
class position of the existing communist parties, all determine the
inevitability of internal splits occurring within these parties. However, rather than allowing these splits to manifest themselves
through shady conspiracies carried on behind the palace curtain – a
course of action which would indeed end contention and rivalry, but
only by destroying the revolution itself – it would be far preferable to
seek a legitimization of the revolution by means of an open and
above-board appeal to the facts and through the public expression of
political views, and by means of a ballot of the citizenry. The latter
would serve both as a final judgement as to what is right and wrong,
and as a means of determining who is to be in power and who in
opposition.

The third such indicator is that, during the Great Proletarian
Cultural Revolution, the masses in all areas generally split into two
major factions. Far from being merely accidental, this in fact served
likewise as an inevitable reflection of the change in actual class
relations. Other factors apart from this determining one of class
relations should also be considered: the mutual hostility of the two
factions reflected a strong sense of self-confidence – albeit one lacking as yet the justification of a popular mandate – while the armed
struggle waged between the two factions reflected a deep sense of
frustration at the lack of any credible democratic system of resolving
disputes.

The fourth such indicator is: the revolutionary committees created
during the Great Proletarian Cultural Revolution. Both the cadre
delegate and the masses' delegate to these committees were recommended to office by the two distinct factions within the masses as a
whole, with only the military delegate being appointed by the higher-
level authorities. However, this recommendation had to operate
within the constraints of the one-party system, and so candidacy
tended to depend upon whether or not one was a party member, and

upon whether or not one could pass the stringent tests relating to class origin. Moreover, it resulted not in the creation of responsible leadership groups composed of those delegates enjoying the support of a majority of the people, but rather in two equal delegates from the distinct factions simply being thrown together in a situation of mutual wrangling and antagonism, and hence being able to achieve very little of real service to the people. The nature of political power, therefore, could still not be said to have undergone any fundamental revolutionary transformation, and dissension, discord and inefficiency formed the inevitable outcome. Nonetheless, the creation of revolutionary committees composed of those recommended by the two mass factions provided certain indications of an incipient two-party system based upon universal suffrage.

The fifth, and perhaps most conspicuous real-life portent of the proletarian two-party system is: the 'May 7th' cadre schools which emerged in the course of the Great Proletarian Cultural Revolution. The 'May 7th' cadre schools were not merely a manifestation of the fact that cadre ranks had become so swollen and overblown as to have produced an actual surplus; in themselves, they expressed a situation tantamount to one section of the Communist Party cadre being in office whilst another went into opposition. The question of who was to hold office and who was to be in opposition was, however, determined not by the people but by the power-holding faction within the party. Then again, there is the whole question of 'tempering through labour'. Because of the one-party system, such a method of tempering the opposition kept those concerned far divorced from the people as a whole; rather than being sent down to suffer weal and woe alongside the people, they were instead isolated from the people, and sent off to live on special farms.

As an integral part of the proletarian-democratic system, the proletarian two-party system, like the proletarian-democratic revolution itself, constitutes a necessary tendency of historical development and therefore will assuredly become a reality. The proletariat is both fully justified in and fully capable of mastering and applying the two-party system. It must no longer permit any single political party to place its own factional and cliquish interests before the interests of the people as a whole. Only by first liberating itself from its enslavement under the political party will the proletariat be able ultimately to liberate all mankind; and, as Marx long ago said, only by liberating all mankind will the proletariat be able to achieve its own ultimate liberation.

3. The Basis of Power under the Proletarian-Democratic System

Whereas, under the proletarian-democratic system, the written Marxist constitution would, represent the supreme leadership of the state, a people's-democratic republican system of universal suffrage, whereby every worker would enjoy the right to vote and the right to stand for election, would constitute the basis of state power as a whole. Under the proletarian-democratic system, state sovereignty would rest with the entire working people headed by the proletariat. Consent and ratification by all workers would have to be sought on any matter concerning the creation of structures of power, the formulation of laws, and the appointment and dismissal of bearers of office.

As Marx pointed out: 'The workers demand the republic, for they no longer see it as a political distortion of the old system of class rule, but as a revolutionary means for the abolition of class rule itself.'[10] And as Engels pointed out: 'Universal suffrage is the gauge of the maturity of the working class.'[11] 'Democracy has become the proletarian principle, the principle of the masses. The masses may be more or less clear about this, the correct meaning of democracy, but all have at least an obscure feeling that social equality of rights is implicit in democracy.'[12] 'The republic . . . is the *ready-for-use* political form for the future rule of the proletariat.'[13] 'If one thing is certain, it is that our Party and the working class can only come to power under the form of a democratic republic. This is even the specific form for the dictatorship of the proletariat . . .'[14]

Quite clearly, since the means of production are now publicly owned, power therefore rightfully belongs, both in name and in reality, to the people themselves. 'All power to the people!' is the principle which must be upheld within the power structure of the proletarian-democratic system.

4. The Upper-Level Structure of Power under the Proletarian-Democratic System

i) The legislature:
The system of conferences of people's delegates

The conferences of people's delegates (people's conferences) of the proletarian-democratic system would, in essence, be quite different from the congresses of people's delegates (people's congresses) of the despotic one-party system of revisionism. Under the proletarian-democratic system: the people's conference would be, both in name and in fact, an organ of legislative power; all citizens of 18 years of age and above would have the right to elect people's delegates, and to stand for election as a people's delegate. Delegates to grassroots, sub-county level people's conferences would be determined entirely through direct popular election. Delegates to people's conferences above county level would be determined through indirect popular election; that is, they would be elected by lower-level people's conferences.

The first session of the National People's Conference held under the proletarian-democratic system would be charged with the mission of formulating a new constitution, together with a new electoral law and other such urgently-required laws and decrees. Quotas of delegates would be apportioned on the basis of present administrative divisions, with a minimum of one delegate from each county. (At a future date, China should be divided into 60 provinces, municipalities and autonomous regions, and the district-level administrative division should be abolished.) Counties and munici-palities with a population of over one million could, after delibera-tion, be allowed one extra delegate, and special attention would be given to quotas of national minority delegates and also women's delegates.

Delegates to the National People's Conference would be nomi-nated by the people's conferences at county level, would then be determined through direct election by the entire population of the country, and would hold office for a period of two years. They would have each year of their term of office apportioned as follows: two months within the electoral ward, continuing to work at their original work-unit and in their former occupation; a further two months within the electoral ward, carrying out wide-ranging social investigation, and being obliged, if the delegate's own occupation had been non-manual, to participate in grass-roots manual labour; two months away, making outside visits and interviews; a further two months engaging in political and legal work, of which one month would be spent as a juror and the other as a defence counsel; two months pursuing theoretical studies, investigating problems and preparing motions and proposals; the final two months would be devoted to participation in the annual preparatory and official conferences.

Delegates' wages would, without exception, be the same as that accorded to them in their original work-unit, occupation, and occupational grade. (All administrative expenses, including non-statutory travel expenses, boat and train fares, would, however, be met by the state treasury.)

During periods of session of the National People's Conference, delegates from universities, middle-schools and primary-schools could, by special arrangement and as the occasion demands, be allowed to attend as observers; such delegates would have the right to speak but not to vote.

The Standing Committee of the National People's Conference would be composed of three to five delegates, and these could either be elected by and from the various delegations to Conference from all the provinces, municipalities and autonomous regions, or else determined by the electorate as a whole, through universal suffrage and on the basis of a system of proportional representation; the Standing Committee would serve as the permanent body of the National People's Conference. Members of the Standing Committee would hold office for a period of six years at a time, with one third of the members coming up for re-election every two years. No-one holding executive office in the government would be permitted, during the period of that office, to serve as a delegate to, or member of the Standing Committee of, the National People's Conference.

The National People's Conference would be empowered to revise the constitution and to draft laws; to investigate, appoint and dismiss, on the advice of the elected president, the ministers and other personnel of the various government departments; to formulate and ratify the national economic plan, the national budget, and foreign policy; to supervise and impeach the executive branch of government, and to perform any other functions which it might deem appropriate. The Standing Committee of the National People's Conference would be empowered, by Conference, to convene the National People's Conference, interpret the law, draft decrees, handle day-to-day foreign affairs, conduct all impeachment proceedings, and so forth.

However, all draft laws and decrees drawn up by the National People's Conference and by its Standing Committee would only come into effect once they had been passed on to, and had received the signature of, the elected president. In cases where the president assented to the proposed law, he would sign it; alternatively, he could express disagreement with the proposed law by rejecting it, and would then be obliged to explain his reasons for so doing. If, after giving reconsideration to a proposed law that had been thus rejected by the president, the delegates to the National People's Conference were to decide, by more than a two-thirds majority, that the item in question should after all stand, the matter could then either be passed on for discussion and deliberation by the people as a whole, and settled by referendum; or else be passed on for resolution by the total membership of the people's conferences at levels higher than that of the county. If the law or decree were, by either method, to receive majority support, it would then be formally instituted. Any proposed laws which, having been submitted to the president, were then delayed or suppressed by him for more than one month, would come into force automatically at the end of that period.

The National People's Conference would not, however, be permitted to draft any law depriving the people of freedom of speech, publication, assembly, association, petition, and so forth.

Under the proletarian-democratic system, full local autonomy would be exercised, and all appointment of senior local officials by the Centre would be totally abolished. All rules, therefore, regarding the requisite credentials for becoming a delegate to the National People's Conference or to its Standing Committee, the limitations upon the power of such delegates, and the method of determining such delegates, may be extended to cover all the people's conferences, from provincial, municipal and autonomous regional levels, right down to the district and county levels. The basic principles involved are just as applicable to people's conferences at the grass-roots of society.

The local people's conference would exercise those powers of office stipulated in the constitution; it would be responsible for examining and approving the personnel of the local administrative organs, on the basis of nominations provided by the elected head of the local administration; it would be able, in line with the principle of 'suiting measures to local conditions', to draft laws and decrees appropriate to specific local circumstances (but only within the limits stipulated in the constitution and in the laws and decrees of the Centre); it would supervise the legal rectitude, proper functioning, and working efficiency of the local administrative authorities, and would have full powers of impeachment. The Standing Committee would deal with any work with which it had been entrusted by the people's conference, and would have full powers of trial and impeachment.

ii) The executive:
The presidential system

Under the proletarian–democratic system, the executive power of the state would be vested in a president. The term 'president' is on the face of it clearly superior, as a description, to either 'chairman' or 'premier'. The term 'chairman', despite having the democratic connotations of 'presiding over a meeting' and 'allowing everyone to have their say', nonetheless appears to be limited to the sphere of meetings alone, and to lack the idea of action. The term 'premier',[15] on the other hand, despite having the authoritative implications of 'being occupied with a multiplicity of day-to-day affairs of state' and 'having more than enough power to act', is nonetheless suggestive of the general failing of taking everything upon oneself and encroaching upon the masses' own sphere of responsibility. By contrast, the term 'president'[16] would seem to achieve a felicitous integration of the twin ideas of debate and action, democracy and centralism, the leader and the great mass of the people. Under the proletarian-democratic system, the president, wielding the executive power of the state, would be charged with the lofty responsibilities of maintaining an intimate link with the masses, establishing a reliance upon them and providing them with a commanding leadership, of remaining faithful to Marxism, of respecting the constitution, of steadfastly adhering to the path of socialism, of struggling ardently for the realization of communism, and of carrying out permanent revolution.

The president would have a four-year term of office, and would not be permitted more than two consecutive terms in office. The holding of the office for life, and the shouting of 'long live the president'[17] would be prohibited.

The procedure for the presidential election would be as follows: candidates would be put forward by each of the two parties at their respective conferences, and these presidential candidates would then choose vice-presidential candidates from amongst their own aides. The state would provide the candidates from both parties with full and equal access to all propaganda organs, thus allowing them to expound their own political views and policies before the people of the nation as a whole, and allowing the people to make their own choice.

The method of indirect election would be used for the presidency. All those citizens eligible to vote would, within a specified period of time applicable to all parts of the nation, and in a manner determined by the people's conferences of all the various provinces, municipalities and autonomous regions, select a certain number of electors to form an electoral college for each province; these electoral colleges would then assemble in their respective provincial capitals and cast their votes. Each electoral college would then sort out and count up the result of the ballot, document this result in certificate form, furnish an official seal, and send the certificate by aeroplane to the Chairman of the National People's Conference. The said chairman would have the responsibility of opening, in front of the assembled delegates, all the sealed certificates, and of publicly registering the ballot counts upon a screen; the assembled delegates would thereupon calculate the outcome of the ballot counts, and the candidate with the greatest number of votes would then become the elected president. However, the candidate concerned would have to have received the vote of more than half the total number of electors. If no-one were to receive the required number of votes, then a re-election would have to be carried out by the National People's Conference itself, and whoever received the greater number of votes would then become president. If the two candidates were to receive an equal number of votes, then the National People's Conference would again have to vote immediately to elect one of the two.

Delegates to the current session of the National People's Conference, and personnel currently working in the administrative organs of the state, would not be eligible to serve as electors.

Any citizen of more than 35 years of age, and who had been resident in China for over 15 years, would be eligible to stand for election to the presidency. Any citizen of more than 30 years of age, and who had been resident in China for over ten years, would be eligible to stand for election to the vice-presidency.

Should the president be dismissed, die while in office, resign, or become incapable of fulfilling the functions of the presidency, then the duties of the office would be carried out by the vice-president. Should both the president and the vice-president be dismissed, die while in office, resign, or become incapable of holding office, then the National People's Conference would have the responsibility of electing an acting president who would hold the office until such time as either the president had recovered his abilities or a new president had been elected.

As for the president's wage, a supply system would be operated according to statutory criteria laid down by the National People's Conference, and no arbitrary increase or reduction would be allowed. Upon relinquishing office, the president would be free to choose any occupation that accorded with his own interests, but would retain a natural responsibility to serve as a high-level adviser to the state. The state would have the duty of preserving the safety of the former president, of guaranteeing his material welfare, of supplying him with funds for research, of providing him with appropriate conditions for engaging in writing activities, and so forth.

For the assumption of office, a ceremony would be held at which the president-elect would take an oath of office and make an inaugural declaration.

The president would be commander-in-chief of the armed forces of the entire nation. The president would put forward his own choice of personnel, and, having secured the approval of a majority in the National People's Conference, would appoint ministers for the various departments and so form a responsible cabinet; he would also appoint ambassadors, consuls, supreme court judges, and other high-level state cadres. The procedures to be followed for such nominations and appointments would be laid down by the National People's Conference in accordance with the stipulations of the law.

The president would report on the state of the nation to the

National People's Conference whenever necessary, and any measures or policies which he himself might deem necessary to adopt would have to be submitted to the National People's Conference for its examination and final decision. The president would be empowered to convene extraordinary sessions of the National People's Conference and of the Standing Committee in times of emergency. He would hold audiences with his diplomatic envoys, and instruct the heads of all branches of the administration to report to him at specific intervals, either in person, or in letters composed by their own hand, regarding the state of work in their respective branches, and raising any suggestions they might have. He would monitor the proper implementation of all laws, and supervise the execution of policy by, and the working efficiency of, the state organs. He would, moreover, bear full responsibility for the above items.

The president, vice-president, and all the cadres of the state organs would be fully obliged to submit to supervision by the masses, and would, if ever impeached for crimes such as violating the constitution, engaging in the factional pursuit of private gain, perpetrating revisionism, engendering division, and indulging in conspiracy and ingrigue, be stripped of office and replaced.

On the basis of this description of the state administrative organs, the method of determining those in leadership thereof, and the limitations upon the power of those leaders, one can readily form an analogous description of the administrative organs at provincial, district, county, and grass-roots levels.

iii) The judiciary:
The Marxist legal system

Under the proletarian-democratic system, the judicial power of the state would rest with the Supreme People's Court, with Higher, Intermediate, and Primary People's Courts devised and instituted by the people's conferences, and with the Court of Appeal.

Judges would attain office through election. They would have to be proficient in law, well versed in the basic principles of Marxism, and in possession of considerable powers of logical deduction. They would be required to be fair and impartial, upright of character, and not susceptible to flattery. Provided they discharged their duties faithfully, judges could remain in office for life, and would be held in high esteem by society; those who proved to be defective of character would be liable to immediate dismissal by the people's conference.

Under the proletarian-democratic system, the state should, as a priority, establish schools of political science and law; such institutions would be, in effect, schools of Marxism. Under the proletarian-democratic system, those who had no understanding of Marxism and lacked the dialectical-materialist conception of history would be able to accomplish very little in political life. The progressive world-view would establish itself amongst the population as never before, and this would inevitably prove of enormous assistance to mankind in its efforts to transform the objective world.

Such a system of law would involve the use of legal counsel, people's jury and open trial. However, the profession of lawyer would not be a fixed and specialized one: anyone, from any walk of life, would, if entrusted to act as counsel by either party in litigation, be held to have lawyer status.

In order to ensure the promotion of justice, secret trials would be utterly abolished. Defendants would have the right either to conduct their own defence, or to entrust their defence to a people's delegate or some other personage in society. Defendants would be permitted to confront the plaintiff or other witnesses in court, and to present evidence in their own favour. In the absence of completion of the statutory procedure, the accused could not be arrested, and his personal security and place of residence would be inviolable. The hearing of cases should not be delayed over lengthy periods of time. Trials would be conducted publicly – and at the administrative level for which the particular details of the case had the greatest significance – in the administrative centre of the area in which the case had arisen.

In order that erroneous judgements and improper verdicts might be avoided, or, where they arose, be rectified, a convicted person would be permitted, indeed guaranteed the opportunity to lodge an appeal, and would be assured a conscientious consideration of that appeal. Courts of Appeal should be instituted in all places with Higher Courts. The court, the procuratorate and the public security bureau should be distinct and separate from one another. Law-enforcement officials who were to employ private methods of investigation, obtain confessions by coercive means, or bind, beat or otherwise illegally interrogate suspects, would, on account of having exploited their position in order to violate the law, be punished with correspondingly greater severity.

The National People's Conference would necessarily have to devise, on the basis of the fundamental principles of Marxism, civil laws, criminal laws, economic laws and regulations, and so forth, to serve as a yardstick for making judgements in court. It would no longer be permissible to invoke 'the needs of the situation' – in reality, the free play of the capricious moods and whims of the bureaucrat, and the manipulation of social connections – for such would be an insult to the courts and would threaten the interests of the people!

Under the proletarian-democratic system and the Marxist system of law, every citizen would have the right to criticise those in power, and would in turn have the duty to undergo self-criticism and accept criticism from others. Slander and libel would be socially quite unacceptable. The right to criticize a serving president would, in the interests both of the state and of the people as a whole, be not only guaranteed by law, but actually supported by society. Criticism of the president would under no circumstances be regarded as constituting a crime; and it would be utterly unthinkable that anyone might ever deserve a cruel death for daring to contradict the president. Under the Marxist legal system, military-bureaucratic fascist tyranny would be buried once and for all.

5. The Grass-roots Structure of Power under the Proletarian-Democratic System

i) The factory

The Great Proletarian Cultural Revolution saw the emergence within the factory not only of the revolutionary committee, but also of such phenomena as the election of team and group leaders by the workers, the institution of workers' management committees, cadres going down to the grass-roots of society, and workers being stationed in the administrative organs. These portents offered a clear and ample indication of the desire for democracy on the part of the working class, and of its demands for mastery over its own affairs.

Under the proletarian-democratic system, the workers of each factory would exercise their powers of legislation and supervision through a conference of workers' delegates (workers' conference).[18] The workers' conference would be responsible for formulating production quotas and plans for its own factory, supervising the work of the factory director and of the entire management structure, and so forth. The factory workers' conference would gather, at regular intervals, to hear reports from the factory director concerning the work of the factory, would keep a check on the overall work of the factory revolutionary committee, etc.

The total quota of delegates in each factory would be apportioned rationally amongst the various workshops in accordance with the specific circumstances of the factory concerned. Delegates to the factory workers' conference from each workshop would be determined through direct election by the workers of each workshop. The factory director, the members of the factory revolutionary committee, persons in charge of the various departments of the administration, and workshop foremen, would not, however, during their period in office, be allowed to serve as factory delegates. Delegates would hold office for a period of two years.

Factory delegates would not be released from production duties for reasons other than attendance at workers' conferences or pursuit of necessary study. Unified arrangements could, however, be made by either the factory workers' conference or the factory revolutionary committee for delegates to spend time in other workshops working at a variety of different jobs and gaining on-the-spot experience in the various departments of management (the administrative organs, canteens, shops, hospitals, etc.), for this would allow them to acquire a grasp of the situation as a whole, carry out their supervisory functions, and promote improvements in the work of management.

Administrative power within the factory would be vested in the factory director, and in a factory revolutionary committee composed of persons nominated by the factory director and approved by a majority vote in the workers' conference (the factory director being the head of the said committee). The factory director would be determined through direct election by the entire workforce of the factory. The factory workers' conference would charge the elected factory director, and the factory revolutionary committee under him, with the responsibility of ensuring (by the employment of capable personnel, streamlined administration, and the maintenance of a high level of efficiency) the proper execution of political and ideological work, production and vocational work, work on finances and wages, social welfare work, and cultural and educational work within the factory as a whole. The elected factory director would bear full responsibility for the above items. A two-year period would be the most appropriate term of office for both the factory director and the revolutionary committee.

If either the factory director or the working personnel of the revolutionary committee office were to show dereliction of duty, or to infringe the law or the code of conduct, the factory workers' conference would be empowered to dismiss and replace them immediately. (The revolutionary committee might, alternatively, be termed the committee of management.)

Under the tyrannical order of privilege resulting from coercive monopolization of power by the minority, the system of having a party secretary in charge, and that of having a factory director in charge, both amount to forms of dictatorship. However, Lenin's statement that 'It is true . . . management is the job of the individual administrator,'[19] *would* indeed be true and applicable in the context of a system of people's democracy.

Team and group leaders, section leaders and workshop foremen would all be directly elected by the workers. Any team or group leader, section leader or workshop foreman thus elected could not be removed from office by the higher authorities without the approval of a two-thirds majority at the factory workers' conference.

Any factory director who was found to be engaging in activities of a devious or conspiratorial nature would forfeit all claim to the title. Such activities would include the utilization of welfarism as a lure to facilitate the misapportionment of state funds and equipment to the production of items not included in the state plan, and the pursuit of alterations in the orientation and nature of production for purposes of deriving illegal profits with which to gain favour with the work-force and secure a majority vote in the election. Any person would be able to lodge a complaint against the factory director, either with their local workers' conference, with the higher administrative authorities or workers' conference, or directly with the courts at any level. Neither the higher leadership authorities nor the courts would be permitted to make verdicts on the basis of the numbers of those

186

supporting the respective parties to litigation. Rather, their standard for determining the truth of the matter should be the Marxist constitution, the relevant laws deriving from the latter, and the actual facts of the matter itself. The minority would be protected, and it would be recognized that the truth sometimes lies with the minority. The securing of votes by illegal means, the formation of cliques for selfish purposes, and corruption and fraud would necessarily be dealt with as representing acts of a criminal nature, and be punished most severely.

ii) The countryside

Although, at present, the basic accounting unit in the countryside is the production team, nevertheless a transition will take place, over not too long a period of time, to a system under which the brigade would form the basic accounting unit.

The post of production team leader would be subject to annual election. After the concluding of accounts and distribution of profits at the end of each year (that is to say, after the annual summing-up session), different draft proposals for the new plan for the coming year would be compared, and all commune members over 18 years of age would then cast their votes to determine the new team leader. Following this, the elected team leader would form, on the basis of nominations put forward by himself and approved by a majority vote of team members, a new revolutionary committee for the production team. Should any of those selected for nomination by the elected team leader be rejected in the course of a vote by all the commune members of the team concerned, the elected team leader would then have to put forward further nominations for the team members to consider. If, for example, the elected team leader were to propose A for the post of team work-point recorder for the year in question, but that nomination were to be rejected, the elected team leader would then propose B for the post instead, and if the latter nomination were to be passed by a majority vote, B would then assume office as the approved team work-point recorder for that year. All candidates for the post of team leader should, at the time of the election, put forward explicit quotas, norms and plans for production for the whole of the coming year. If, after being elected, the successful candidate deemed it necessary to modify his plan, then the changes in question would have to be passed at a general meeting of all team members. The team leader would be obliged to make known, whenever so requested, the situation regarding revenue and expenditure, and the state of affairs regarding work-points and distribution. Any team leader failing to carry out his duties, or engaging in illegal activities, would be liable to immediate dismissal at a general meeting of all team members.

Since the production team constitutes the basic economic accounting unit of the rural collective ownership system, people's natural sense of their own best interests would suffice to produce within them both a burning desire for democracy and a genuine ability to make a proper choice of 'good housekeepers' for the team. With the establishment of the proletarian-democratic system, the intimate sense of economic self-interest engendered by the public-ownership base would undoubtedly serve to assist the countless millions of the peasantry to break free from their traditional clannish and patriarchal ideas, and to overcome the limitations imposed by their low cultural level. The unfolding of proletarian-democratic revolution at the basic rural level would, unquestionably, proceed in a most vigorous and powerful manner.

Whereas the production team is the basic cellular unit of the organization of rural labour, the brigade is its very foundation. The 'poor and lower-middle peasant-managed schools', the 'poor and lower-middle peasant-managed shops', the 'brigade co-operative medical services' and other such 'new-born things' of the Great Proletarian Cultural Revolution have all served to demonstrate clearly the importance of taking the brigade level as the foundation. However, when such new-born things as these come into existence in the context of reformism, and are dominated and controlled by the forces of privilege, they cannot possibly proceed to grow and develop in such a way as would allow the poor and lower-middle peasants to become the true masters of their own affairs; indeed, they have little prospect of surviving in anything but name alone.

Under the proletarian-democratic system, the supreme legislative powers of the brigade would rest with the brigade-level conference of people's delegates (people's conference). The brigade-level people's conference would be fully empowered to supervise the overall managerial work of the brigade's administrative cadre, to arbitrate in any disputes which might arise within the brigade and its various constituent teams; to determine recommendations for college entrance; and to inspect prospective personnel for, and determine work allocations to, the spheres of military service, administration, and productive labour. The total quota of delegates to the brigade people's conference would be apportioned amongst the various teams in accordance with the size of their respective memberships, and delegates would be determined through direct election at general meetings of the various team memberships. However, no brigade leader, team leader, or member of the brigade or team revolutionary committee would, during their period in office, be eligible for election to the brigade people's conference. A conference chairman would be elected by the brigade people's conference to act as its convenor. The term of session of the conference would be two years.

Under the proletarian–democratic system, the executive power of the brigade would rest with the brigade leader. The office of brigade leader would be subject to re-election every two years. Both the brigade leader and the team leader could be elected to consecutive terms in office, without limitation on the number of terms. The brigade leader would be determined through direct election by all brigade members of 18 years of age or more with rights of citizenship, at a special assembly. The brigade revolutionary committee would be formed on the basis of nominations put forward by the elected brigade leader and passed by a majority vote at the brigade people's conference.

A brief description of the brigade revolutionary committee will suffice here: the brigade leader should spend at least half of each year participating in collective productive labour, but not necessarily within his own production team; there would be an assistant brigade leader who would deal with clerical work, and who would likewise only be released from production for half of each year; the brigade revolutionary committee would take care of the overall work of managing agriculture, forestry, animal husbandry, non-staple food production, fishing, cultural activities, education, health services, and the brigade-run general store; brigade health workers, marketing workers and those in charge of schools would be nominated by the elected brigade leader from amongst local people or persons who had been local residents for more than three years, and would be determined by election at a general meeting of brigade members. The brigade leader would bear full responsibility for all the above items of work.

The brigade people's conference would be empowered to dismiss and replace, at any time, any brigade leader failing to carry out his duties or engaging in illegal activities.

As in the case of factories, any irregularities in an election would render the election in question illegal; any person would be able to lodge a complaint, either with their local people's conference, with the higher administrative authorities or people's conference, or directly with the courts. Malpractices of this variety would be dealt with severely by the state.

The National People's Conference should lay down, in law, explicit stipulations designed to ensure the socialist nature of the basic economic accounting unit in the countryside. The various levels of the leadership in the countryside must likewise serve as models of obedience to the laws and regulations of the state.

iii) The military

Under the proletarian-democratic system, both democratic principles and the system of officer responsibility must be resolutely implemented within the armed forces. However, in view of the special nature of the armed forces, the ways in which this would be done would be somewhat different as compared to the factory or the countryside.

The military and the political should on no account be administered separately and made into two distinct systems. The principles of army-building of the proletarian-democratic revolution would entail a high degree of integration between military work on the one hand, and political and ideological work on the other — an integration to which the two are, in any case, entirely susceptible.

Squad and platoon leaders would be determined through direct election by the rank-and-file soldiers. Deputy squad leaders and deputy platoon leaders would be appointed by the elected squad and platoon leaders themselves. The elected squad and platoon leaders would together form the company soldiers' committee, which would in turn elect the company commander. The deputy company commander and general affairs officer would then be determined on the basis of nominations put forward by the company commander and approved by a majority vote in the company soldiers committee.

The elected platoon leaders and company commanders would together form the battalion soldiers committee, which would in turn elect the battalion commander. The deputy battalion commander and other essential cadres would then be determined on the basis of nominations put forward by the battalion commander and approved by a majority vote in the battalion soldiers committee.

The elected company commanders and battalion commanders would together form the regimental soldiers committee, which would in turn elect the regimental commander. The deputy regimental commander, the chief of staff, and other essential cadres would then be determined on the basis of nominations put forward by the regimental commander and approved by a majority vote in the regimental soldiers committee. Staff officers would then be nominated by the chief of staff and appointed by the regimental commander.

Election to the above posts would be for a two-year term of service.

The appointment of all commanders at levels higher than the regiment would be carried out by the Ministry of Defence, which would, in turn, be under the direct control of the elected president.

All commanders at levels higher than the regiment would have to have undergone a systematic, modern military training, or else have proved in an examination that they possessed both a sound general knowledge with regard to modern military warfare, and would have to have a certain amount of experience of life at the basic levels of the armed forces.

If a commander at squad, platoon, company, battalion or regimental level were either killed in battle, or else so seriously wounded as to have lost the capacity to command his soldiers, then his place would be filled immediately either by someone directly appointed by a senior officer or by one of the original candidates for the post, in accordance with a prior arrangement. All those under the command of the new officer would be obliged to offer him their total obedience. Once the troops had had sufficient time for rest and recuperation, the appointment would be revised in accordance with the democratic principles outlined above.

The overall military competence and acumen of the commander has a profound bearing upon the performance in battle, and, indeed, upon the personal fate of the troops under his command; thus, the implementation at basic levels of the military of a combination of democratic principles and a militarily and politically integrated system of officer responsibility, would be entirely feasible and appropriate. For this would not only greatly enhance the fighting capacity of the military; it would also make the military function as a staunch and reliable defender of the proletarian–democratic system, and would remove all sanctuary for warlords.

Following the worldwide victory of socialist revolution, the state, under the proletarian–democratic system, would gradually abolish the standing army, and would carry out the transition to universal military service and the arming of the whole people.

6. The Rights of the Individual Citizen under the Proletarian-Democratic System

Just as distribution is dependent upon production, and yet at the same time able to advance production, so too, the question of human rights is subordinate to, and yet at the same time able to advance, the economic relations and political system of society.

The bourgeoisie declares: 'Men are born free, and remain free and equal in their rights'.[20] This is nothing more than a deceitful lie. One simply has to look at the bourgeois system of ownership to verify this: '. . . bourgeois private property . . . is based on class antagonisms, on the exploitation of the many by the few.'[21] Under the bloodsucking rule of the bourgeoisie, human beings are merely 'the personification of economic categories, the bearers of particular class-relations and interests.'[22] The great differences in wealth between one family and another endure from one generation to another. In fact, therefore, under the private-ownership system man is neither born, nor does he always remain, free and equal.

Marxism, however, has offered us the glorious vision of a communist future, and has announced quite plainly: people should and indeed can be free and equal from birth. And how may this be achieved? As Marx and Engels said — '. . . the theory of the Communists may be summed up in the single sentence: Abolition of private property.'[23] Does the transformation of private ownership of the means of production, then, mean the abolition of private ownership? Our analysis would suggest that this is not in fact the case. Coercive monopolization of power by the minority means that public ownership soon ceases to exist in anything other than purely nominal form. 'Nationalization' and 'collectivization' are nothing more than newly disguised versions of private ownership, for they involve merely a transformation from ownership of capital by the capitalist to ownership of privilege by the bureaucrat! Moreover, privilege-ownership gives rise to far, far greater social inequality than ever existed in the context of capital-ownership, and serves to reduce the working people as a whole to an extreme condition of unfreedom.

Privilege-ownership involves the stripping from the working people as a whole of all human rights, as the bureaucrat class strives with might and main to reduce these to such 'rights' as are commonly enjoyed only by beasts of burden. Such a reduction of rights is utterly intolerable! Gradually, steadily, there is arising within the proletariat and working people as a whole, the most powerful call-to-arms of our time: Give us back democracy! Give us back freedom! Give us back equality! Give us back human rights! We want to live as human beings — we *will not* be beasts of burden!

Democracy, freedom, equality and human rights will not, however, simply fall from heaven, nor will they ever be graciously bestowed upon us by the reactionary ruling class. The proletariat and working people as a whole will only secure liberation through their own efforts. 'Political freedom, the right to assembly and association, and freedom of publication are our weapons; if any should attempt to disarm us of these weapons, are we to fold our arms, stand to one side, and discard politics?'[24] Only by way of proletarian-democratic revolution, and only under a proletarian-democratic system, will the proletariat and working people as a whole ever attain to true democracy, freedom, equality and human rights! Moreover, only by way of the storms of proletarian-democratic revolution and by instituting a proletarian-democratic system will it ever become possible to establish a firm and enduring guarantee for any of these things!

Public ownership, under the proletarian-democratic system, would be truly socialist in nature. The people would be producers, and at the same time their own masters, and all would be equal with respect to the ownership of the means of production!

The proletarian–democratic two–party system and system of people's conferences would truly, and forever, free the people from all threat of a life of servitude under the lash of the slave-driving party; it would give them the democratic rights that they require in order to become the real masters of their own affairs: the right to vote, and the right to stand for election!

Under the proletarian–democratic system, the people would enjoy genuine freedom of speech, publication, assembly and association. Not only the central organs of either party, but also their local organs at provincial, district and county level would be able to publish different newspapers and journals. The party in power would be able to express an official point of view and understanding of events; but the party in opposition would be similarly free to express its own political views and proposals, and thus to exercise, alongside and as a part of the people, the proper functions and powers of supervision. The reporting of news would recover its sacred authenticity, and would serve as a timely mirror of the richness and diversity of real life. The people are highly discerning, and would quickly reject any deceitful propaganda and any irresponsible attempts to attack or slander individuals. A fresh and vigorous style of writing would inevitably arise in place of the various lifeless and stilted 'eight-legged' styles characteristic of party literature both past and present.

The proletarian–democratic system would firmly promote the policy of letting 'a hundred flowers blossom and a hundred schools of thought contend', and would provide reliable guarantees for such a policy; it would stimulate diversity, improvement and development within scientific investigation and within the fields of literature and art; it would give all those engaged in these fields the freedom not only to extol the bright side of things, but also to expose the dark side of things. The state would provide any support necessary for scientific investigation, and would respect and encourage all individual creative endeavour in the fields of science, literature and art. The state would lay great stress not only upon the extensive popularization of education but also upon the conscientious improvement of educational quality. The principle of determining selection and appointment solely on the basis of worth, talent and ability would be earnestly applied throughout the entire educational system and system of personnel allocation.

Under the proletarian–democratic system, ceaseless efforts would be made to abolish the ossification afflicting the social division of labour. To this end, people would have, as far as could be managed, freedom to choose their occupation and also their place of residence. Coercive transference of residence and division of labour by administrative means should be gradually abolished. The state would strive hard, by means of all measures and channels at its disposal, to reduce the 'three great differences',[25] to improve all aspects of the treatment accorded to relatively backward regions and lower types of work, and to extend the development of production in an all-round way. A person's work-card, bearing details added by the people's conference, would serve both as a curriculum vitae and as a reference when seeking employment, and would be retained and used directly by the person concerned.

The proletarian–democratic system is itself the product of history. For this reason, the approach which would be adopted under such a system towards all those rational elements which have accumulated in the course of history to date would by no means be one of metaphysical exclusion. On the contrary, all things posited during the course of history which were found to be still of progressive significance, and to contain aspects worthy of consideration, would, under the proletarian–democratic system, undergo the requisite process of sublation and receive historical affirmation. On the question of human rights, for example, this approach would be applied in dealing with certain of the proposals put forward by the bourgeoisie in the anti-feudal programmatic document *The Declaration of the Rights of Man and of the Citizen* [1789]:

> 'The principle of all sovereignty is vested in the nation. No form of collective power and no individual can exercise authority that does not directly emanate from the nation.'
>
> 'The law should only forbid actions that are to the detriment of society. No man must prevent what is not prohibited by law, and no one can be forced to do what is not demanded by the law.'
>
> '. . . All citizens have a right to take part in framing the laws either personally or by means of their representatives. The law must be equal for all. Every citizen, being equal before the law, is equally eligible, according to his capacity, for all dignities, offices or posts in the public administration, without distinction, save that due either to character or talent.'

'No one may be accused, imprisoned or held under arrest except in such cases and in such a way as is prescribed by law. Those who solicit, give, or carry out, or who cause others to carry out, arbitrary orders, shall be punished; but every citizen who is summoned or arrested in virtue of the law, must obey instantly; if he resists he is guilty.'

'The law can only establish such penalties as are strictly and obviously necessary, and it can not be retroactive.'

'Every man is presumed innocent until he is proved guilty.[26] Therefore if his imprisonment is held to be indispensable, all severity exceeding that which is necessary for securing his person must be strictly repressed by law.'

'No one may be molested for his opinions, religious or otherwise, provided that the manifestation of these does not disturb public order, as established by the law.'

'Free expression of thought and opinion is one of the most precious rights of mankind: every citizen may therefore speak, write and publish freely, but must be held responsible for abuse of this freedom in such cases as are determined by the law.'

'The defence of man's natural and civic rights renders a public police force necessary; this force is therefore constituted in the common interest and not for the particular use of those to whom it is entrusted.'

'Society has the right to demand from its public servants an account of their work.'

'That society is which there is no guarantee of rights, and in which the separation of rights is not determined, has no constitution.'[27]

The course of historical development is now propelling the human rights issue into a position of great prominence, and it is an issue which the proletariat can by no means afford to ignore. For as Marx pointed out, the wrong suffered by the proletariat '. . . is not a *particular wrong* but wrong in general; a sphere of society which can no longer lay claim to a *historical* title, but merely to a *human* one . . . the *total loss* of humanity and which can therefore redeem itself only through the *total redemption of humanity.*'[28] And for the proletariat, moreover: 'The only liberation . . . which is *practically* possible is liberation from the point of view of *that* theory which declares man to be the supreme being for man.'[29] If this be so in the context of capital-ownership, then it becomes still more so in the context of privilege-ownership. Under the system of privilege-ownership, the brutal and bloodthirsty rule of the bureaucrats is forcing countless millions of proletarians and working people in general to take up the most powerful call-to-arms of our time:

We want to live as human beings — we *will not* be beasts of burden!

Give us back democracy! Give us back freedom! Give us back equality! Give us back human rights!

7. This Great New Social Need Can and Will Be Fulfilled

The above plan of action, describing the proletarian-democratic system that is to be established in the course of proletarian-democratic revolution, is directed at the very roots within the mode of production of the evolution from socialist society to revisionist society, and delineates the measures to be adopted for eradicating those roots. As is clear from the nature of these measures, proletarian-democratic revolution in no way constitutes a panacea for all the problems – past, present and future – with which society is faced; it merely constitutes a means of tackling the central issues, and of providing the proletariat and working people as a whole with a rational basis upon which to pursue, on their own account, the proper solutions to their own problems. It should on no account be thought that all this is mere pie in the sky, some insubstantial fantasy that can never be realized. It belongs entirely to the realm of the possible, and will begin to become a reality as soon as the proletariat and working people as a whole both recognize it and begin to act upon it. As has been demonstrated time and again, in various in- stances of social change throughout the course of history, a new social need always surfaces as the end result of a lengthy process of incubation within society as a whole, and the actual recognition of that need by people foretokens its imminent fulfilment. The proletarian-democratic system is predicated upon the great new social need which has been formed in the course of development of the previous mode of production and previous social relations. The successful definition of this great new social need shows, precisely, that the objective conditions and moment for its fulfilment are now upon us. The countless millions of those now enduring oppression and exploitation at the hands of the bureaucrat class, those cast aside with nowhere to appeal, those languishing in the darkness of their unbearable sufferings, will one day rise up and march towards the light! This great new social need can and will be fulfilled!

11
Proletarian Dictatorship

1. The Revisionist 'Proletarian Dictatorship'

'The dialectics of history were such that the theoretical victory of Marxism compelled its enemies to *disguise themselves* as Marxists.'[1] In countries where the conquest of political power by the proletariat has already been accomplished, the agents of revisionism – in deference to Lenin's famous dictum 'only he is a Marxist who *extends* the recognition of the class struggle to the recognition of the *dictatorship of the proletariat*'[2] – perform a reversal of their former stance of repudiating, opposing and attacking proletarian dictatorship. Transforming themselves overnight into 'Marxists', they espouse more resoundingly than anyone the slogan of 'proletarian dictatorship'; again and again, they declare themselves to be implementing and defending 'proletarian dictatorship', again and again they proclaim themselves to be struggling pitilessly against the 'class enemy' in order to consolidate and strengthen this 'proletarian dictatorship'.

Let us consider, however, just what this revisionist 'proletarian dictatorship' actually amounts to. The 'proletarian dictatorship' of revisionism means the despotic, untrammeled pursuit of self-interest, and the arbitrary exercise of a brutally oppressive and exploitative rule over the people by the bureaucrat class; it means the tyranny of bureaucratic class privilege. It means the coercive monopolization of power by a slave-driving minority, and, in varying degrees, a hereditary, monarchistic system of autocracy. It means the blatant implementation by the bureaucrat class, against the proletariat and working people as a whole, of a policy of savage cruelty and bloody terror. It means the vilification, persecution, seizure, imprisonment and murdering of proletarian revolutionaries by the bureaucrat class. It means the expropriation of the rights of the proletariat and working people as a whole to vote, and to stand for election. It means the expropriation of the various freedoms – of speech, publication, assembly, association, change of residence and choice of occupation – of the proletariat and working people as a whole: the turning of society into a prison for the confinement of their physical and intellectual liberty. It means the fascist tyranny of the bureaucrat class – the wanton jeopardization of citizens' personal security, the arbitrary entering and searching of residences and confiscation of possessions, the indiscriminate slandering, tying up, beating, taking into custody and arresting of citizens – and the exploitation of its powers of office for purposes of settling, in manifold ways, private scores against citizens.

In short, the 'proletarian dictatorship' of revisionism means the summary expropriation by the bureaucrat class of the freedom, democracy and human rights of the proletariat and the entire working people, the creation of a heaven for the bureaucrat class and a hell for the proletariat and working people as a whole.

Proletarian dictatorship? Nothing of the sort! On the contrary, this is out-and-out social-fascist dictatorship, out-and-out dictatorship by the bureaucrat class, out-and-out dictatorship *over* the proletariat. The revisionist 'proletarian dictatorship' is, in fact, utterly bogus.

The time has come for a thorough clarification of the whole question of proletarian dictatorship. As Chairman Mao said: 'Why did Lenin speak of exercising dictatorship over the bourgeoisie? It is essential to get this question clear. Lack of clarity on this question will lead to revisionism. This should be made known to the whole nation.'[3] Let us now turn to consider the question: what constitutes genuine Marxist proletarian dictatorship?

2. Marxist Proletarian Dictatorship

i) The origin, the aim, and the timing of proletarian dictatorship

Marx, in 1852, declared, 'What I did that was new was to prove: —
1) that the *existence of classes* is only bound up with *particular historical phases in the development of production;* — 2) that the class struggle necessarily leads to the *dictatorship of the proletariat;* — 3) that this

dictatorship itself only constitutes the transition to the *abolition of all classes* and to a *classless society*.'[4]

In this passage, Marx not only makes clear the aim of proletarian dictatorship, but also, and even more importantly, shows that proletarian dictatorship, far from having its source in the subjective thinking of any individual or in the inventions of any school of thought, stems in fact from the necessary development of the historical, objective class struggle, and from the material productive activities of mankind. Engels, in his *Preface to the 1883 German Edition of 'The Communist Manifesto'*, develops this point further:

> 'The basic thought running through the Manifesto [is] — that economic production and the structure of society of every historical epoch necessarily arising therefrom constitute the foundation for the political and intellectual history of that epoch; that consequently (ever since the dissolution of the primeval communal ownership of land) all history has been a history of class struggles, of struggles between exploited and exploiting, between dominated and dominating classes at various stages of social development; that this struggle, however, has now reached a stage where the exploited and oppressed class (the proletariat) can no longer emancipate itself from the class which exploits and oppresses it (the bourgeoisie) without at the same time forever freeing the whole of society from exploitation, oppression and class struggles.'[5]

The historical position of the proletariat determines that the proletariat can only achieve final liberation itself by liberating the whole of society, the whole of mankind, and also, thereby, determines the necessity of the proletarian dictatorship. 'Between capitalist and communist society lies a period of revolutionary transformation from one to the other. There is a corresponding period of transition in the political sphere and in this period the state can only take the form of a *revolutionary dictatorship of the proletariat*.'[6]

ii) The original conception of proletarian dictatorship

I. The definition given by Marx

'This socialism is the *declaration of the permanence of the revolution*, the *class dictatorship* of the proletariat as a necessary intermediate point on the path towards the *abolition of class differences in general,* the abolition of all relations of production on which they are based, the abolition of all social relations which correspond to these relations of production, and the revolutionizing of all ideas which stem from these social relations.'[7]

This sentence, written in 1850, represents the most substantial, condensed and clear definition of proletarian dictatorship ever given by the founder of Marxism, the founder of the doctrine of proletarian dictatorship. All of Marx and Engel's later expositions on proletarian dictatorship merely elaborate upon or further supplement this definition. In considering this definition, particular regard should be paid to the three parts stressed by Marx himself.

II. A socialism of permanent revolution* – against the idealization of existing society by petty-bourgeois socialism

According to Marx's definition, the first item of substance in proletarian dictatorship is the declaration by the proletariat of a socialism of permanent revolution. Here, Marx gives a clear indication as to the nature both of the economic base and political stance of proletarian dictatorship. Proletarian dictatorship depends upon the socialist economic base, and its political stance – aimed at 'forever freeing the whole of society from exploitation, oppression and class struggles' – is that of 'the declaration of the permanence of the revolution.' It is worth taking a closer look at the question of against

* *Translator's Note:*
There has been much controversy as to how this term *'buduan geming',* which I have rendered as 'permanent revolution', may best be translated into English. Many writers on China prefer to render it as 'uninterrupted' or 'continuous' revolution, in order to distinguish it clearly from Trotsky's theory of permanent revolution. In my view, this obscures rather than clarifies the underlying problem – in both linguistic and political senses. Stuart Schram summarizes the nature of the problem as follows: 'Mao Tse-tung [stated in a] speech of 28 January 1958, to the Supreme State Conference . . . 'I advocate the theory of the permanent revolution. You must not think that this is Trotsky's theory of the permanent revolution". Quite obviously, if Mao were not deliberately using the same term as Trotsky, and thus inviting confusion, there would be no need for him to warn his listeners against confusion. Moreover, the Chinese used in 1958, and still use today, *buduan geming* to translate Marx's expressions *"die Revolution in Permanenz"* or *"die Permanenzerklärung der Revolution".'* ('Mao Tse-tung and the Theory of the Permanent Revolution, 1958–69', by Stuart R. Schram, in *The China Quarterly* of Jan–March 1971, p.222.) The point to be made here is that Chen is using the term strictly (if that is the right word, considering the foregoing remarks) in its Maoist sense. Indeed, it is most improbable that Chen had ever read or had access to the works of Trotsky prior to writing this book.

whom, precisely, Marx's phrase 'the declaration of the permanence of the revolution' was directed.

Directly before giving this definition of proletarian dictatorship, Marx indicates quite explicitly that the declaration of the permanence of the revolution is directed, not against the bourgeoisie, but against *petty-bourgeois socialism*. For the bourgeoisie, already reactionary, the question of the permanence or otherwise of the revolution simply doesn't arise, but for the petty-bourgeoisie, the fellow-travellers of the proletarian revolution, such a question certainly does arise. Marx describes the socialism of the petty-bourgeoisie as being a 'utopia', 'doctrinaire socialism'. Even today, in those countries where the proletariat has already seized political power, this petty-bourgeois socialism not only continues to exist but has become still more rampant; indeed, it has come to represent a most pernicious threat to proletarian dictatorship. Let us note carefully the incisive observations made by Marx with regard to this petty-bourgeois socialism:

> 'The *utopia, doctrinaire socialism,* subordinates the total movement to one of its elements, substitutes for common social production the brainwork of individual pedants and, above all, in its fantasy dispenses with the revolutionary struggle of classes and its requirements by means of small conjuring tricks or great sentimentalities; fundamentally it only idealizes the existing society, takes a picture of it free of shadows and aspires to assert its ideal picture against the reality of this society.'[8]

It follows from this that proletarian dictatorship in fact means: a socialism of permanent revolution, a revolutionary dictatorship opposed to the idealization of existing society by petty-bourgeois socialism. Proletarian dictatorship represents a persistent standpoint of development, change, and seeking truth from facts, and thus accords with the basic principles of the Marxist, dialectical-materialist conception of history.

This follows in direct descent from the position adopted by Marx and Engels as early as 1845–46: 'We call communism the *real* movement which abolishes the present state of things.'[9] It is also consistent with the view proclaimed by Marx and Engels in March 1850 (approximately contemporary with Marx's above definition of proletarian dictatorship) in another article, *Address of the Central Com-*

mittee to the Communist League: 'Our concern cannot simply be to modify private property, but to abolish it, not to hush up class antagonisms but to abolish classes, not to improve the existing society but to found a new one.'[10] '[The proletariat's] battle-cry must be: The Permanent Revolution.'[11]

It is, moreover, in full accordance with the core thinking of Marxism, expressed so consummately in Marx's 1873 Postface to the Second Edition of *Capital:* '[The dialectic] includes in its positive understanding of what exists a simultaneous recognition of its negation, its inevitable destruction; because it regards every historically developed form as being in a fluid state, in motion, and therefore grasps its transient aspect as well; and because it does not let itself be impressed by anything, being in its very essence critical and revolutionary.'[12]

Quite clearly, Marxist proletarian dictatorship is both in essence and in terms of fundamental standpoint quite incompatible with – indeed diametrically opposed to – on the one hand, the ossified political situation arising from coercive monopolization of power by the minority, and on the other, petty-bourgeois socialism which 'subordinates the total movement to one of its elements', 'idealizes the existing society', and 'hopes to bribe the workers with a more or less disguised form of alms and to break their revolutionary strength by temporarily rendering their situation tolerable.'[13] In complete contradistinction to this stands Marxist proletarian dictatorship, which is, both in essence and in terms of fundamental standpoint, fully concordant with the proletarian–democratic revolution and with the system of democracy to be established thereby.

III. A *class* dictatorship: proletarian democracy as its life-force, Marxist legality as its soul

According to Marx's definition, the second item of substance in proletarian dictatorship is that it constitutes a *'class dictatorship'* of the proletariat. Here, Marx is stressing not merely that all political power should belong to the proletariat, but also that it would be quite unacceptable for proletarian dictatorship to assume, in any way, the monarchistic form of dictatorship by party bosses or warlords, sectarian dictatorship, or dictatorship by a minority over the majority.

This accords with the fundamental Marxist principle holding the mass of the people to be the creators of history. In 1844, some time before Marx had given his definition of proletarian dictatorship, he and Engels declared: 'The emancipation of the working class must be the work of the working class itself. We cannot ally ourselves, therefore, with people who openly declare that the workers are too uneducated to free themselves and must first be liberated from above by philanthropic big bourgeois and petty-bourgeois.'[14]

It follows from this, that the exercise of proletarian dictatorship is a right belonging *to all members of the proletariat in common*. It is a right which the bureaucratic minority must never be allowed either to usurp, or to hegemonize and monopolize in the borrowed name of the proletariat.

But how, given that the proletariat is composed of such a vast multitude of individuals, is this dictatorship which can only be that of the class as a whole actually to be accomplished? Clearly, in order to carry out class dictatorship it is first of all necessary to carry out class democracy. In essence, dictatorship and democracy form, as far as a single class is concerned, a single entity. Or rather, dictatorship and democracy form the two mutually complementary aspects of the political power of a single class, with dictatorship being exercised externally and democracy being applied internally. The dictatorship of any class must be founded on the basis of a high degree of mobilization of the overall resources of that class. Any class dictatorship, in order to be powerful and effective, must mobilize and utilize the energy, sense of responsibility, zeal, and fighting spirit of each individual element within the ruling class. The more complete this class mobilization within the ruling class becomes, the greater will be the strength of the dictatorship; and the most effective means of achieving this class mobilization is, moreover, through the full utilization of democracy within the ruling class itself.

Lenin, discussing the relationship between proletarian dictatorship and democracy, comments: 'How then, is this dictatorship related to democracy? As we know, *The Manifesto of the Communist Party* places together the two concepts of "the raising of the proletariat to the position of ruling class" and "the winning of the battle of democracy".'[15] Lenin also remarks that proletarian dictatorship ensures 'democracy for the poor, for nine-tenths of the population';[16] for the proletariat, 'democracy [is] almost complete, limited only by the *suppression* of the resistance of the bourgeoisie.'[17] Chairman Mao, in a speech made in 1962 to a meeting of 7,000 cadres in which he summarized the 13 years since the founding of the People's Republic, expressed the point very clearly: 'Without a broad people's democracy, proletarian dictatorship cannot be consolidated and political power would be unstable.'[18]

Clearly, therefore, proletarian democracy is the very life-force of proletarian dictatorship: without it, there *is* no proletarian dictatorship. But the proletariat lives in a class society and at existing levels of production, on the one hand unavoidably joined to the petty-bourgeoisie and to petty production by a whole complex of connections; and on the other hand unavoidably subject to the influence of old traditional conceptions and old force of habit, and to the vestigial influence of the exploiting class. How, then, may such class democracy be steered consistently along the path of socialism, how may its communist orientation and purity be maintained? Clearly, the essential prerequisite for an assertion of proletarian class democracy is the creation of a Marxist legal system embodying the will of the proletariat. The placing of Marxist legality in a position of command over proletarian class democracy represents the sole means by which such democracy may be steered consistently along the entire path of socialism, may avoid losing its communist orientation and purity, may express the class nature, organization and discipline of the proletariat, restrict bourgeois right in an effective manner, and eliminate the threat posed by non-proletarian ideologies and tendencies such as petty-bourgeois individualism, aversion to discipline, and anarchism.

Hence, Marxist legality is the very soul of proletarian dictatorship. Without it, proletarian democracy lacks correct orientation and criteria, and proletarian dictatorship lacks breadth of vision.

In sum: Marxist proletarian dictatorship and the revisionist oligarchical tyranny imposed by the party of privilege are like fire and water: they can never be reconciled; while on the contrary, the connection between proletarian-democratic revolution and Marxist proletarian dictatorship is as natural, and as harmonious, as that between the fish and water.

IV. The abolition of class differences in general – not mainly through the use of force, but through a new and higher mode of social production.

According to Marx's definition, the third item of substance in proletarian dictatorship is that it represents merely an intermediate point on the path towards 'the *abolition of class differences in general*'. It is here that Marx reveals to us the very essence of proletarian dictatorship.

Marx not only gives an indication of the general timing of proletarian dictatorship, but also delineates the aim of proletarian dictatorship as being '[the transition to] the abolition of all classes and to a classless society'. Morever, the task of proletarian dictatorship and the orientation of permanent revolution both lie, as we have seen Marx explicitly point out, in the abolition of 'the three alls' and the revolutionizing of 'the one all'. It is this aim, this task, and this orientation which together form the essence of proletarian dictatorship. If dictatorship does not serve to accomplish the abolition of these 'three alls', and the revolutionizing of this 'one all', if it does not serve the fundamental interests of the proletariat and the realization of the great goal of communism; or if, on the contrary, having once abolished the exploitative order of capital, it then replaces it with the still worse one of privilege, then in no way is it *proletarian* dictatorship.

We would by no means deny absolutely that, for purposes of abolishing things belonging to the category of class differences and social relations, and for purposes of revolutionizing things belonging to the category of ideas, a certain useful and effective role may indeed be performed by the use of force (for example, in the nationalization of bureaucrat-capital during the process of abolition, or transformation, of private ownership). But the decisive point is, nonetheless, that the use of force by itself cannot be a *sufficient* means of fully accomplishing such objectives. Quite obviously, 'the abolition of class differences in general' is by no means as simple and straightforward as the mere physical matter of annihilating an enemy or killing a chicken. And 'the revolutionizing of all ideas which stem from these social relations' is something which it is still less possible to accomplish by the use of force — iron bars can be bent by force, but not ideas. These are all objectives which one cannot hope to achieve at a single stroke – or indeed, to achieve properly at all – by the use of force. As Lenin remarked: 'When the old society perishes, its corpse cannot be nailed up in a coffin and lowered into the grave. It distintegrates in our midst; the corpse rots and infects us.'[19] How, pray tell, could one ever eliminate by force this infection transmitted to us from the corpse of the old society? Or how, for that matter, could one ever remove by force the soil from which class exploitation and class oppression arises? Even if one were the commander-in-chief of a global Red Army, with the most massive of forces at one's disposal, with the greatest iron fist imaginable, one still could not accomplish these things.

As Lenin pointed out: '. . . The dictatorship of the proletariat is not only the use of force against the exploiters, and not even mainly the use of force. The economic foundation of this use of revolutionary force, the guarantee of its effectiveness and success is the fact that the proletariat represents and creates a higher type of social organization of labour compared with capitalism. This is what is important, this is the source of the strength and the guarantee that the final triumph of communism is inevitable.'[20] And, '. . . in the last analysis, the deepest source of strength for victories over the bourgeoisie and the sole guarantee of the durability and permanence of these victories can only be a new and higher mode of social production, and substitution of large-scale social production for capitalist and petty-bourgeois production.'[21]

The aim, task, and orientation of proletarian dictatorship, therefore, determine that '. . . the essence of proletarian dictatorship does not lie in force alone, or even mainly in force.'[22] *The essence of proletarian dictatorship lies precisely in the creation of a higher type of social organization of labour, in the adoption of a new and higher mode of social production, in the vigorous expansion of socialist production!*

This accords with the principles of the force theory of Marxism: 'Always and everywhere it is the economic conditions and instruments of power which help "force" to victory and without which force ceases to be force.'[23]

It can thus be observed that those formulations or courses of action which indiscriminately regard the essence of proletarian dictatorship as consisting mainly or entirely in force, are all distortions of Marxist proletarian dictatorship; they are merely low-grade reproductions of either bourgeois or pure fascist dictatorship, reproductions of the nonsense spouted by petty-bourgeois socialists of the Dühring variety, about how 'the *primary factor must* be sought *in direct political force* and not in any indirect economic power.'[24]

It is therefore evident that Marxist proletarian dictatorship, and revisionist social-fascist rule by force and terror, with its ugly and superstitious fascination with knives, cudgels and shackles, are fundamentally dissimilar, as different as two things could possibly be. By contrast, the proletarian–democratic system which will be established in the course of proletarian–democratic revolution is the one system which can provide the proletariat with the most favourable conditions for permanent revolution, for the continuous creation of higher types of social organization of labour and the continuous adoption of new and higher modes of social production. It is, hence, the one system which can provide the most favourable conditions for proletarian dictatorship — indeed, *the proletarian-democratic system is none other than the mature form of the proletarian dictatorship itself.*

V. The role of force – as midwife, and as subsidiary instrument

According to Marx's definition, the three points which we have been considering are organically interlinked:

a) a socialism of permanent revolution – against the idealization of existing society by petty-bourgeois socialism;

b) *class* dictatorship – with proletarian democracy as its life-force and Marxist legality as its soul;

c) abolition of class differences in general – not mainly through force, but through a new and higher mode of social production. These three items together form the principal and fundamental content of proletarian dictatorship.

It should, however, be noted that it is only under circumstances whereby the proletariat has already established its political power, has already seized state power and established a socialist economic base, that the full realization of this principal and fundamental content of proletarian dictatorship actually becomes feasible. As Chairman Mao said, 'The fundamental issue in revolution is political power. With political power, we have everything; without it, all is lost.'[25] And furthermore, 'Unless we secure political power, we cannot mobilize for revolution, we cannot defend the revolution, we cannot complete the revolution.'[26] However: ' "I grant you everything except power", tsarism declares. "Everything is illusory except power", the revolutionary people reply.'[27] There has never once, in the whole of world history, been a single reactionary who has voluntarily withdrawn from the stage of history and relinquished, of his own accord, his own fundamental interests. Before the advent of a high tide in the seizure of political power through world-wide socialist revolution, before the imposition of a state of total siege against the bourgeoisie by the proletariat, it is quite inconceivable that the bourgeoisie, armed to the teeth as it is, would ever agree to surrender obediently either state political power or the means of production to the proletariat.

Manifestly, 'winning power' is quite a different matter from 'wielding power', for, unless one wins political power, one cannot wield it, let alone exercise dictatorship. How, then, is the proletariat to win the right to exercise its own dictatorship?

As *The Manifesto of the Communist Party* points out, 'The proletariat of each country must, of course, first of all settle matters with its own bourgeoisie.'[28] 'The violent overthrow of the bourgeoisie' declares the *Manifesto,* 'lays the foundation for the sway of the proletariat'.[29] Following the Paris Commune uprising of 1871, Marx proceeded to make a timely summary of the Commune experience, and, in so doing, enriched and developed the content of the theory of proletarian dictatorship which he himself had first brought into being. 'The conquest of political power', declared Marx, 'becomes the great duty of the proletariat.'[30] And, precisely because of such a duty, precisely in the context of such a duty: '. . . the first condition [of proletarian dictatorship] was a proletarian army. The working classes would have to conquer the right to emancipate themselves on the battlefield.'[31] Following the conquest of political power by the proletariat, '. . . so long as the other classes, especially the capitalist class, still exists, so long as the proletariat struggles with it (for when it attains government power its enemies and the old organization of society have not yet vanished), it must employ *forcible* means, hence governmental means. It is itself still a class and the economic conditions from which the class struggle and the existence of classes derive have still not disappeared and must forcibly be either removed out of the way or transformed, this transformation process being forcibly hastened.'[32]

It is thus quite clear that '. . . force, however, plays yet another role in history, a revolutionary role; that, in the words of Marx, it is the midwife of every old society pregnant with a new one, that it is the instrument by means of which social movement forces its way through and shatters the dead, fossilized political forms.'[33] While the proletariat is still struggling for that conquest of political power which would enable it to establish its own class dictatorship, and even in the initial stage after the conquest of political power – during the period of transformation from private ownership of the means of production – the force factor inevitably tends to predominate and form the primary aspect of proletarian dictatorship. Even subsequently, force is not abolished; it is merely withdrawn from primary to secondary position, with the form of force changing from that of bullets and bayonets to that of governmental means and laws, and the role of force changing from that of midwife to that of subsidiary instrument.

We see, therefore, that proletarian dictatorship can only be established after the conquest of state political power through violent revolution, and that force then continues to function as a mutually co-existent aspect of dictatorship.

Consequent upon the division of the socialist revolution into two stages, and because of the differences in the principal target and task of the revolution during these two stages, proletarian dictatorship must also, of necessity, pass through two stages. Furthermore, the proletarian–democratic revolution simply represents the conclusion of the first stage, and the inauguration of the second stage of proletarian dictatorship. It signifies merely a tendency towards maturity on the part of proletarian dictatorship. This point will be further analyzed later.

3. The Prototype of the Dictatorship of the Proletariat

The founders of Marxism not only laid down in theory the original conception of proletarian dictatorship; they also affirmed the occurrence, in practice, of a prototype of the proletarian dictatorship.

For as Engels remarked, in his 1891 Introduction to Marx's *The Civil War in France*: '. . . the Social-Democratic philistine has once more been filled with wholesome terror at the words: Dictatorship of the Proletariat. Well and good, gentlemen, do you want to know what this dictatorship looks like? Look at the Paris Commune. That was the Dictatorship of the Proletariat.'[34]

What actually, then, was the nature of the Paris Commune? That is to say, what was the nature of that which the founders of the

Marxist doctrine of proletarian dictatorship affirmed as its prototype? As the best way of elucidating this question, let us now recall
the series of extracts from Marx's main work of discussion on the
Paris Commune, *The Civil War in France,* as presented by Lenin in
his *Marxism on the State.*

Lenin compiled the following series of summaries and expositions
by Marx (Lenin's emphases):[35]

'(1) "The first decree of the Commune, therefore, was the *suppression of the standing army,* and the substitution for it of the armed
people . . ."

(2) ". . . The Commune was formed of the municipal coun-
cillors, chosen by universal suffrage in the various wards of the
town, responsible and *revocable at short terms.* The majority of its
members were naturally working men, or acknowledged representatives of the working class."

(3) ". . . The Commune was to *be a working, not a parliamentary,
body,* executive and legislative at the same time . . ."

(4) ". . . Instead of continuing to be the agent of the central
government, the police was at once stripped of its political attributes, and turned into the responsible and at all times revocable
agent of the Commune."

(5) ". . . So were the officials of all other branches of the administration."

(6) ". . . From the members of the Commune downwards, the
public service had to be done at *workmen's wages.*" (Marx's
emphasis)

(7) ". . . The vested interests and the representation allowances of
the high dignitaries of state disappeared along with the high dignitaries themselves . . ."

(8) ". . . Having once got rid of the standing army and the police,
the physical force elements of the old Government, the Commune
was anxious to break the spiritual force of repression, the 'parson-
power' . . ." (by the disestablishment and disendowment of all
churches as proprietary bodies).

(9) ". . . The judicial functionaries were to be divested of that
sham independence . . ." They were thenceforth "to be elective,
responsible, and revocable . . ."

(10) ". . . In a rough sketch of national organization which the Commune had no time to develop, it states clearly that the Commune was to be the political form of even the smallest country hamlet . . ." The communes were also to elect the "national delegation in Paris . . ." [The original text of *The Civil War in France* also mentions here: ". . . Each delegate to be at any time revocable and bound by the *mandat imperatif* (formal instructions) of his constituents." – *Chen*].

(11) ". . . The few but important functions which still would remain for a central government were not to be suppressed, as has been intentionally mis-stated, but were to be discharged by Communal, and therefore strictly responsible, agents . . ."

(12) ". . . The unity of the nation was not to be broken, but, on the contrary, to be organized by the Communal constitution and to become a reality by the *destruction of the state power* which claimed to be the embodiment of that unity independent of, and superior to, the nation itself, from which it was but a *parasitic excresence.* While the merely repressive organs of old governmental power were to be *amputated,* its legitimate functions were to be wrested from an authority usurping pre-eminence over society itself, and restored to the responsible agents of society . . ."

(13) ". . . Instead of deciding once in three or six years which member of the ruling class was to misrepresent the people in parliament, universal suffrage was to serve the people, constituted in communes, as individual suffrage serves every other employer in the search for the workmen and managers in his business."

(14) ". . . It is generally the fate of completely *new historical* creations to be mistaken for the counterpart of older and even defunct forms of social life, to which they may bear a certain likeness. Thus, this *new Commune, which breaks the modern state power,* has been mistaken for a reproduction of the mediaeval communes . . . for a federation of small States (Montesquieu, the Girondins) . . .for an exaggerated form of the ancient struggle against over-centralization . . ."

(15) ". . . The Communal constitution would have restored to the social body all the forces hitherto absorbed by *that parasitic excrescence, the 'state',* feeding upon, and clogging the free movement of, society. By this one act it would have initiated the regeneration of France . . ."

(16) ". . . In reality, the Communal constitution brought the rural producers under the intellectual lead of the central towns of their districts, and these secured to them, in the working men, the national trustees of their interests. – The very existence of the Commune *involved, as a matter of course, local self-government,* but no longer as a check upon the, *now superseded, state power."*

(17) "The Commune made that catchword of bourgeois revolutions, cheap government, a reality, by *destroying* the two greatest sources of expenditure – *the standing army and state functionarism."*

(18) *"The multiplicity of interpretations* to which the Commune has been subjected, and the multiplicity of interests which construed it in their favour, show that it was a *thoroughly expansive political form,* while all previous forms of government had been emphatically repressive. Its true secret was this. It was essentially a *working-class government* (Marx's emphasis), the produce of the struggle of the producing against the appropriating class, *the political form at last discovered under which to work out the economical emancipation of labour."*

(19) ". . . Except on this last condition, the Communal constitution would have been an impossibility and a delusion . . ."

. . . [The Commune's] special measures could but betoken the tendency of a government of the people by the people." '

As will be observed, our indication of what constituted Marx's own definition of proletarian dictatorship, and also our subsequent interpretation of that definition and the inferences we then drew from it, are indeed in accordance with the original conception of Marxist proletarian dictatorship.

It follows, therefore, that proletarian–democratic revolution and the system of democracy to be established thereby merely represent a direct continuation of the revolutionary cause of the Paris Commune, merely a fulfilment of that cause which the Paris Commune left unfulfilled.

4. The Elementary Form of Proletarian Dictatorship

i) The lessons of the Paris Commune

Why was it that the Paris Commune was defeated after lasting for only 72 days? The Commune, Marx says, 'should have marched at once on Versailles . . . They missed the opportunity because of conscientious scruples. They did not want *to start a civil war*, as if that mischievous abortion Thiers had not already started the civil war with his attempt to disarm Paris! Second mistake: The Central Committee surrendered its power too soon, to make way for the Commune. Again from a too "honourable" scrupulosity!'[36] According to Lenin: '*Both* mistakes consist in an insufficiency of the offensive, in an insufficiency of consciousness and resolution to *smash* the bureaucratic-military state machine and the rule of the bourgeoisie.'[37] And, as Engels points out: 'Would the Paris Commune have lasted more than a day if it had not used the authority of the armed people against the bourgeoisie? Cannot we, on the contrary, blame it for having made too little use of that authority?'[38] Lenin points out, on the basis of the analysis by Marx and Engels, that the Commune had committed these further errors: '. . . It did not capture the Bank of France, did not undertake an offensive on Versailles, did not have a clear programme, etc.'[39] The mistakes of the Commune also included its lack of any political party to serve as a nucleus, and its failure to form an alliance with the peasantry.

The lessons of experience, drawn both from the failure of the Paris Commune and from the successes of the October Revolution and the Chinese Revolution, demonstrate the necessity for proletarian dictatorship to pass through an initial or preparatory stage.

ii) The initial stage of proletarian dictatorship

What is the nature of this stage, what does it comprise? It comprises the struggles waged by the proletariat first of all to capture state political power and then to carry out an initial consolidation of that power; it represents the stage of transition from capitalist society or from colonial or semi-colonial/semi-feudal society to socialist society, the stage of modification within the economic base, of transformation from private to public ownership of the means of production. In China, this stage spanned two periods chronologically: The New Democratic Revolution, and the first stage of socialist revolution.

There exists, therefore, somewhat parallel to the transitional period between capitalist society and communist society, a stage of transition between bourgeois dictatorship and proletarian dictatorship, namely the initial or preparatory stage of proletarian dictatorship. The primary, most immediate task of proletarian revolution during this initial stage is the capture of state political power and the transformation from private ownership of the means of production; that is to say, the overthrow of the rule of capital and the establishment of a socialist economic base, together with the laying of a foundation for, and creation of conditions necessary to, the comprehensive implementation of the original conception of Marxist proletarian dictatorship.

During this initial stage, the main target of the proletarian revolution is an external one: namely the old exploiting classes, the landlords and capitalists. This initial stage is itself, therefore, the pioneering part of proletarian dictatorship; and the beginning of anything is of course always the most difficult part. It is a stage of life–and–death struggle waged between proletariat and bourgeoisie for the control of state political power, one of intense conflict between the proletariat and the propertied classes headed by the bourgeoisie over the issue of carrying out the transformation to public ownership of the means of production.

During this initial stage, therefore, the smell of gunpowder is everywhere apparent. It serves to demonstrate that: 'Dictatorship is a big, harsh and bloody word, one which expresses a relentless, life–and–death struggle between two classes, two worlds, two historical epochs. Such words must not be uttered frivolously.'[40] There is, moreover – corresponding to its initial stage – an initial or elementary *form* of proletarian dictatorship.

iii) Characteristics of the elementary form of proletarian dictatorship

I. Force occupies a position of primacy

The first characteristic of the elementary form of proletarian dictatorship is that force occupies a position of primacy. Why should this be so?

First and foremost because, during the period of the conquest of political power:

'There has never once, in the entire history of the world, been a ruling class which has given in of its own accord and without a struggle.'[41] 'History does not know any cases of the ruling and oppressing class voluntarily relinquishing their right to rule and oppress, their right to huge incomes from enslaved peasants and

216

workers.'⁴² 'It is very probable – even most probable – that the bourgeoisie will not make peaceful concessions to the proletariat and at the decisive moment will resort to violence for the defence of its privileges. In that case, no other way will be left to the proletariat for the achievement of its aim but that of revolution.'⁴³

Prior to the advent of a high tide in the seizure of political power through world-wide socialist revolution, therefore, prior to a condition of total collapse within international capitalism, there can be no possibility of the proletarian revolution in any one country being able to smash the bureaucratic-military state machine of the bourgeoisie and capture and consolidate state power, except by force. Clearly, therefore, during this period of the conquest of political power by means of armed force, but *only* during this period, proletarian dictatorship is subject to no legal restriction whatever — for all laws hitherto have been those of the exploiting classes.

Secondly, once the proletariat has already seized political power, but before it has brought about the consolidation of that power, namely (as Lenin remarks)

'. . . *During every transition* from capitalism *to socialism* dictatorship is necessary for two main reasons, or along two main channels. Firstly, capitalism cannot be defeated and eradicated without the ruthless suppression of the resistance of the exploiters, who cannot at once be deprived of their wealth, of their advantages of organization and knowledge, and consequently for a fairly long period will inevitably try to overthrow the hated rule of the poor; secondly, every great revolution, and a socialist revolution in particular, even if there is no external war, is inconceivable without internal war, i.e. civil war, which is even more devastating than external war, and involves thousands and millions of cases of wavering and desertion from one side to another, implies a state of extreme indefiniteness, lack of equilibrium and chaos. And of course, all the elements of disintegration of the old society, which are inevitably very numerous and connected mainly with the petty bourgeoisie (because it is the petty bourgeoisie that every war and every crisis ruins and destroys first), are found to "reveal themselves" during such a profound revolution. And these elements of disintegration *cannot* "reveal themselves" otherwise than in an increase of crime, hooliganism, corruption, profiteering and outrages of every kind. To put these down requires time and requires an iron hand.'[44]

Because the proletariat has, during this period, seized but not yet consolidated political power, because 'The class of exploiters, the landowners and capitalists, has not disappeared and cannot disappear all at once (under the dictatorship of the proletariat . . .) . . . Because they have been defeated, the energy of their resistance has increased a hundred- and a thousandfold.'[45] Because the proletariat is, during this period, confronted by 'the resistance always offered by the exploiters — a resistance that is most desperate, most furious, and that stops at nothing';[46] because it is confronted, moreover, by the resistance and the challenge posed by the forces and traditions of the old society as a whole, and faces the dangers of encirclement by international capital and invasion and subversion by imperialist re-actionaries – it follows that while force is used less prominently during this period than in the preceding one (namely the period of armed seizure of political power) it does, nevertheless, continue to play a conspicuous role. For without the powerful deterrent of proletarian force, the proletariat may well lose once more that political power over which it has only just gained possession, and would thus be rendered incapable of enforcing its programme for the transformation of society as a whole.

It should be noted, however, that although force occupies a position of primacy during the struggle for the conquest and consoli-dation of political power, it is nevertheless the movement of the economy, the adoption of a new and higher mode of production which remains fundamental. For without the slogans and activities of the Agrarian Revolution there would have been no Workers and Peasants Red Army; without the policy of rent reduction and return of tenancy deposits, without land reform, without mutual-aid teams and co-operativization, without joint state-private ownership, with-out socialism . . . it would have been impossible to achieve the mobilization and organization of the great mass of the people.

II. Monopolization of power through the single-party system.

The second characteristic of the elementary form of proletarian dictatorship is that the only agency fitted to occupy the core position in the struggle during the period from the conquest of power to the consolidation of public ownership, the only agency fitted to play the leading role and to exert a monopoly of power, is the party-organization of a single communist party. Why should this be so?

The reason is, that the conquest of political power by the proletariat differs from that undertaken by any previous class. Hitherto, the aim in conquering political power, whether by the landlord class or by the bourgeoisie, has invariably been the mere substitution of new relations of exploitation in place of the old. Whereas the aim of the proletariat in conquering political power is, in fact, the permanent deliverance of the whole of society from exploitation, oppression, and class struggle. In the old society, however, with its private-ownership relations of production and its enslavement and ideological poisoning by the reactionary classes, the proletariat in its entirety is not capable of perceiving this fact. Only a few advanced elements are, in the last analysis, capable of recognizing the doctrine of Marxism and, therefore, of taking the path of conscious resistance to class exploitation and class oppression.

It is only these few elements who, under the bloody and dictatorial rule of the old society, possess the capacity to brave death in the cause of forming the kind of party which will fight valiantly for the fundamental interests of the proletariat, the kind of party which will not be tolerated by the reactionaries in power. The hardship and danger which constitute the objective conditions and environment of the party during its early days, suffice to ensure the party's ability to rid itself of any political speculators as a matter of course. The communist party is born into misery and suffering; it forms, because of that context, the newly-emergent core force of the revolution, a vigorous vanguard organization deeply imbued with the spirit of revolution and self-sacrifice, an organization capable of leading the proletariat and revolutionary masses into battle against the class enemy.

Because of the nature of the balance between reactionary class forces and revolutionary forces at this time, and because the proletariat, prior to its conquest of political power, does not as yet hold the power of initiative in the struggle, the revolutionary forces of the proletariat must, if they are to succeed in disposing of the reactionary classes, be concentrated within a single party. Even after the conquest of political power, only the communist party, tried and tempered in the course of the long struggle towards the conquest of political power, remains capable of applying and upholding Marxist principles. It alone can carry through the socialist transformation from private ownership of the means of production.

During its initial stage 'The dictatorship of the proletariat means a persistent struggle – bloody and bloodless, violent and peaceful, military and economic, educational and administrative – against the forces and traditions of the old society. The force of habit in millions and tens of millions is a most formidable force. Without a party of iron that has been tempered in the struggle, a party enjoying the confidence of all honest people in the class in question, a party capable of watching and influencing the mood of the masses, such a struggle cannot be waged successfully'.[47] — Therefore, the only agency fitted to occupy the core position in the proletarian revolution during the initial or preparatory phase of proletarian dictatorship, the only force fitted to exert a monopoly of power and play the leading role during this period, is the communist party, and, what is more, the *single* communist party. 'Since we desire revolution, we must have a revolutionary party, for without a party of revolution, without a revolutionary party established in accordance with Marxist-Leninist revolutionary theory and revolutionary style, it would be impossible for us to lead the working class and the broad mass of the people to triumph over imperialism and its running-dogs.'[48]

It should, however, be noted that while this initial phase of proletarian dictatorship meant the implementation of a single-party system in China, it also meant the establishment, under party leadership, of a united front of all revolutionary classes and all revolutionary factions; it should also be noted more particularly that, during the period of the conquest of political power, it was only during and by means of the stage of New Democratic Revolution, by raising high the banner of winning democracy and opposing autocracy, that the Chinese Communist Party was in fact able to secure the reputation amongst the general populace of having 'the great advantage of being democratic'. Only thus was it able to establish a broad united front for people's democracy, to isolate the reactionaries and, finally, to achieve the conquest of political power. 'Only in the name of the universal rights of society can a particular class lay claim to universal domination.'[49] In its struggle towards the conquest of political power, the proletariat too must submit to this law.

III. Dictatorship through the concentration of power

The third characteristic is that during this initial phase of proletarian dictatorship, the functions of political power are exercised, in obedience to the requirements both of violent revolution and of the single-party system, by means of an all-encompassing concentration of power, a concentration which, in reality, entails a fusion of the legislature, executive and judicary, and which, furthermore, falls under the unified leadership and control of the party. The necessity for this is self-evident, and we need labour the point no further.

One point is, however, well worth noting here. During the implementation of such dictatorship through concentration of power under a single-party system, there exists an antithesis — the political power and political party of the reactionaries (or at the very least, the residual influence of such.) Objectively, this represents a driving force for competition. This driving force makes the party, which is striving to secure popular allegiance, accept, in a willing and sensitive manner, overall supervision by the mass of the people; and this in turn helps the party to avoid internal ossification. Thus, the mass of the people exercise an *effective* power of supervision during this period. Conversely, the weakening or disappearance of this antithesis brings about a corresponding weakening or disappearance, both of the driving force for competition and of the effective power of supervision.

The main characteristics of the elementary form of proletarian dictatorship are, then, the conquest and consolidation of political power through violent revolution; the implementation of dictatorship through concentration of power under a single-party system; and the overthrow of the rule of capital.

5. The Advanced Form of Proletarian Dictatorship

i) *The second stage of dictatorship*

The advent of the second stage of socialist revolution, that comprising the socialist transformation of the superstructure, signals also the advent of the second stage of proletarian dictatorship. By this stage, as compared with the previous one, massive changes have taken place in the objective situation, primarily in terms of class relations and relations of production.

The old economic base has already been changed: the proletariat has carried out, by means of the resources of political power at its disposal, the rapid completion and preliminary consolidation of the transformation to public ownership of the means of production. The establishment of public ownership, the expansion of social produc- tion, and the progress made in terms of social consciousness, all now militate against any straightforward recurrence of the capitalist mode of production as characterized by private ownership. More- over, in the course of time, all the overthrown exploiters, the land- lords and capitalists will, in obedience to the laws of nature, end up in their graves. The exploiters are now of a different kind, as are the roots from which exploitation arises. The main enemy of the pro- letariat is no longer an external but an internal one, and is located, moreover, within the core leadership group itself. The main target of proletarian revolution is no longer the old exploiting classes, but, instead, a new-style exploiting class – the bureaucrat class, or those known as 'the capitalist-roaders within the party'.

With the arrival of this stage, therefore, it becomes necessary to carry out a thorough and comprehensive implementation of Marx's theory of proletarian dictatorship. It becomes necessary, that is to say, to pursue a socialism of permanent revolution, to oppose the idealization of existing society by petty-bourgeois socialism, to create a class dictatorship of the proletariat and to abolish class differences in general. And, in the main, these things must be accomplished through the vigorous expansion of socialist produc- tion by means of a continuous adoption of new types of organization of labour and new modes of production.

The primary, most immediate aim and task of proletarian revolu- tion becomes, at this stage: the winning of victory in the struggle against revisionism, the smashing of that coercive monopolization of power by the minority which fetters the social productive forces, the overthrowing of enslavement to the forces of privilege, the transformation of the superstructure, the establishment and gradual perfecting of a system of proletarian democracy, the all-round imple- mentation, down to the grass-roots and down to every quarter of society, of the original conception of Marxist proletarian dictator- ship, the rapid and vigorous expansion of socialist production, and the preparation of an abundant material basis for the transition to communism.

Corresponding to this, its second stage, there emerges also an advanced *form* of proletarian dictatorship. Moreover, in the process of changing from the lower to the higher form, proletarian dictatorship must pass through a process of transition. This process of transition is, precisely, the proletarian–democratic revolution.

Provided that state political power remains in the hands of genuine Marxists, then the elementary form of proletarian dictatorship may well undergo a direct and relatively tranquil and harmonious transition towards the advanced form. By the same token however, if state political power has fallen into the hands of revisionists, then, in order for this transition to take place, an interim period of armed struggle for the conquest of power will be necessary: one of even greater complexity, one still more cruel and bloody, than that whereby political power was wrested from the hands of the bourgeoisie — in other words, the unfolding of violent revolution at a still higher level.

ii) Characteristics of the advanced form of proletarian dictatorship

A general outline of the advanced form of proletarian dictatorship was put forward in the previous chapter, and in earlier chapters we considered in some detail the various factors underlying its development. We shall therefore confine ourselves here to giving a short account of those characteristics which distinguish this advanced form from the elementary form of proletarian dictatorship.

I. The legal system

Owing to specific circumstances deriving from the course of social development thus far — namely, the need to protect the socialist economy and prevent public ownership from evolving into ownership by the bureaucrat-monopoly privileged class; the necessity for a socialism of permanent revolution; the fact that the abolition of class differences in general is to be accomplished not mainly through force, but through the adoption of a new and higher mode of production; that despite the gradual dying out of the old exploiting class elements, the influence and residues of such classes nonetheless persist; the continued existence of bourgeois right, petty production, and petty-bourgeois socialism; the continuous emergence of a new-style exploiting class – the bureaucrat class, and of new-born bourgeois elements; the need to prevent the bureaucrats from arbitrarily inverting right and wrong in pursuit of their own selfish aims; and, lastly, the need to abolish the indiscriminate use of force by privilege — it now therefore becomes necessary to devise and institute a comprehensive and authoritative system of Marxist law. *Fundamental to this Marxist legality would be:* its *legitimization* of revolution, and its provision of safeguards for *permanent* revolution; its preservation of the socialist economy; and its defence of any revolutionary action opposed to the idealization of existing society and directed towards the adoption of new and higher modes of production.

II. Democracy

Because of the pressing need to eliminate from the superstructure the intensely corrosive function exerted jointly therein by the system of appointment, the hierarchical order, the autonomization of the state organs, and the sanctification of the party; in view of the urgent necessity for a transformation of the relations of production whereby power is coercively monopolized by the minority; and in virtue of the prior creation, during the transformation to public ownership, of the requisite basis and conditions for an ever more profound and extensive dissemination of Marxist ideas amongst the people — the present single-party system would therefore, during the second stage of proletarian dictatorship, be replaced by a proletarian two-party system. By this means, political parties would be converted from being instruments of privilege, means whereby the bureaucrat class exercises dictatorship *over* the proletariat, into instruments of true, authentic proletarian dictatorship. The written Marxist constitution would be placed in the core position and would constitute the supreme leadership of the state, and power would emanate from a proletarian-democratic republican system of universal suffrage. *The fundamental aim and principle of proletarian democracy* would be: the implementation of a *class* dictatorship of the proletariat, one which would establish the latter, in its own right rather than through any paternalistic agency, as the true, direct master of society, and would thus bring about the liberation of both the workers and the productive forces.

III. Dictatorship through the separation of powers

Since the main enemies of the revolution in its second stage are generated not only by relations of production whereby power is coercively monopolized by the minority, but also by the highly concentrated *structure* of power characteristic of the (still-existent) elementary form of dictatorship, through the highly corrosive influence exerted upon those in power by the privilege to which that structure gives rise, it thus follows that in terms of power-structure the advanced form of proletarian dictatorship must consist in the exact *opposite* of its previous form. No longer would dictatorship be exerted by means of an all-encompassing concentration of power subsuming the sovereignty of the legislature, executive and judiciary, through coercive monopoly by the minority. Instead, it would be exerted through the 'separation of powers', in a tripartite division between legislative, executive and judiciary, so that power would govern power, with the whole being integrated through the Marxist legal system. *The fundamental aim of this dictatorship through the separation of powers* would be: to abolish *all class exploitation,* to forestall the privilegization of power, and to prevent the mechanism of state power becoming bureaucratized and so acquiring, by virtue of its inertial tendency, a negative role in relation to the people. Thus would be safeguarded the democracy and freedom of the working masses.

IV. The safeguarding of human rights

Whereas proletarian democracy forms the *life-force* of proletarian dictatorship, the provision of safeguards for basic human rights, such as freedom of speech, publication, assembly and association, and the right to vote and to stand for election, forms its indispensable *prerequisite*. The founding of the new superstructure and the consolidation of the public-ownership base would establish this prerequisite condition. Under the advanced form of proletarian dictatorship, citizens would enjoy a genuine, extensive, and ever fuller degree of democracy and freedom. *The fundamental orientation in this provision of safeguards for proletarian human rights* would be: towards ensuring that labour-power casts off its contradictory-aggregate status, towards the abolition both of its commodity nature and of its slave-like role, and towards the firm establishment of its position as subject.

In sum: the proletarian-democratic system is, itself, the advanced form of proletarian dictatorship. Comprehensive expression and embodiment of Marxist legality, democracy, dictatorship through separation of powers, and respect for human rights — such would be the fundamental content of the proletarian-democratic system, and, equally, the main characteristic of the advanced form of proletarian dictatorship.

iii) In reply to the howls of the bureaucrat class

I. A predictable complaint*

'Legality, democracy, dictatorship through the separation of powers, the safeguarding of human rights — that's all bourgeois stuff!' The best reply to those who spout such nonsense is this sentence from Marx: 'It is generally the fate of completely new historical creations to be mistaken for the counterpart of older and even defunct forms of social life, to which they may bear a certain resemblance.'[50] I would inform you good people that it is precisely *because* proletarian legality, democracy, dictatorship through the separation of powers, and safeguarding of human rights 'bear a certain resemblance' to their bourgeois counterparts that these things do indeed constitute progress, and do indeed amount to new and pioneering historical creations! For this is in complete conformity with the law of dialectics which holds that the development of things proceeds in a spiral of ascent, from the simple to the complex, and from the lower to the higher. It accords precisely with that which Engels refers to as: '. . . processes which in their nature are antagonistic, contain an internal contradiction; transformation of one extreme into its opposite; and finally, as the kernel of the whole thing, the negation of the negation;'[51] and, also, with that which Lenin describes as: '. . . from coexistence to causality and from one form of connection and reciprocal dependence to another, deeper, more general form . . . the repetition at a higher stage of certain features, properties, etc. of the lower and . . . the apparent return to the old,'[52] and which he terms '. . . the essence of dialectics'. To be sure, the same words – legality, democracy, separation of powers, human rights – are used in both cases, but what these words denote is fundamentally different in either case! The same thing as belongs, in the one, to the bourgeoisie, belongs, in the other, to the proletariat; for one is based upon capitalist private ownership while the other is based upon socialist public ownership. Just as the elementary form of proletarian dictatorship is bound to be somewhat 'similar' to feudal despotism, so too is the advanced form of proletarian dictatorship bound to be somewhat 'similar' to the bourgeois democratic republic. Such is the dialectic of history, and so must it be! It would be absurd if one had to regard every individual state as being identical to, for example, the slave-owning state, simply by virtue of their identical descriptions as 'states'; or if, by the same token, one had to regard the glorious communism of the future as being identical to the primitive communism of the past.

II. A dangerous conjuncture – a rare opportunity

For the past century and more, the whole issue of proletarian dictatorship has been subjected, by the bourgeoisie and by the old-style revisionist elements following it, to an unbridled offensive, to torrents of abuse and a frenzy of opposition, and still they have been unable to halt the forward march of the proletarian dictatorship.

The modern revisionists, however – the bureaucrat class in power and government within states of the proletarian dictatorship – have accomplished with ease what the bourgeoisie and the old-style revisionists never, for all their wishes and efforts, managed to accomplish.

Flaunting the banner of proletarian dictatorship, they make use of the state apparatus nominally under such dictatorship as a means of exercising dictatorship *over* the proletariat and the great mass of the people. This, a typical social-fascist dictatorship, they attempt to pass off as proletarian dictatorship. Proletarian dictatorship is defiled and trampled underfoot, distorted beyond recognition and turned into a thing of ugly notoriety.

Within the state this performance has the direct and disastrous consequence of promoting an evolution from socialism to revisionism. As the facts demonstrate, the great majority of socialist states in which proletarian dictatorship was once established have now, in essence, evolved into revisionist states under social-fascist dictatorship. This has meant not merely the cancelling out of the initial victories of the proletarian revolution, but also the complete extinguishing, through trickery and coercion, of the proletarian revolution itself; not simply the destruction of proletarian dictatorship, but also the degeneration of the proletariat to a level where it itself has become the object of a most savage and barbarous dictatorship of terror.

Externally, this performance has the direct effect of making the working peoples of the contemporary capitalist world, when comparing the capitalist system with that of socialism, frequently but mistakenly regard the revisionist system as being representative of socialism, and the social-fascist dictatorship of the former as being representative of proletarian dictatorship. This misconception greatly impedes the development of the proletarian revolutionary movement within the capitalist world. At the same time, the immense productive and competitive capacity of unicorporate publisocial production, with its high degree of organization, concentration and monopoly, is bound to appear enormously attractive to those countries in the process of being plundered, oppressed and exploited by the industrialized nations of imperialism, social-imperialism and capitalism. However, it is the dictatorship of the bureaucrat-monopoly privileged class of the revisionist system which most precisely suits the appetites and requirements of the highly-individualistic political activists of the bourgeoisie and petty-bourgeoisie within these same countries. They are delighted to avail themselves of the golden banner of socialism, for this allows them to exploit the conditions for revolution which have already formed within their country; following the path of the national liberation movements, they carry out extensive state capitalism, and, in the aim of securing hereditary positions of privilege for themselves and their families, they steer society towards the dark abyss of revisionism. Competition between productive forces is unprecedentedly intense in the contemporary world, and there is thus a great necessity for productive monopoly. Quite a few so-called developing countries may therefore be expected to develop not towards a system of *laissez-faire* capitalism, but rather, through a system of state capitalism, towards the social-fascist dictatorship of the bureaucrat-monopoly privileged class. Such a course of development is, in essence, one whereby the 'national liberation movement' is steered along a dead-end path towards a system of super-enslavement and super-exploitation, and it results in the proletarian revolutionary movement being prematurely brought to an end.

Quite clearly, therefore, because of revisionism, socialism descends once more to the level of a utopia. In fact, revisionism, has brought the proletarian revolution, the proletarian dictatorship, and the international communist movement to a conjuncture so perilous that the future of all three now hangs in the balance. All the activities of modern revisionism, whose social basis is the bureaucrat class, constitute, in this sense, a crime of historic proportions — for in consequence of these activities, the whole of human society may now be plunged into the utter darkness of an era of revisionism and social-fascist dictatorship, a disaster which would postpone the advent of true socialism and true proletarian dictatorship until some far distant future.

However, just at this gravely perilous conjuncture, Chairman Mao has given us important instructions on matters of theory. Furthermore, world historical development as a whole has now reached, as we described earlier, a stage at which all social systems presently in existence are, as a result of the worsening of their own internal disorders, coming to a dead-end.

Plunged into the basic contradiction arising from the incompatibility between the socialized nature of production on the one hand, and ownership by private individuals on the other, profoundly riven by the continual eruption of periodic economic crises, and under attack by the theory of surplus value and by people's revolution, the capitalist system totters precariously.

Plunged into the basic contradiction between unicorporate publisocial production and coercive monopolization of power by the minority, and confronted with the step-by-step total usurpation of party and state power by the bureaucrat class, the system of crossroads socialism hovers perilously on the brink of revisionism.

Plunged into the basic contradiction between highly-socialized production under the signboard of socialism on the one hand, and ownership by the bureaucrat-monopoly privileged class on the other, profoundly riven by grave periodic political crises and afflicted by internal ossification, pounded and imperilled by the human rights movement, strong in appearance but inwardly brittle, and confronted at all times with the possible outbreak of sudden violent incidents, the system of revisionism faces imminent collapse.

Furthermore, class contradiction and class struggle, with the proletariat at one pole and all manner of exploiting classes at the other, are now in an extensive state of development within these social systems. In the capitalist world, the contradiction and struggle between proletariat and bourgeoisie is becoming ever more acute; in the crossroads-socialist world, the contradiction and struggle between proletariat and bureaucrat class is reaching an unprecedented level of sharpness and intensity; while in the revisionist world, the contradiction and struggle between proletariat and bureaucrat-monopoly privileged class is now white-hot, and becoming more explosive with each passing day.

Moreover, the mutual contradiction and struggle between one state and another, arising from the different nature of their social systems, have reached a point whereby the whole world is now caught within a vortex of contradiction and struggle from which it is unable to free itself. The contradiction and struggle between imperialism on the one hand, and social-imperialism on the other, are particularly severe; indeed, conditions are now being engendered which may lead to the outbreak of a new world war, one which would, furthermore, be based upon modern levels of science and technology and would therefore constitute a totally new type of warfare. Mankind is thus placed under more intense pressure than ever before over the question of war and peace.

At the same time, all these factors provide excellent conditions and opportunities for the world-wide victory of proletarian revolution and proletarian dictatorship. If, however, we remain committed to previous forms and halt at previous levels, it will not be possible for us to exploit these conditions and opportunities. Proletarian-democratic revolution is the sole means by which such conditions and opportunities may be exploited to the full.

The elucidation of elementary and advanced forms of proletarian dictatorship, and the system of proletarian democracy to be established through proletarian-democratic revolution, will inevitably provoke a powerful response from all countries and from prominent figures throughout the world.

Only when we have mastered the enemy's all will we be able to destroy all enemies. In order to completely expropriate the exploiters, we must expropriate even their methods of expropriation.

Until such time as we make room for whatever portion of truth is contained within viewpoints opposed to our own, then such opposing viewpoints will, as a matter of course, have the right to continue to exist.

In view of the mutual interconnection, the mutual constraint and interpenetration of objective reality, no man may defy the require-

ments of a development expressing necessity, or deny the demands
of an existence still imbued with necessity. Therefore, once the
proletariat has carried out not only a revolutionary critique of the
bourgeois dictatorship, but also a critical revolution within its own
dictatorship; once the proletariat has proclaimed a genuine democratic revolution and a genuine system of democracy; once it has in
addition proclaimed that the proletarian–democratic system will
expropriate and utilize (in the same way as the means of production
of the bourgeoisie are expropriated and utilized) that last remaining halo worn by the bourgeoisie, the rationality contained within
the bourgeois–democratic system — then no man will be capable
either of saving the international capitalist system from total collapse, or of preventing the revisionist system from rapidly disin-
tegrating.

Only by way of proletarian–democratic revolution will the
socialist revolutionary movement of the proletariat be able to make a
rapid advance in the many countries of the world now searching for
liberation. Most significant of all, in the sourcelands of world war, in
the social–imperialist and imperialist nations, the hurricane force of
proletarian–democratic revolution is certain to 'roll back the enemy
like a mat'! In the imperialist nations, the people's demand for a
transformation of the private ownership system, together with the
democratic tradition and monopoly capital, all form ready-made
ladders by means of which these nations may, in the course of this
revolution, undergo a direct transition to socialism. And in the
social–imperialist nations, an economic base has already been prepared such as may, in the course of this revolution, be restored
immediately to public ownership; furthermore, the great mass of the
people in the social–imperialist nations have already acquired
Marxist revolutionary consciousness, and have an ardent desire for
true socialism and for a form of human rights, democracy, freedom
and legality expressing the interests of the proletariat.

In today's world, only by way of proletarian–democratic revolution can socialism replace capitalism, can new world war be prevented by new world revolution, can proletarian dictatorship be
established throughout the world, and Marxism triumph over
revisionism.

The advent of proletarian–democratic revolution will unquestionably mean the opening of a new chapter in the socialist revolution

and the proletarian dictatorship, and will hold out the radiant prospect of world-wide victory in both.

If the opportunity is seized firmly, and proletarian-democratic revolution carried out without delay, the effect upon the entire world and upon the whole of mankind will be of a most powerful, profound and far-reaching nature.

China has a great contribution to make to mankind — the opportunity must on no account be missed, the revolution must on no account be delayed or forsaken!

★ *Translator's Note:* The original parts I–III of section iii) were deleted from Chen's manuscript in the *April 5th Forum* edition.

12
Policy and the Evaluation of History

1. The New Criterion Distinguishing Revolution from Counter-Revolution

The concept of 'the people' and the concept of 'revolution' each assume a different meaning at different stages in the development of the forces and relations of production, in different historical periods and under different historical circumstances. During the period of proletarian–democratic revolution – the present stage – it is the nature of the stance adopted towards that revolution which provides the new criterion for distinguishing between the people and the enemy, between revolution and counter-revolution. All classes, strata, social groups and individuals which endorse, support and participate in the proletarian–democratic revolution, and struggle for the establishment of a proletarian–democratic system, belong to the category of the people, represent the standpoint of revolution and are our comrades. Conversely, all social forces, social groups and individuals which oppose the proletarian–democratic revolution, and are hostile towards and sabotage the establishment of a proletarian–democratic system, constitute the enemies of the people, represent the standpoint of counter-revolution and are reactionaries.

2. Policy Towards the Existing Leadership Cadre

The policy of the proletarian–democratic revolution towards the existing leadership cadre would be: removal from office, but retention of present salary and living circumstances, and full entitlement to such citizen's rights as the right to vote and the right to stand for election. For example, ministers of the various departments of the Centre would, under such a policy, have the following options open to them:

(1) They could compete for election as president and, if elected, would be accorded, in terms of salary and so forth, the treatment appropriate to that office.

(2) They could compete, under preferential conditions, for nomination by the elected president to continue to serve in their former ministerial capacity.

(3) If, having attained retirement age, they should indeed decide to retire, then they would still enjoy the pension remuneration accorded to a present-day minister upon retirement.

(4) They could compete for election as head of the local administration of their native province or of a province or district where they had worked for many years, or for election as a people's delegate to, or member of the Standing Committee of, the District, Provincial, or National Conference of People's Delegates. If, upon election, the salary remuneration were to be lower for the elected post than for that of an incumbent minister, then remuneration would be uniformly maintained at the original higher level. But if remuneration were to be higher for the elected post than for the former ministerial post, then remuneration would be provided at the new, higher level.

(5) If, being no longer inclined towards an active participation in politics but having not yet attained retirement age, they should wish to revert to ordinary citizen status, then they would be allowed free choice of a job and workplace appropriate to their own interests. The state would make suitable arrangements for their family and children in accordance with the wishes of the individual concerned. Their circumstances, in terms of remuneration, standard of living and political treatment would be identical to those of an existing minister, and would remain so for the rest of their days. All further matters would be dealt with by extension of the same principles.

A firm endorsement by the existing leadership cadre of these and other policies of the proletarian–democratic revolution would, without doubt, be most warmly welcomed by the people. By supporting and participating in the proletarian–democratic revolution, the leadership would demonstrate, in the clearest possible terms, its continued loyalty and continuing value to the revolution as a whole, and the people would support it once more as in former years. Any errors of one kind or another which members of the leadership cadre may have committed in the past, even the most serious ones, would without exception be forgiven, both by the state and by the people. For these would be regarded, not as errors on the part of the individual, but rather as errors of history, as errors attributable to a worsening of the fundamental disorder which dominates the mode of production. For as Marx declared:

> 'I do not by any means depict the capitalist and the landowner in rosy colours. But individuals are dealt with here only in so far as they are the personifications of economic categories, the bearers of particular class-relations and interests. My standpoint, from which the development of the economic formation of society is viewed as a process of natural history, can less than any other make the individual responsible for relations whose creature he remains, socially speaking, however much he may subjectively raise himself above them.'[1]

The state and the people would, therefore, on no account show prejudice towards or apportion individual blame to any member of any level of the existing leadership cadre who accepted and supported the policies of the proletarian-democratic revolution. A historical and magnanimous attitude would be adopted towards the past mistakes of such people, and full affirmation and acknowledgement would be given to their past contributions and achievements.

3. Policy Towards the Chinese Nationalist Party (Guomindang)

In talking of proletarian-democratic revolution in China today, one cannot ignore the continued existence, as a political force, of the Chinese Nationalist Party.

The Chinese Nationalist Party is the political party of the bourgeoisie. Hence, the relationship between the Nationalist Party on the one hand, and the proletariat and working people as a whole on the other, is one permeated with antagonistic contradiction.

At one time, the Nationalist Party held the reins of state power and had great military strength; nonetheless, it forfeited the support of the people, and suffered defeat at the hands of the Communists. Such are the historical facts. But with the Nationalist Party having subsequently undergone more than twenty years of self-renovation, and the Communist Party for its part having undergone the immense process of evolution described above, might not there now exist the possibility of the Nationalist Party turning defeat into victory and staging a comeback?

The answer is no. For China is no longer the China of yesteryear. In the course of the past two decades and more, and with the exception of Taiwan Province, China has by and large achieved public ownership of the means of production; the people have become deeply imbued with socialist ideology, Marxism has been disseminated on an extensive scale, and the population is now fast approaching one billion. The people suffered bitterly under the corrupt politics and degenerate officials of the Nationalist Party, and memories of such suffering remain strong even today. It is one thing to win trust in the first place, but quite another to regain it once lost. The kind of democracy and freedom preached by the Nationalist Party, namely democracy and freedom founded on the basis of private ownership, can only ever apply to the landlords and capitalists, not to the working masses. Furthermore, the vaunted democracy and freedom of Nationalist Party politics remain in fact, even within the bourgeoisie itself, the prerogative of a single body. By comparison with the multi-party democratic politics of the bourgeoisie in countries such as America or Japan, Nationalist Party politics amounts to nothing more than single-party autocracy. In view of the situation in China today and the present overall trend in world history, it would be manifestly unrealistic of the Nationalist Party to think of trying to restore its rule over China. Overseas foreign policy towards China from Nixon's time onwards has served clearly to underline this point.

At the same time, however, let us not forget that the man who founded the Chinese Nationalist Party was none other than the great revolutionary forerunner, Dr. Sun Yatsen. His doctrine of the Three People's Principles was of progressive significance for China then, and contains many rational elements that are still of relevance today. As Chairman Mao said, Sun Yatsen has left much that can be of value to us in terms of politics and ideology. Indeed, the Chinese of today are all, with the exception of a tiny handful of reactionary elements, the successors to Sun Yatsen's revolutionary cause.

Let us not forget either that, even though a certain section of the upper stratum of the Nationalist Party belongs to the bureaucrat-comprador bourgeoisie, the main class basis of the Nationalist Party is nonetheless the national bourgeoisie and the petty bourgeoisie.

Finally, let us not forget that the Nationalist Party has in recent years opposed any action that might lead to the breaking-up of the motherland. Whatever else may be said, the Nationalist Party's standpoint of opposing the idea of 'two Chinas' – namely, that of making China and Taiwan distinct and separate, with Taiwan as an independent state – is certainly to be commended.

The great revolutionary forerunner, Sun Yatsen, is the eternal pride and joy of the Chinese nation. Without any thought of self, he devoted all his energies and resources, wholeheartedly, unstintingly and until his dying day, to the task of transforming Chinese society. His revolutionary spirit is worthy of our eternal respect. He observed the dictates of objective reality, and succeeded in carrying out permanent revolution. The progressive character of the statements and policies put forward by Sun Yatsen in his later years, during the first period of cooperation between the Nationalist Party and the Communist Party, has long been acknowledged. But indeed, he had been rebuking the opponents of socialism since as far back as the days of the Alliance Party,[2] and in no uncertain terms: 'Those who express these views are of such narrow vision that it is simply not worth trying to persuade them otherwise.'[3] He held that '. . . the capitalist sees it as his *right* to oppress the common people, and accepts no responsibility at all for their sufferings. In a word: the capitalist is without conscience.'[4] In his view, the gap between poor and wealthy classes in the European and American democracies was excessively large, and, until socialist revolution was carried out there: '. . . the people as a whole cannot know contentment; only a small number of capitalists enjoy happiness, while the majority of people, the workers, endure suffering; inevitably, the two cannot live in peace with each other.'[5] In the immediate aftermath of the 1911 Revolution, he therefore proclaimed the following: 'The principle of nationalism, as espoused by our party, is directed towards defending our national independence against the incursions of foreigners; the principle of democracy is directed towards eradicating the evil phenomenon of the monopolization of politics by a minority; the principle of people's livelihood is directed at the expulsion of the capitalist minority, and will allow the people to enjoy freedom of production in common. The principle of people's livelihood is thus state socialism. Many of our comrades have shed their blood in order that we might enjoy our present success with respect to the first two principles, and this makes it all the more appropriate that we should now give all our thought and exert ourselves to the utmost in order to achieve our final aim. I place my deepest hopes, in this regard, in all of our comrades.'[6] Later on he declared: 'The principle of people's livelihood is communism and socialism.'[7]

In short, for a whole range of reasons both historical and contemporary, it is our sincere hope that the Chinese Nationalist Party may continue to advance in the direction indicated by Sun Yatsen, and that it will participate in the proletarian–democratic revolution and thereby assist in the cause of the peaceful reunification of China. The policies which would be adopted towards the Chinese Nationalist Party in the proletarian–democratic revolution would be as follows:

(1) Any Nationalist who was to endorse, support, and participate in the proletarian–democratic revolution, strive for the establishment of a proletarian–democratic system and assist in the peaceful reunification of the motherland would (in accordance with the criterion earlier advanced) be considered as one of the people, and as a revolutionary, and any discrimination against such a person – by no matter whom – would be forbidden.

(2) Any leading cadre of the Nationalist Party who were to choose such a path would be accorded the same treatment – politically, professionally, and in terms of living standard – as that accorded to similarly progressive members of the Communist leadership cadre.

(3) Under the proletarian–democratic system, Taiwan would exercise local autonomy as an inseparable province of China.

(4) Should the people of Taiwan decide, autonomously, to carry out the socialist transformation of private ownership, then the state would pay compensation for any portion of privately-owned property intended for nationalization.

(5) Any Nationalist or Taiwanese resident who wished to emigrate and live elsewhere would be at liberty to do so, and

238

would suffer no let or hindrance.

(6) If, however, the Nationalist Party were to reject these policies and proceed to adopt a hostile and disruptive attitude towards the proletarian–democratic revolution, then, inevitably, it would meet with the armed critique of popular revolution and suffer total destruction!

The storms of the proletarian–democratic revolution will, we believe, provoke a powerful response within Taiwanese society and will assuredly serve to hasten the reunification of the motherland.

Is the path finally taken going to be that of peaceful reunification, or that of reunification through armed liberation and violent revolution? The Nationalist Party should consider this question most carefully.

In the celebrated words of Sun Yatsen: 'The trends of the world are vast and mighty — those who comply with them will prosper, but those who resist them will perish.' And, moreover, 'It is essential that we cast our sights farther afield, several decades and several centuries ahead, and extend our view to all the countries of the world.'[8]

It is our sincere hope that all Nationalists loyal to the revolutionary thought and spirit of Sun Yatsen will comply with the trend of history, embark upon the shimmering path ahead, and, in the course of the proletarian–democratic revolution, perform meritorious service to the nation and mankind as a whole.

4. Considerations on the Failure of Napoleon and the Success of Washington

The great bourgeois hero Napoleon, at the sound of whose name the whole world once trembled, passed his last days in banishment upon an island. We need hardly speculate as to the nature of his thoughts and feelings at this time, as death drew near. However, certain of the elements underlying his failure are clearly worthy of our present consideration.

These should be approached not from a narrowly nationalistic point of view, but from the point of view of the productive forces and historical development as a whole. Certainly, it was the war with Russia that brought about the downfall of Napoleon and determined the failure of his historical enterprise. However, the main source of Napoleon's failure lay neither in his having launched an offensive against the greatest bastion of European feudalism, in his having had the audacity to aim his cannon at the all-powerful Tsar, nor in the fact of the Russian forces having had one such as Kutuzov as their commander-in-chief — nor even in such factors as the great fire of Moscow and the dreadful cold of the Russian winter. No, his direct attack on Moscow, the lair of the Tsar himself, was an act of great courage.

The main source of Napoleon's failure consisted rather in the fact that he did not proceed forthwith to proclaim the emancipation of the serfs. For such an act would, given the intensity of class contradictions and class struggle within Russia at the time, have assuredly dealt a mortal blow to the Tsarist state, and have resulted in the latter simply collapsing of its own accord. The serfs within the Tsarist army and throughout society as a whole so longed for emancipation that they would have greeted the news of such an act with firm action in support of Napoleon, and the entire social and military basis of Tsarist Russia would then have crumbled and fallen apart.

It could well be remarked that this failure derived from the bourgeois limitations of Napoleon. However, it must also be recognised that, contrarily, the chief representative of the forces of feudalism, Tsar Alexander, contrived to emerge from the situation as somehow being on the side of 'French republicanism'. By virtue of this paradox, the choice then seeming to confront the French nation at the time of the onslaught against it by the allied armies of European feudalism, was not one between Napoleon and the Bourbon monarchy, but rather one between Napoleon and the Republic! Furthermore, despite bitter personal experience (in the course of his own attempts at aggressive domination in the case of Spain) of the repeated setbacks and difficulties arising from a people's war of resistance, Napoleon nonetheless remained, at a time when the outbreak of a people's war within France itself was what the invading allied armies dreaded most of all, fearful of ordering the mobilization of the French population as a whole! This failure too derived from his bourgeois limitations.

How utterly contradictory then is it not, that Napoleon, a representative of the bourgeois revolution, should have proceeded in the end to institute a feudal autocratic system and have himself crowned and proclaimed emperor! Undoubtedly, revolutionary autocracy by a single individual is, as far as the people are concerned, always greatly preferable to counter-revolutionary autocracy exercised collectively by an entire ruling class. However, such revolutionary autocracy can never prevail in the face of counter-revolutionary *betrayal* by the entire ruling class. Napoleon bestowed generous rewards and favours upon his victorious generals, but in so doing merely succeeded in fostering a new aristocracy! Those whom Napoleon enfeoffed as marshals, dukes, earls and barons soon forgot the arts of war, gave themselves over to pleasure alone, and in the end betrayed both him and their own past honour! Napoleon was, in truth, a most *contradictory* figure. And the true extent of the failure of this contradictory figure may be judged from the fact that the triumphal column of Vendômes, which he had erected as a symbol of France's victory, was in the end torn down by the French themselves, the people having come to regard it as a symbol of chauvinism and national enmity!

Let us now turn our attention to another representative of the bourgois revolution, namely, George Washington, the founding father of the United States of America. In terms of talent and ability, Washington would appear to have been a far lesser figure than Napoleon, and yet his successes outweigh those of Napoleon. Having led the American people to victory in the War of Independence, rather than entertaining any ambitions of having himself crowned and proclaimed emperor, Washington instead declared: 'My greatest pleasure in life is farming', and confessed that he desired only to lay down arms and return to his fields. Following the inauguration of the constitution, Washington was elected as the first president of the United States of America; but again, instead of using his prestige and new-found power to effect a new political order and proclaim himself king or emperor, he remained faithful to the constitution. At the end of his term in office, in a moving farewell address, he declared: 'We must unite — we must be Americans', and therewith went back to his old home village in Virginia.

And yet, Washington's life was one of victory! His success lay, not in the fact that he was able to live out his allotted span in peace, without suffering banishment or imprisonment, free from the threat of assassination, and free from fears of subversion, *coups d'état,* or injury to his own person and his dependents, but, principally, in the profound and far-reaching nature of the influence subsequently exerted, both in his own country and throughout the world as a whole, by the system for whose establishment he was responsible. As Marx said: 'The republic is generally only the *political form for the revolutionizing of bourgeois society,* and not its *conservative form of existence,* as for example in the United States of America.'[9] Thus, Franklin, for his part, could rightly declare: 'Often and often during meetings, in my changing moods of hope and fear for the result, I have gazed at the sun behind the chairman,★ and have been unable to say whether it was rising or setting. But now finally I am content: I know it is a rising, and not a setting sun.'

All these events and individuals – Washington, Napoleon, the Tsar – belong of course to the era of the bourgeois revolutions of the late 18th and early 19th centuries, and now seem remote from our own time. And yet, turning to the present, is it not quite clear that our own era, the era of proletarian revolution, has produced quite similar figures — Lenin, Stalin, Khrushchev and others? And for what, we might enquire, are each of these various individuals commonly remembered nowadays? History judges mercilessly, but at the same time fairly and impartially. One privileged to play a role in history must shape that role with care, for a mere hairsbreadth may separate eternal fame from everlasting notoriety.

For a certain historical figure, only two courses of action lie ahead. Choose the first, and his name will be forever venerated and revered; but choose the second, and eternal loathing and execration will be his! The choice is this: either to remain faithful to Marxism-Leninism, uphold the fundamental aims of the party, strive to liberate all mankind, and in so doing free himself; or else, to betray Marxism-Leninism, defend the interests of the bureaucrats, cast the people still deeper into enslavement, and secure thereby his own eventual overthrow at their hands.

The choice before us is a momentous one, and goes far beyond the historical fate of the particular individual concerned. It is germane both to the destiny of China and to the future of the world as a whole. It is a matter of immense public significance, and deserves

★ i.e., the sun painted on the back of Washington's chair [*Chen*].

our most vigilant consideration.

Let it be firmly borne in mind, that in failing through lack of courage to undergo self-negation, one forfeits all possibility of self-*affirmation*. Justice and revolution are evergreen, and the days of the executioners upon this earth are numbered: the veil of deception will fall!

Truly, he who serves as supreme leader of the revisionist party and state suffers a wretched fate indeed: in terms of power, he is but a temporary god; by his own people, he is viewed as an eternal enemy; in his personal existence, he is but a prisoner, stripped of all freedom; and in the context of history, he stands nailed to the pillar of shame, and is condemned down the ages.

Such then is the fate to which the supreme leader is consigned by relations of production in which power is coercively monopolized by the minority. For when any man, even the most wise and democratic, is placed in the position of holding and accumulating such power over an extended period of time, then – since being determines consciousness – his thinking will become ever more ossified. As he becomes increasingly divorced from life at the grass-roots, as he grows older and acquires an ever-greater monopoly of power, his ideological work-style will inevitably become at best conservative and at worst despotic. Nowhere was this more evident than in the case of the great Stalin during his later years. Such a condition, when it affects the supreme leader, has disastrous consequences for the state, the people and the revolution. The leader himself suffers, but the fundamental cause of the party – Marxist proletarian revolution – suffers still more. Sun Yatsen once remarked that if revolutionaries ever succumbed to the imperial mentality, they would assuredly end up bringing disgrace and ruin upon themselves, and destruction upon the nation. Extending this same principle, we would assert that: *so long as the organizational structure of crossroads socialism continues to provide a basis for the emergence of imperial autocracy, the danger will remain of the party and state leader committing, in his later years, the most profound errors.* It was by no means the subjective factor which supplied the principal source of the errors committed by Stalin in his later years. And, what is more: 'the overturned cart ahead serves as a warning to those behind!' Being determines consciousness — this is an objective law independent of man's subjective will.

Clearly, though, if it should so be that the supreme leader of the party and state were indeed a genuine Marxist – that is to say, a man possessed of breadth of vision and generosity of character, a man deeply imbued with revolutionary ardour and combative spirit, a man with a steadfast commitment to the cause of universal liberation from oppression – then, it is quite certain, he would comply with the trend of history, confront the tide of reaction, and resolve to carry out the proletarian–democratic revolution. Thus would he acquire – as leader of the revolution, and as the founder of proletarian democracy – a clear title to the inaugural presidency of the ascendant proletarian–democratic state. His assumption of leadership would allow the revolution to be carried out in a relatively peaceful manner. He would forestall the outbreak of a new world war by initiating a new world revolution, thus greatly reducing the losses suffered by the state and mankind as a whole, and supplying an enormous impetus to the course of historical development. In this endeavour, he would win the sincere support and heartfelt esteem of the people of the whole world; his illustrious reputation for selflessness and fearlessness would shine forth like the sun and the moon, and his glorious achievements would endure for all time! This, surely, is the *only* destiny worthy of the leader of the party and state under crossroads socialism, and the one to which he must attain.

Once thought breaks free from its bonds, the red light of the sun will illumine the world! As the radiance of Marxism shines forth amongst the people, the theory of proletarian–democratic revolution will gain ever wider support, and be recognized as a timely solution to society's present needs. With the ascertainment by society as a whole of the criterion for distinguishing revolution from counter-revolution in today's world, the people will become capable of charting their future course wisely. Whosoever proves loyal to the people will in turn receive their loyalty and be cherished by them, but he who tries to tyrannize them will be overthrown, and consumed in the flames of their vengeance! 'The people are like the sea, and the ruler a ship which sails thereon': borne afloat by the sea, the ship may also be capsized by it. This is a truth which has been recognized by the Chinese ever since the time of the feudal emperor Tai Zong, in the 7th century AD. 'Now it is exceedingly difficult for the leading men of the nation to be knaves and for the inferior sort of people to be honest; for the former to be cheats, and for the latter to consent to be duped.'[10] Such was the unequivocal conclusion delivered by the bourgeois Enlightenment thinker, Montesquieu, in the mid-18th century.

The theory of marxist proletarian–democratic revolution will be as a spring wind upon the land, blowing, pure and fresh, the length of the Yellow River, within and without the Great Wall, then onwards, across the Pamir Plateau, to embrace the whole world! For truly, the people are capable of both understanding and practising the wise words of their great teacher: 'In this case, therefore, the monarchy was the unreal and the revolution was the real. And so, in the course of development, all that was previously real becomes unreal, loses its necessity, its right of existence, its rationality. And in the place of moribund reality comes a new, viable reality — peacefully if the old has enough intelligence to go to its death without a struggle, forcibly if it resists this necessity.'[11]★

★ *Translator's Note:* The subsequent chapter in Chen's manuscript was deleted by *April 5th Forum* in its *samizdat* edition of the work. Chapter 13 of the present edition thus appeared as Chapter 14 in Chen's manuscript. For some speculative thoughts as to the possible content of the original (missing) chapter 13, see *Introduction*, above, pp. 28-29.

IV. Rationality

13
On sublation

1. The New Metaphysicians

'Just as philosophy finds its *material* weapons in the proletariat, so the proletariat finds its *intellectual* weapons in philosophy.'[1] The foundations of a proletarian philosphy were laid long ago by Marx and Engels. However, in consequence of the development of production, the class struggle, and scientific experimentation, as a result of the whole range of contemporary achievement in the natural sciences, and with the steady deepening of the proletarian revolution, it has become of great importance that proletarian philosophy now be enriched and further developed. History has conferred upon the proletarian–democratic revolution the task of producing – in succession to such works as *Materialism and Empirio-Criticism, On Practice* and *On Contradiction* – a new work of philosophy: an exposition of the theory of sublation.[2]

Such a work would comprise a critique of the neo–metaphysics presently running rampant in our society, namely the metaphysics which manifests itself under the dialectical banner of 'one divides into two'.[3]

The metaphysician, observed Engels, '. . . thinks in absolutely unmediated antitheses. His communication is "yea, yea; nay, nay"; for whatsoever is more than these cometh of evil.'[4] This absolute, isolated, rigid and one-sided way of viewing things in this common attribute of all metaphysicians. However, whereas the metaphysicians of old generally made no attempt at concealment or prevarication when expounding their views, the distinguishing feature of the neo–metaphysicians is their attempt, by invocation of the principle 'one divides into two', to peddle their wares under the signboard of dialectics. They profess to be loyal exponents of the law of the unity of opposites, and of the methodology 'one divides into two', yet they view and apply this law and method precisely from the standpoint of metaphysics. Under their auspices, the unity of opposites itself is 'divided into two': either they absolutize *opposition,* and attempt to arrogate all 'unity' to themselves; or else they absolutize *unity,* and endeavour to eradicate from the course of movement all trace of opposition. The two approaches are different, but share a common objective and achieve the same result. Both exert, by virtue of their one-sided and absolute perspective on things, a most pernicious influence upon society. Though manifested in different form, they derive from the same root: a politics which has become ossified by the workings of bureaucratic privilege.

The neo-metaphysicians who absolutize opposition regard opposites as immutable, as neither interconnected nor interpenetrating, as exerting no mutual influence upon one another: 'right is right, and wrong is wrong'. That which is good is entirely and unsurpassably so, and is thus to be beautified sky-high, while that which is bad is likewise entirely and unsurpassably so, and is therefore to be denounced as the devil. In determining what is correct and what is false, this type of neo-metaphysician shows respect for neither objective facts nor even the principle of seeking truth from facts. Instead, he indulges in wholesale absolutization from a position of idealism, subjectivism and sectarianism: *I* am the incarnation of absolute truth and revolution, while *you* represent absolute falsehood and counter-revolution. Such people speak of struggle, but not of affinity; they speak of the exclusive nature of antagonism, but not of the unitary nature (identity) of contradiction; they speak of the first negation which transforms the other, but not of the second negation which raises the self to a higher level. According to their creed, struggle is everything and there can be no possibility of transformation; the emergence of new things which transcend their own origins is forever impossible, and the *status quo* – being absolutely fixed and immutable, incapable of change – will remain thus for all eternity.

They denounce the viewpoints of others on an *ad hominem* basis, showing not the slightest regard for the rational component of viewpoints which run contrary to their own. Moreover, by depriving people of the possibility of making comparisons and choices, they both preserve the grounds for the existence of the contrary viewpoint, and at the same time render impossible the raising of their own to a higher level. It is self evident that if such neo-metaphysics were to be applied in the sphere of scientific investigation, it would engender such defects as complacency, conservatism and general narrowness of vision. But when spread throughout society at large, such neo-metaphysics gives rise to a state of massive contention wherein one-sidedness, stubbornness and belligerence reign supreme; it places in grave jeopardy the revolutionary unity within the people, and seriously obstructs the revolutionary development of society.

The other neo-metaphysicians, those who absolutize unity, invariably take as their objective the conscious maintenance of the stability of the old order. Focussing their attention purely upon quantitative change, they deny the occurrence of a hiatus interrupting the gradualness of such change, the transformation wrought by qualitative change, and the development of the thing to a new stage as a result of the leap to a new qualitative order. Adopting the slogan 'one divides into two', they purvey an eclecticism which they claim represents dialectics, and – unable to determine the real truth – pursue instead an unprincipled peace, a unity in which there is no opposition. They fail to perceive that contradiction and struggle constitute the form of existence of any dynamic entity, and that stability and equilibrium are always conditional, relative and temporary; they fail to perceive that the conflict intrinsic to the contradiction cannot develop other than through the struggle of opposites, and that the cost of inhibiting the contradiction at the point of relative rest is, therefore, stagnation and underdevelopment. When spread throughout society, this second type of neo-metaphysics results in the following: the denial and concealment of changes in actual class relations, the repudiation and concealment of the real class struggle, and, in general, the creation of an atmosphere of bureaucratic conservatism, inaction and stagnation. Evil is connived at, and spreads by a chain of association; reforms are met with a wall of resistance, and revolution is lowered into the grave.

2. Towards a Reinstatement of the Dialectic

Our prospective work – *On Sublation* – would take as its object of study the revolutionary dialectic of Marxism, and would concern a theory of development through the complete two-aspected and dihedral circular process of 'one divides into two, and two struggle and produce a third'.

'Dialectics', remarked Engels, 'is nothing more than the science of the general laws of motion and development of nature, human society and thought.'[5] And as Lenin indicated: 'In brief, dialectics can be defined as the doctrine of the unity of opposites. This embodies the essence of dialectics, but it requires explanations and development.'[6] Moreover: *'Dialectics* is the teaching which shows how *opposites* can be and how they happen to be (how they become) *identical* — under what conditions they are identical, becoming transformed into one another — why the human mind should grasp these opposites not as dead, rigid, but as living, conditional, mobile, becoming transformed into one another.'[7]

On Sublation would restore the respective concepts of relativity (ascertained by observing rest), the absolute (ascertained by observing motion), and necessity (ascertained by observing development), to the wholeness of their proper mutual and organic interconnection. This establishment of the whole would make apparent that 'one divides into two' signifies the modalities of analysis, dissection, decomposition: from it there would emerge the new principle of 'two struggle and produce a third', signifying the modalities of synthesis, combination and composition. The former serve to locate that which lies within the already formed, but the latter serve to bring into being the as yet unformed. Only by the integration of these two principles do we obtain a relatively comprehensive and revolutionary dialectic of the unity of opposites. For wherever 'one divides into two', we find also that 'two struggle and produce a third'. This 'third' is a 'one' distinct from the old one, a new one, a developed one alien to the former, a one which both differs from the beginning and is itself a beginning.

As the facts of natural, human and intellectual development as a whole demonstrate, neither the combining of the already existent nor the emergence of the new occur through processes of harmonious mediation, devoid of contradiction and struggle. The methodological formula 'two combine into one'[8] both ignores and conceals this law of contradiction and struggle within things. It is inconducive to any conscious and dynamic recognition and resolution of contradictions, and serves to inhibit the forward leap, the revolutionary transformation, producing instead stagnation and retrogression. By contrast, the principle 'two struggle and produce a third' both emphasizes and illuminates the law of contradiction and struggle. It exposes the existence of contradiction in the internal activity and necessary tendency of a thing, and – by allowing a conscious sublation of the contradiction to be carried out – abbreviates the period of struggle within it and leads to its resolution. It stimulates the forward leap, accelerates revolutionary transformation, and permits a clear and timely recognition of the new qualitative order thus produced.

Hence, 'two struggle and produce a third' is entirely different in nature from the proposition 'two combine into one'. 'Two struggle and produce a third' augments, succeeds and develops 'one divides into two'.

However, the *method* of struggle suggested by 'two struggle and produce a third' differs substantially from that advocated by the neo-metaphysicians who absolutize opposition. *On Sublation* would explain opposition as being the initial form of struggle within a contradiction, and a general law governing its motion; and sublation, by contrast, as being an advanced form of struggle and particular law of motion which emerges only when the contradiction has attained a certain stage and level of development. Sublation is the link through which opposition produces transformation, while opposition is the basis upon which sublation proceeds. The purpose of opposition is the transformation of the other. Sublation, however, seeks not merely the transformation of the other, but also, of necessity, the alienation of this transformation of the other; that is to say, through 'the kernel of the whole thing, the negation of the negation',[9] the conscious transformation of the self as well, and hence the development, progression and raising of the thing to a new and higher stage. Clearly then, sublation by no means represents an absolute negation, but rather a negation preserving that which has been affirmed. Or as Hegel put it: 'The negative is to an equal extent positive.'[10]

Thus, in sublation both sides of the contradiction undergo alienation and are raised to a higher level. And as we have seen, sublation is certainly not premissed upon absence of struggle. On the contrary, it itself forms the outcome of fierce confrontation and struggle between the two opposing sides of the contradiction. 'Sublation' merely denotes the particular, advanced form and means of struggle. It is therefore to be clearly differentiated in essence and principle from concepts of an eclecticist origin, and it is quite different in kind from the principles pursued by those neo-metaphysicians who absolutize unity.

Nor does sublation mean the combination of half a pound of one side of the contradiction with eight ounces of the other. For the positive components, the rational elements to be retained on either side of the contradiction, will not actually be equivalent: one of the two sides will necessarily assume the principal aspect, and the other the secondary aspect. Equally, sublation does not entail a preservation of the original nature and form of the two sides of the contradiction; rather, it preserves through transformation. The very existence of a space of mutual coincidence between the two aspects of the contradiction is explained, in part, by the laws of metabolism: because of the interpenetration and interconnection of the old and the new, and the mutual restriction and influence which they exert, the new aspect – though always charged with vitality – nonetheless itself acquires a space which must be repudiated, while the old aspect for its part acquires a certain vitality which must be preserved. The new and the old thus acquire an identity of repudiation, and an identity of preservation. Once, in the course of development of the struggle, this identity of the two sides has attained a certain stage and level – that is, at the moment of the commingling of the two sides in the same direction – there then appears the particular, advanced form of struggle: sublation. Both aspects then undergo instant alienation and, in a leap from simple to complex and from lower to higher, combine to form a contradiction qualitatively different from that of the original process.

Significantly, Rousseau described the transformation to the opposite as: '. . . the extreme point that closes the circle and meets that from which we set out'.[11] This formulation Engels considered to be one of the 'masterpieces of dialectic'.[12] It has its counterpart too in Hegel's remark: 'Science is seen to be a *circle* which returns upon itself';[13] and Lenin, for his part, added as a marginal note to this: 'Science is a circle of circles.'[14] However, neither Rousseau, Hegel, Marx, Engels nor Lenin ever offered any clear and precise explanation of the nature of this 'circle'. Indeed, the world of philosophy has to this very day failed to resolve the issue, and continues to shroud it in mystery. *On Sublation,* with its 'theory of development through the complete two-aspected and dihedral circular process of one dividing into two and two struggling to produce a third', will signal the hour of this mystery's dissolution.

For in truth, the tree of life is eternally green, and the river of development flows ceaselessly onwards. The idea that some 'zenith' can be attained is fallacious![15]

Only by winning liberation in the realm of philosophy will mankind ever achieve true and complete liberation!

The means by which thought is enabled to grasp both contradiction, and, within contradiction, itself – such is the dialectic. Moreover: 'The dialectic . . . includes in its positive understanding of what exists a simultaneous recognition of its negation, its inevitable destruction; because it regards every historically developed form as being in a fluid state, in motion, and therefore grasps its transient aspect as well; and because it does not let itself be impressed by anything, being in its very essence critical and revolutionary.'[16] Mastery of this method will give us foresight, breadth of vision and daring, and its application shall make us invincible!

Let us now, together, engrave upon our minds and proceed earnestly to apply: 'The great basic thought that the world is not to be comprehended as a complex of ready-made *things*, but as a complex of *processes*, in which the things apparently stable no less than their mind images in our heads, the concepts, go through an uninterrupted change of coming into being and passing away, in which, in spite of all seeming accidentality, and of all temporary retrogression, a progressive development asserts itself in the end.'[17]

for assuredly, a most splendid and mighty new vista must then unfold before our eyes!

The light is ahead.

'And thence we came forth,
to see again the stars.'[18]

(Dante: 'The Divine Comedy')

Key to References

References to the works of Marx, Engels and Lenin in the most frequently quoted editions have been abbreviated as follows:

MESW   Marx and Engels, *Selected Works* (three-volume edition), Lawrence and Wishart, 1977.

MECW   Marx and Engels, *Collected Works* (in progress), Lawrence and Wishart.

EWM   Marx, *Early Writings*, Penguin Books, Harmondsworth, 1975.

TRO 1848   Marx, *The Revolution of 1848*, Penguin Books, Harmondsworth, 1974.

SFE   Marx, *Surveys From Exile*, Penguin Books, Harmondsworth 1973.

TFIA   Marx, *The First International and After*, Penguin Books, Harmondsworth, 1984.

LSW   Lenin, *Selected Works* (three-volume edition), Progress Publishers, Moscow, 1970.

LCW   Lenin, *Collected Works*, Progress Publishers, Moscow 1972.

Notes and References

Chapter 1

1. The Chinese term used here – *zhengzhi jingji yitihua* (subsequently abbreviated to *zheng-jing yitihua*) – is, as far as I have been able to ascertain, Chen's own coinage; as with several other of his highly distinctive formulations, its accurate rendering has required, correspondingly, a new English coinage. *Yitihua,* literally translated, means 'to form into a single (homogeneous) body'; the terms 'integration', 'unification', 'fusion', or even 'incorporation' all fail to convey the full impact of the original: an 'active coalescence' of the political and the economic, whereby the two instances come to lose their individual specificity. Metaphors drawn from natural science seem inadequate or even misleading, and I have therefore resorted to the more sociological coinage 'unicorporation'. (*Trans.*) See also *Translator's Note* on p.87

2. 'Goulash welfarism' was the charge levelled by the Chinese against Khruschev in the early 60s, and denotes his 'revisionist' view that the Soviet people would be content with socialism as long as they had enough goulash to fill their stomachs.

3. Marx, 'A Contribution to the Critique of Hegel's Philosophy of Right', in EWM, p. 246.

4. Marx and Engels, 'Manifesto of the Communist Party', in TRO 1848, p. 70.

5. Marx, 'A Contribution to the Critique of Hegel's Philosophy of Right', in EWM, p. 246.

6. Chen's use of the term 'social fascism' invokes only in a very indirect way Stalin's charge against European Social Democracy during the later period of the Third International. The immediate reference is to the official Chinese Communist usage of the term in the anti-Soviet polemics of the early 70s.

7. Lenin, 'Imperialism, the Highest Stage of Capitalism', in LSW vol. 1, p. 686.

Chapter 2

1. Here, and in most subsequent instances, Chen uses the term *fanxiu fangxiu*, which has the twofold meaning of 'opposing existing revisionism' (i.e., primarily, the Soviet Union) and preventing its further emergence (i.e., in China); in order to make the English less cumbersome, I have reduced this to the single term 'the struggle against revisionism'. (*Trans.*)

2. Mao, 'Speech at the Meeting of the Supreme Soviet of the USSR in Celebration of the 40th Anniversary of the Great October Revolution', in *Quotations from Chairman Mao Tsetung,* Peking 1972, p. 24.

3. Lenin, 'Certain Features of the Historical Development of Marxism', in LCW vol.

17, p, 42,

4. Lenin, 'What is to be Done', in LCW vol. 5, p. 369.

5. Ibid., p. 370

6. Mao, no reference.

7. Mao, no reference.

8. In a major article of January 1940 entitled 'On New Democracy', Mao formulated the view that the Chinese revolution, from the time of the October Revolution and more particularly the Chinese 'May 4th Movement' of 1919, had ceased to be of the 'old bourgeois-democratic' variety, leadership in the democratic revolution having henceforth passed to the hands of the proletariat owing to the weakness of the Chinese national bourgeoisie. The 'New Democratic Revolution' extended into the first half decade or so of the People's Republic, and there was much controversy within the CPC as to the most appropriate timing and speed for the subsequent 'transition to socialism', which Mao eventually pushed through as early as the mid-50s.

9. Hegel, *Philosophy of History*, no page ref., translated from the Chinese.

Chapter 3

1. Engels, *Anti-Dühring*, Peking 1976, p. 343. N.B: Quotations from Engel's *Anti-Dühring* are cited, in the present translation, from the Peking 1976 English translation of Engel's work, in preference to the Lawrence and Wishart/Progress Publishers 1975 translation. There are numerous points of divergence between the Peking and Moscow translations; since the former correlates with the Chinese edition used by Chen Erjin, it conveys to the English reader a more accurate picture of Chen's reading of Engels.

Chapter 4

1. Marx, *Capital* Volume 1, Penguin Books 1979, p. 450.

2. Ibid., p. 449.

3. Lenin, 'Economics and Politics in the Era of the Dictatorship of the Proletariat', in LSW vol. 3, p. 289.

4. Mao, *Red Flag*, Issue No. 13, 1967.

Chapter 5

1. Marx and Engels, 'Manifesto of the Communist Party', in TRO 1848, p. 98.

2. Engels, 'Letter to C. Schmidt', in MESW vol. 3, p. 491.

3. Engels, *Anti-Dühring*, Peking 1976, p. 233.

4. Ibid., p. 364.

5. Rousseau, 'A Discourse on the Origin of Inequality', in *Rousseau's Social Contract and Discourses* (trans. by G.D.H. Cole), J.M. Dent/Everyman's Library 1930, p. 231.

6. Ibid., p. 232.

7. Mao, *People's Daily*, 16/10/68.

8. Han Fei Zi (philosopher of the 3rd century BC), 'Book 4, Chapter 11: Solitary Indignation', in *Han Fei Tzu – Works from the Chinese*, London 1959.

9. Note the close similarity between this passage and an official pronouncement made some 18 months later, in Nov. 1977, in *People's Daily:*

'The Soviet bureaucrat-monopoly capitalist group has transformed a highly centralized socialist state-owned economy into a state-monopoly capitalist economy without its equal in any other imperialist country and has transformed a state under the

dictatorship of the proletariat into a state under fascist dictatorship.'
(see King C. Chen, ed., *China and the Three Worlds: A Foreign Policy Reader*, p. 108).

10. Translated from the Chinese; the book referred to by Chen – 'Marx, Engels, Lenin and Stalin on the Paris Commune' – has not been located.

11. Marx and Engels, 'Manifesto of the Communist Party' in TRO 1848, p. 68.

12. Marx, 'The Civil War in France' (first draft), in TFIA, p. 251.

13. One Chinese *yuan* is equivalent to approximately ¹/₃ of a pound Sterling, and there are 100 *fen* in a *yuan*.

14. Marx, *Capital* Volume 1, Penguin Books 1979, pp. 874–5.

15. Translated from the Chinese: see note 10, Chapter 5.

16. Rousseau, 'A Discourse on the Origin of Inequality', op. cit. p. 165.

17. Marx, 'Moralising Criticism and Critical Morality', in MECW vol. 6. p. 5.

18. Engels, 'Ludwig Feuerbach and the End of Classical German Philisophy', in MESW vol. 3, p. 339.

19. Engels, 'The American Workers' Movement' (26 Jan. 1887: no English translation found, present translation from the Chinese).

Chapter 6

1. Wrong reference given; translation from the Chinese.

2. Lenin, 'A Great Beginning', in LCW vol. 29, p. 432.

3. Lenin, 'The Workers' State and Party Week', in LCW vol. 30, p. 63.

4. Lenin, reference not found; translation from the Chinese.

5. The term 'capitalist-roaders' (full form: "party persons in authority taking the capitalist road') was put forward by Mao in the early to mid-60s; during the Cultural Revolution, Liu Shaoqi was denounced as the 'No. 1 capitalist-roader', and Deng Xiaoping as the 'No. 2 capitalist-roader'. Chen's redefinition of the term as 'revisionist-roaders' involves, as his subsequent dicussion suggests, an extension of the underlying charge to cover not only the right-wing of the party, but also and perhaps even primarily the party's ultra-left wing.

6. Marx, *Capital* Volume 1, Penguin Books 1979, p. 134.

7. Eugène Pottier, *The Internationale*.

8. Marx, *Capital* Volume 1, p. 874.

9. Marx, Letter to Engels, 24 August 1867, *Marx-Engels Selected Correspondence*, (no date) p. 180.

10. Marx, 'Letter to Engels (Jan. 1868), in *Marx-Engels Selected Correspondence* p. 239.

11. Lenin, 'Deception of the People with Slogans of Freedom and Equality', in LCW vol. 29, p. 364.

12. This article of March 1926 appears at the very beginning of Volume One of *The Selected Works of Mao Tse-Tung* (Peking 1967). For a later analysis by Mao of the classes in Chinese society, see *Selected Works* Volume Two, pp. 319–326 ('The Chinese Revolution and The Chinese Communist Party', December 1939).

13. Marx and Engels, 'Feuerbach. Opposition of the Materialistic and Idealistic Outlook', in MESW vol. 1, p. 35.

14. Engels, *Anti-Dühring*, Peking 1976, p. 364.

15. Marx and Engels, 'Feuerbach. Opposition of the Materialistic and Idealistic Outlook', in MESW vol. 1, p. 34.

16. Engels, 'Letter to C. Schmidt', in MESW vol. 3, p. 491.

17. Lenin, 'A Great Beginning', in LSW vol. 3, p. 231.

18. Marx, 'Letter to J. Weydemeyer', in MESW vol. 1, p. 528.

19. Marx and Engels, 'Manifesto of the Communist Party', in TRO 1848, p. 68.

Chapter 7

1. Lenin, 'Marxism and Reformism', in *Against Revisionism*, Moscow 1959, p. 167.
2. Lenin, ' "Left-Wing" Communism – An Infantile Disorder', in LCW vol. 31, p. 85.
3. Engels, *Anti-Dühring*, Peking 1976, p. 342.
4. Engels, 'Letter to C. Schmidt', in MESW vol. 3, pp. 491-2.
5. *Anti-Dühring*, p. 405.
6. Mao, in *Marx, Engels and Lenin on the Dictatorship of the Proletariat*, Peking 1975, p. 2.
7. Mao, in *The Tenth National Congress of the Communist Party of China (Documents)*, Peking 1973, p. 20.
8. The reference is to the Incantation of the Golden Hoop used by the monk Tripitaka, in the classical novel *Pilgrimage to the West*, to keep the Monkey King under control.
9. Marx and Engels, 'Manifesto of the Communist Party', in TRO 1848, p. 79.
10. This is a quotation from the classical Chinese philosopher *Han Fei Zi* (translation by James Legge).
11. Marx and Engels, 'Address of the Central Committee to the Communist League', in TRO 1848, p. 323.
12. Marx and Engels, 'Manifesto of the Communist Party', in TRO 1848, p. 88.
13. Mao, in *The Tenth National Congress of the Communist Party of China (Documents)*, p. 20.
14. Marx, *Capital* Volume 1, Penguin Books 1979, p. 557.
15. Engels, 'The Origin of the Family, Private Property and the State', in MESW vol. 3. pp. 324–5.
16. Marx and Engels, 'Manifesto of the Communist Party', in TRO 1848, p. 87.
17. Stalin, *Economic Problems of Socialism in the USSR*, Peking 1976, pp. 40-1.
18. Engels, 'Letter to A. Bebel', in *Marx and Engels – Selected Correspondence*, Moscow 1975, p. 334.
19. Marx, 'Preface to "A Contribution to the Critique of Political Economy" ', in MESW vol. 1, p. 503.

Chapter 8

1. Engels, 'Letter to C. Schmidt', in MESW vol. 3, p. 491.
2. Marx, 'Preface to "A Contribution to the Critique of Political Economy" ', in MESW vol. 1, p. 504.
3. Engels, *Anti-Dühring*, Peking 1976, p. 34.
4. Marx, 'Preface to "A Contribution to the Critique of Political Economy" ', in MESW vol. 1, pp. 503-4.
5. *Anti-Dühring*, p. 382.
6. Marx, 'The Civil War in France: Address of the General Council', in TFIA, p. 212.
7. Ibid., p. 210.
8. Marx, 'Letter to L. Kugelmann', in MESW vol. 2, p. 420.
9. Marx, 'A Contribution to the Critique of Hegel's Philosophy of Right', in EWM, p. 257.
10. Marx, 'The Civil War in France' (first draft), in TFIA, p. 253.
11 . Marx, 'Preface to "A Contribution to the Critique of Political Economy" ', in MESW vol. 1, p. 504.
12. Marx and Engels, 'Address of the Central Committee to the Communist

League', in TRO 1848, p. 323 and p. 324.

13. Marx, 'The Eighteenth Brumaire of Louis Bonaparte', in SFE, p. 153.

14. Marx, 'The Class Struggles in France: 1848 to 1850', in SFE, p. 35.

15. Ibid., p. 35.

16. Engels, 'Revolution and Counter-Revolution in Germany', in MESW vol. 1, p. 301.

17. Montesquieu, *The Spirit of the Laws*, D.W. Carrithers (ed.), University of California Press 1977, p. 107.

18. Marx, 'The Class Struggles in France: 1848 to 1850', in SFE, p. 131.

19. Engels, 'Revolution and Counter-Revolution in Germany', in MESW vol. 1, p. 300.

Chapter 9

1. Marx, 'The Civil War in France: Address of the General Council', in TFIA, p. 217.

2. Engels, *Anti-Dühring,* pp. 343-4.

3. Lenin, 'On Co-operation', in LSW vol. 3, p. 766.

4. Lenin, 'How We Should Reorganise the Workers' and Peasants' Inspection', in LSW vol. 3, p. 771.

5. Lenin, 'Better Fewer, But Better', in LSW vol. 3, p. 776.

6. Ibid., p. 777.

7. The Cultural Revolutionary interpretation of the 1960 'Angang Charter' (an abbreviation for the Charter of the Anshan Iron and Steel Company), is contained in the following remarks by a leading cadre of the Peking General Knitwear Factory (as quoted by Charles Bettelheim in *Cultural Revolution and Industrial Organization in China,* Monthly Review Press 1974, p. 17): 'Implementing [the Charter] means always to put politics in command, strengthen party leadership, launch vigorous mass movements, systematically promote the participation of cadres in productive labour and of workers in management, reform any unreasonable rules, assure close co-operation among workers, cadres and technicians, and energetically promote the technical revolution'.

8. The 'revolutionary committee', an institution established throughout China both at work-unit level and at various state-administrative levels during the late 1960s, was originally intended to be of a provisional nature, but remained as a permanent feature for the entire subsequent decade. An administrative body under the political leadership of the party committee, it comprised a twofold 'three-in-one combination' of personnel: 1) representatives of the masses, party cadres, and PLA; 2) young, middle-aged and older members.

9. Marx, 'Resolutions of the Meeting Held to Celebrate the Anniversary of the Paris Commune', in MESW vol. 2, p. 287.

10. Marx, 'The Civil War in France: Address of the General Council', in TFIA, p. 212.

11. Lenin, 'The State and Revolution', in LSW vol. 2, p. 327.

12. Ibid., p. 367.

13. Engels, 'Introduction of 1891 to Marx's "The Civil War in France" ', in MESW vol. 2, p. 189.

14. Lenin, 'A Fly in the Ointment', in LCW vol. 33, p. 368.

15. Lenin, 'Better Fewer, But Better', in LSW vol. 3, p. 781.

16. Lenin, 'Second Congress of the Communist International', in LCW vol. 31, p. 253.

17. Engels, 'A Critique of the Draft Social-Democratic Programme of 1891', in MESW vol. 3, p. 436 and p. 437.

18. Lenin, 'The State and Revolution', in LSW vol. 2, p. 339.
19. *American Declaration of Independence*
20. Ibid.
21. Montesquieu, *The Spirit of the Laws*, op. cit., pp. 201-202.
22. Engels, 'Origin of the Family, Private Property and the State', in MESW vol. 3, p. 329.
23. Marx, 'Critique of the Gotha Programme', in MESW vol. 3, p. 27.
24. Lenin, 'The State and Revolution', in LSW vol. 2, pp. 343-4.
25. Marx and Engels, 'Feuerbach. Opposition of Materialistic and Idealistic Outlook', in MESW vol. 1, p. 38.
26. Engels; wrong reference given, translated from the Chinese.
27. Mao, 'On the Correct Handling of Contradictions Among the People', in *Selected Works of Mao Tsetung* vol. 5, p. 420.
28. Engels, 'Letter to F. Mehring', in MESW vol. 3, p. 497.
29. Lenin, ' "Left-Wing" Communism – An Infantile Disorder', in LSW vol. 3, pp. 415-6.
30. Ibid., pp. 416-7.
31. Ibid., p. 410.
32. Ibid., p. 410.
33. Mao, in *The Ninth National Congress of the Communist Party of China (Documents)*, Peking 1969, p. 27.
34. Ibid., pp. 106-7.

Chapter 10

1. Mao, 'Opening Address at the First Session of the First National People's Congress of the People's Republic of China', in *Quotations from Chairman Mao Tsetung*, Peking 1972, p. 1.
2. Wrong reference given.
3. Mao, 'On the Correct Handling of Contradictions Among the People', in *Selected Works of Mao Tsetung*, vol. 5, p. 409.
4. Marx and Engels, 'Manifesto of the Communist Party', in TRO 1848, p. 79.
5. Engels, 'Letter to A. Bebel', in MESW vol. 2, p. 431.
6. Lenin; wrong reference given, translated from the Chinese.
7. Engels, 'Letter to F.A. Sorge', in MESW vol. 2, p. 434.
8. Ibid., p. 433.
9. Engels, 'Letter to F.A. Sorge', in MESW vol. 2, pp. 431-3.
10. Marx; wrong reference given, translated from the Chinese.
11. Engels, 'The Origin of the Family, Private Property and the State', in MESW vol. 3, p. 329.
12. Engels, 'The Festival of Nations in London', in MECW vol. 6, p. 5.
13. Engels, 'Letter to P. Lafargue', in *Marx-Engels – Selected Correspondence*, p. 555.
14. Engels, cited in Lenin, *Marxism on the State*, Moscow, p. 15.
15. Premier: *zongli* 'arranger-in-general'.
16. President: *zongtong* 'ruler-in-general'. The element 'tong' in this term has two meanings: 1) to rule, and 2) to unify or integrate; Chen's conception of the term stresses the second of these meanings.
17. The Chinese for 'long live' is *wan sui* ('10,000 years'): this term was applied not only to the emperors of old, but also, during the Cultural Revolution, to Mao himself.
18. Chen abbreviates the term 'conference of workers' delegates' to 'delegates' conference'; I have altered the latter to 'workers' conference', in order to make clearer the distinction between it and the 'people's conference' (*Trans.*)

19. Lenin, 'Ninth Congress of the RCP(B)', in LCW vol. 30, p. 465.

20. *Declaration of the Rights of Man and of the Citizen* (1789), in *The French Revolution*, Gaetano Salvemini, 1954, p. 144.

21. Marx and Engels, 'Manifesto of the Communist Party', in TRO 1848, p. 80.

22. Marx, *Capital* Volume 1, p. 92.

23. 'Manifesto of the Communist Party', in TRO 1848, p. 80.

24. Translated from the Chinese; see note 10, Chapter 5.

25. 'The three great differences' (*san da chabie*): the distinctions between town and country, industry and agriculture, and physical and mental labour.

26. This principle is not recognised in the Chinese judicial process; however, the issue is currently under debate in legal circles.

27. *Declaration of the Rights of Man and of the Citizen* (1789), in *The French Revolution*, Gaetano Salvemini, 1954, pp. 144–6.

28. Marx, 'A Contribution to the Critique of Hegel's Philosophy of Right', in EWM, p. 256.

29. Ibid., p. 257.

Chapter 11

1 Lenin, 'The Historical Destiny of the Doctrine of Karl Marx', in LCW vol. 18, p. 584.

2. Lenin, 'The State and Revolution', in LSW vol. 2, p. 310.

3. Mao, in *Marx, Engels and Lenin on the Dictatorship of the Proletariat*, Peking 1975, p. 1.

4. Marx, 'Letter to J. Weydemeyer', in *Marx – Engels – Selected Correspondence*, p. 86.

5. Engels, 'Preface of 1883 to "Manifesto of the Communist Party" ', in MESW vol. 1, p. 101.

6. Marx, 'Critique of the Gotha Programme', in TFIA, p. 355.

7. Marx, 'The Class Struggles in France', in SFE, p. 123. N.B.: Marx's word 'revolutionizing' is rendered in the Chinese edition as simply 'changing' (*gaibian*); I have maintained the former translation in Chen's subsequent invocations of this quote, for the sake of consistency. (*Trans.*)

8. Ibid., p. 122.

9. Marx and Engels, 'Feuerbach. Opposition of the Materialistic and Idealistic Outlook', in MESW vol. 1, p. 38.

10. Marx and Engels, 'Address of the Central Committee to the Communist League', in TRO 1848, p. 323.

11. Ibid., p. 330.

12. Marx, *Capital* Volume 1, p. 103.

13. Marx and Engels, 'Address of the Central Committee to the Communist League', in TRO 1848, p. 323.

14. Marx and Engels, 'Circular Letter to Bebel, Liebknecht, Bracke *et al*', in TFIA, p. 375.

15/16/17. Lenin, *Marxism on the State*, Moscow, pp. 20 and 30.

18. Mao, 'Talk at an Enlarged Central Work Conference', in *Mao Tsetung Unrehearsed*, Stuart R. Schram (ed.), Penguin Books 1974, p. 169.

19. Lenin, 'Session of CEC, Moscow Soviet and Trade Unions', in LCW vol. 27, p. 434.

20. Lenin, 'A Great Beginning', in LSW vol. 3, p. 230.

21. Ibid., p. 233.

22. Lenin, 'Greetings to the Hungarian Workers', in *Against Revisionism*, Moscow

1959, p. 500.

23. Engels, *Anti-Dühring*, p. 219.

24. Ibid., p. 202.

25. Mao, *People's Daily*, 13 August 1967.

26. Mao, *People's Daily*, 23 January 1967.

27. Lenin, 'The Dénouement is at Hand', in LCW vol. 9, p. 449.

28. Marx and Engels, 'Manifesto of the Communist Party', in TRO 1848, p. 78.

29. Ibid., p. 78.

30. Marx and Engels, 'From the Resolutions of the General Congress Held in the Hague,' in MESW vol. 2, p. 291.

31. Marx, 'Speech on the Seventh Anniversary of the International', in TFIA, p. 272.

32. Marx, 'Conspectus of Bakunin's "Statism and Anarchy" ', in TFIA p. 333.

33. Engels, *Anti-Dühring*, pp. 235-6.

34. Engels, 'Introduction of 1891 to Marx's "The Civil War in France" ', in MESW vol. 2, p. 189.

35. Marx, 'The Civil War in France', as cited by Lenin in *Marxism on the State*, Moscow, pp. 43-8; present version drawn from TFIA pp. 209-21.

36. Marx, 'Letter to L. Kugelmann', in *Marx-Engels — Selected Correspondence*, pp. 318-9.

37. Lenin, *Marxism on the State, p. 9*.

38. Engels, 'On Authority', in MESW vol. 2, p. 3.

39. Lenin, The Paris Commune and the Tasks of the Democratic Dictatorship' in *Lenin: On the Paris Commune*, Progress Publishers, Moscow 1974, p. 120.

40. Lenin, 'A Publicist's Notes', in LCW vol. 30, p. 355.

41. Wrong reference; translated from the Chinese.

42. Lenin, 'Draft Speech on the Agrarian Question in the Duma', in LCW vol. 12, p. 277.

43. Lenin, 'A Retrograde Trend in Russian Social-Democracy', in LCW vol. 4, p. 276.

44. Lenin, 'The Immediate Tasks of the Soviet Government', in LCW vol. 27, p. 264.

45. Lenin, 'Economics and Politics in the Era of the Dictatorship of the Proletariat', in LCW vol. 30, p. 115.

46. Lenin, 'The First Congress of the Communist International: Theses and Report on Bourgeois Democracy and the Dictatorship of the Proletariat', in LCW vol. 28, p. 458.

47. Lenin, ' "Left-Wing" Communism – An Infantile Disorder', in LCW vol. 31, pp. 44-5.

48. Mao; wrong reference.

49. Marx, 'A Contribution to the Critique of Hegel's Philosophy of Right', in EWM, p. 254.

50. Marx, 'The Civil War in France: Address of the General Council', in TFIA, p. 211.

51. Engels, *Anti-Dühring*, p. 179.

52. Lenin, 'Conspectus of Hegel's "Science of Logic" ', in LCW vol. 38, p. 222.

Chapter 12

1. Marx, *Capital* Volume 1, p. 92.

2. The 'Alliance Party', or 'United League' (Tongmenghui), was the main force behind the 1911 Revolution, and the forerunner of the Chinese Nationalist Party

(founded in the following year).

3. Sun Yatsen, in *Sun Zhongshan Xuan Ji* (vol. 1), p. 94.

4. Ibid., p. 95.

5. Ibid., p. 85.

6. Ibid., p. 93.

7. Ibid., (vol. 2), p. 797.

8. Ibid., (vol. 1), p. 85

9. Marx. 'The Eighteenth Brumaire of Louis Bonaparte', in SFE. p. 155.

10. Montesquieu, *The Spirit of the Laws*, op. cit., pp. 120-1.

11. Engels, 'Feuerbach and the End of Classical German Philosophy', in MESW vol. 3, p. 338.

Chapter 13

1. Marx, A Contribution to the Critique of Hegel's Philosophy of Right', in EWM, p. 257.

2. 'Sublation': the Hegelian/Marxian dialectical principle of *Aufhebung* (synthesis, and the reconstitution of things at a higher level of development).

3. See accompanying *Introduction*, p. 24, for an explanation of the political significance of the term 'one divides into two'.

4. Engels, *Anti-Dühring*, p. 26.

5. Ibid., p. 180.

6. Lenin, 'Conspectus of Hegel's "Science of Logic" ', in LCW vol. 38, p. 223.

7. Ibid., p. 109.

8. See accompanying *Introduction*, p. 24, for an explanation of the term 'two combine into one'.

9. Engels, *Anti-Dühring*, p. 179.

10. Hegel, as cited in Lenin's 'Conspectus of Hegel's "Science of Logic" ', in LCW vol. 38, p. 97.

11. Rousseau, 'A Discourse on the Origin of Inequality', op. cit., p. 235.

12. Engels, *Anti-Dühring*, p. 24.

13. Hegel, as cited in Lenin's 'Conspectus of Hegel's "Science of Logic" ', in LCW vol. 38, p. 233.

14. Lenin, ibid., p. 233.

15. The 'zenith' or 'pinnacle' theory (*dingfenglun*) was Lin Biao's doctrine that Mao Zedong Thought represented the acme of contemporary marxism, and that Mao himself was infallible. It is associated closely with Lin Biao's other 'contribution' to knowledge, namely the 'theory of genius' (*tiancailun*).

16. Marx, *Capital* Volume 1, Penguin Books 1979, p. 103.

17. Engels, 'Feuerbach and the End of Classical German Philosophy', in MESW vol. 3, pp. 362-3.

18. Dante, *The Divine Comedy, 1: Inferno*, Oxford University Press 1971, p. 427.